FRED KARLSSON

FINNISH
GRAMMAR

Translated by Andrew Chesterman

WERNER SÖDERSTRÖM OSAKEYHTIÖ
PORVOO - HELSINKI - JUVA

The second edition
This edition can be used together with the first edition.

ISBN 951-0-11627-0

WSOY Printing plants, Juva 1987

ISBN 951-0-11627-0

Preface

Finnish Grammar is a translation of the Finnish book *Suomen peruskielioppi* published in 1982. The Swedish original *Finsk grammatik* appared in 1978. These versions were published by the Finnish Literature Society (Suomalaisen Kirjallisuuden Seura), Helsinki.

Finnish Grammar is primarily intended for foreigners wanting to learn the basics of the language. The book covers the grammatical core; rare forms and constructions have not been included. I have tried to formulate the grammatical rules as precisely as possible using "reasonable" terminology. At the same time, all essentials should be readily seen from the numerous examples.

The book relies on some basic insights of modern linguistics and might therefore serve as an introduction to the structure of Finnish for professional linguists as well.

Chapters 3 and 7 contain surveys of the word and clause structure, respectively, and should therefore be read before the others.

My sincere thanks are due to Andrew Chesterman, who skilfully and critically made the translation, and to the Finnish Ministry of Education for financially supporting the undertaking.

Helsinki, July 1982
F.K.

Preface to the second edition

I am endebted to Maija-Hellikki Aaltio for valurable comments on the first edition of the book. In the second edition, some 70 minor corrections have been included.

Helsinki, March 1986
F.K.

Contents

Notational conventions

/   An oblique stroke marks the division between the root and the ending of a word, and between different endings. E.g. **auto/ssa** 'in the car', **äiti/ni/kin** 'my mother, too', **sano/isi/n** 'I would say', **ole/mme lähte/neet** 'we have left'. In the glosses an oblique stroke indicates an alternative: 'he/she'.

'   Single quatation marks include the meaning of a word or example: **auto** 'car', **lähte/ä** 'go, leave', **minä matkusta/n Helsinki/in** 'I am travelling to Helsinki'.

"   In the glosses, double quotation marks indicate a literal but unidiomatic or ungrammatical translation: **auto/ni** "car my".

[ ]   Square brackets are used for the actual pronunciation of a word: **rengas** [re$\eta\eta$as] 'ring' means that the word is pronounced with a long [-$\eta\eta$-] sound in the midle.

á   An acute accent marks the main stress: **tálo** 'house', **tálo/on** 'into the house', both with stress on the first syllable.

:   The colon separates inflected forms of a given word, thus: **käsi** 'hand' : **käde/n** 'of a hand', **tul/la** 'come' : **tule/n** 'I come'.

~   The tilde shows variants of the same form: **-ssa** ~ **-ssä** 'in', **-vat** ~ **-vät** (3rd person plural ending).

-n   A preceding hyphen indicates an ending, to be added to a stem. A following
tule-   hyphen marks a stem, to which an ending is added.

1   **Introduction**

§1. *THE RELATION OF FINNISH TO OTHER LANGUAGES*

Finno-Ugrian languages

The Finnish language is a member of the Finno-Ugrian language family; this is quite different from the Indo-European family, to which e.g. English, French, German and Russian belong. Only three of the Finno-Ugrian languages are spoken outside the Soviet Union: Finnish, Hungarian, and the Lapp dialects of the north of Scandinavia. These dialects are in some respects so varied that they could also be regarded as separate languages.

Baltic-Finnic languages

The languages most closely related to Finnish are Estonian, Karelian, Veps, Lude, Vote and Livonian, which are all spoken around the south and east of the Gulf of Finland. Of these Baltic-Finnic languages Finnish and Estonian are spoken most widely. These two are so similar in grammar and vocabulary, so closely related, that after a little practice Finns and Estonians can understand each other's languages fairly well.

If we group together the other Finno-Ugrian languages according to their relations to each other and to Finnish, we have the following picture:

Finnish (Estonian etc.)	Lapp (dialects)	Mordvinian Cheremiss	Zyryan Votyak	Hungarian Ostyak Vogul

increasing distance from Finnish →

Finnish and Hungarian are thus quite distant from each other, and the relation between these two languages can really only be established on historical linguistic grounds. Roughly speaking, Finnish is as far from Hungarian as English or German is from Persian.

Uralic languages

The Finno-Ugrian languages and the Samoyed languages spoken in Siberia constitute the Uralic language family.

§2. *FINNISH PAST AND PRESENT*

Finnish is the native language of approximately 93% of Finland's population of 4.7 million. The population also includes a minority group of about

300,000 Swedish-speaking Finns, the Finland Swedes, who are guaranteed the same basic rights as the Finnish-speaking majority by the country's constitution, about 4,500 Lapps (of whom 2,900 speak Lapp), 6,000 gypsies (the number of Romany speakers is not known), about 5,000 deaf people whose first language is sign language, and about a thousand Tatars.

Finland is officially a bilingual country, whose national languages are Finnish and Swedish. Waves of emigration have resulted in large Finnish-speaking minorities particularly in North America (both the USA and Canada) and in Sweden. In Sweden today there are approximately 300,000 Finns, i.e. about the same number as there are Swedish-speaking Finns in Finland.

colon-
ization

According to the traditional theory Finland was settled from three directions: the Finns themselves came over from the south across the Gulf of Finland and from the east across the Karelian Isthmus, and the Scandinavians came from the west. The first major wave of immigration was that of the Häme Finns, who came over the Gulf of Finland and occupied parts of South-West Finland in the early centuries of the Christian era. The Scandinavians came to Finland during and after the time of the Crusades; the Swedish-speaking Finns of today are their descendants.

According to a recently proposed alternative theory there were Finno-Ugrian settlements in Finland as long ago as 4000 BC. This population incorporated Baltic elements around 2000 BC and Germanic elements as early as c. 1500 BC. The original population thus formed then absorbed the Baltic Finns from across the Gulf of Finland about 2000 years ago.

Politically, Finland was a part of Sweden until 1809, and an autonomus Grand Duchy within Tsarist Russia from 1809 to 1917. Finland has been an independent republic since 1917.

During the Swedish period Finnish was very much a secondary language. The language of the administration and the intelligentsia was Swedish. It was not until 1863 that Finnish was decreed to have equal status with Swedish "in all matters directly concerning the Finnish-speaking population of the country".

the
written
language

The earliest actual texts in Finnish date from the beginning of the 16th century. The father of written Finnish is considered to be Mikael Agricola, the Bishop of Turku (Åbo), who started the Finnish translation of parts of the Bible during the Reformation.

Finnish was greatly influenced by Swedish for a long time, especially as regards its vocabulary, which was quite natural considering that the authorities were generally Swedish-speaking. Since Turku was the capital city until 1827, it is understandable that standard Finnish developed primarily out of south-western dialects. In the 19th century there was increasing influence

Kalevala

from Eastern Finland, mostly owing to the national epic Kalevala, the first *part* of which was published in 1835. The Kalevala is based on the folk poetry of Eastern Finland and Karelia, and it was an important source of inspiration for the 19th century nationalist movement, whose central figure was Johan Vilhelm Snellman.

The nationalist movement also had a variety of linguistic effects. Many language scholars wanted to "finnicize" Finnish by getting rid of Swedish loanwords and a number of grammatical structures borrowed directly from Swedish.

Language is not a uniform system: it varies in different ways, e.g. regional dialects. Finland's main dialect areas are shown on the following map.

FINLAND'S
DIALECT
AREAS

regional dialects

1. South-western dialects
2. South-western transition dialects
3. Häme dialects
4. Southern Ostrobothnian dialects
5. Central and northern Ostrobothnian dialects
6. Northern dialects
7. Savo dialects
8. South-eastern dialects
▧ Swedish-speaking areas

the standard language

However, this book does not deal with regional dialects and their differences. Instead, we shall be concerned with the official norm of the language, *standard Finnish*, one important variant of which is normal written prose. But even the standard language is not completely uniform. Its grammatical structures and also (in spoken standard Finnish) its pronunciation both vary slightly depending on the speech situation and a number of other factors. The standard language spoken in official or formal situations is grammatically very close to the written norm; but colloquial spoken Finnish differs to some extent from more formal usage in both pronunciation and grammar. The differences between everyday and more formal Finnish are discussed in more detail in chapter 22.

§3. *THE BASIC CHARACTERISTICS OF FINNISH*

endings

The basic principle of word formation in Finnish is the addition of endings (bound morphemes, suffixes) to stems. For example, by attaching the endings -i 'plural', -ssa 'in', -si 'your', and -kin 'too, also' to the stem *auto* 'car' in different ways, the following words can be formed.

auto/ssa	in the car	(car/in)
auto/i/ssa	in the cars	(car/s/in)
auto/ssa/si	in your car	(car/in/your)
auto/si	your car	(car/your)
auto/kin	the car too	(car/too)
auto/si/kin	your car too	(car/your/too)
auto/ssa/kin	in the car too	(car/in/too)
auto/i/ssa/kin	in the cars too	(car/s/in/too)
auto/i/ssa/si/kin	in your cars too	(car/s/in/your/too)

Finnish verb forms are built up in the same way. Using the verb stem *sano-* 'say', and the endings **-n** 'I', **-i** 'past tense', and **-han** 'emphasis', we can form e.g. these words:

sano/**n**	I say	(say/I)
sano/**n**/**han**	I do say	(say/I/emphasis)
sano/**i**/**n**	I said	(say/past/I)
sano/**i**/**n**/**han**	I did say	(say/past/I/emphasis)

The adding of endings to a stem is a morphological feature of many European languages, but Finnish is nevertheless different from most others in two respects.

case endings

In the first place Finnish has more case endings than is usual in European languages. Finnish case endings normally correspond to prepositions or postpositions in other languages: cf. Finnish *auto*/**ssa**, *auto*/**sta**, *auto*/**on**, *auto*/**lla** and English *in* the car, *out of* the car, *into* the car, *by* car. Finnish has about 15 cases; English has only one, the genitive, as in *Bill*/**'s**.

possessive suffixes

The second difference is that Finnish sometimes uses cases where Indo-European languages generally have independent words. This is also true of the Finnish possessive suffixes, which correspond to possessive pronouns, e.g. **-ni** 'my', **-si** 'your', **-mme** 'our', cf. *kirja*/**ni** 'my book', *kirja*/**mme** 'our book'.

enclitic particles

Another set of endings particular to Finnish is that of the enclitic particles, which always occur in the final position after all other endings. It is not easy to say exactly what these particles mean; their function is often emphasis of some kind, similar e.g. to that of intonation in some other languages. The particles include **-kin** 'too, also', **-han** 'emphasis' (often in the sense 'you know, don't you?'), and **-ko** 'interrogative', cf. *kirja*/*ssa*/**kin** 'in the book too', and *On*/**ko** *tuo kirja?* 'Is that a book?'.

derivatives

Another characteristic feature of Finnish is the wide-ranging use made of endings in the formation of new independent words. Compare the basic word *kirja* 'book' with the derived forms *kirj*/*e* 'letter', *kirja*/*sto* 'library', *kirja*/*lli-nen* 'literary', *kirja*/*llis*/*uus* 'literature', *kirjo*/*itta(a)* '(to) write', and *kirjo*/*it-ta*/*ja* 'writer'. Derivational morphemes (derived words) can also be followed by other endings, for nouns e.g. case endings, possessive suffixes and particles. We can then form such words as:

kirja/sto/**ssa**	in the library
kirjo/ita/**n**/**ko**	shall I write?
kirjo/itta/ja/**n**/**kin**	of the writer, too
kirja/sto/**sta**/**mme**	out of our library

Learning the endings is not as difficult as is often thought. Since the endings are often piled up one behind the other rather mechanically, Finnish wordforms are usually easy to analyse if one knows the endings.

no gender

Finnish nouns differ from those of many Indo-European languages in that there is no grammatical gender. In German there is the "der — die — das" difference, French has "le — la", Swedish "en — ett", and so on, but these distinctions do not occur in Finnish.

no articles

Finnish does not have articles, either (cf. *a* car — *the* car). The semantic function of articles is often expressed by word order in Finnish:

13

Kadulla on auto.   There is *a car* in the street.
Auto on kadulla.   *The car* is in the street.

concord　　　When adjectives occur as attributes they agree in number and case with the head-word, i.e. they take the same endings.

iso auto   the big car
iso/ssa auto/ssa   in the big car
iso/n auto/n   of the big car
iso/t auto/t   the big cars
iso/i/ssa auto/i/ssa   in the big cars

sound
structure　　　There are 21 phonemes (basic sounds) in Finnish: 8 vowels and 13 consonants. The number is noticeably smaller than in most European languages. The main stress always falls on the first syllable of a word. The writing system is systematic in that a given phoneme is always written with the same letter. The converse is also true: a given letter always corresponds to the same phoneme.

§4. *WHAT ARE THE SPECIAL DIFFICULTIES?*

vocab-
ulary　　　It is also worth briefly mentioning the areas of Finnish grammar which can cause most learning difficulty. Since Finnish is not an Indo-European language it is to be expected that the basic vocabulary differs from Indo-European — as indeed it does. The 20 most frequent words in Finnish are the following:

1. *olla*	(to) be		11. *kun*	when, as
2. *ja*	and		12. *niin*	so
3. *se*	it		13. *kuin*	than
4. *ei*	no		14. *tulla*	(to) come
5. *joka*	which		15. *minä*	I
6. *hän*	he, she		16. *voida*	can
7. *että*	that		17. *kaikki*	all
8. *tämä*	this		18. *ne*	they
9. *mutta*	but		19. *me*	we
10. *saada*	(to) get		20. *myös*	also

loan-
words　　　It is immediately clear that learning Finnish words requires an effort. The burden is lightened, however, by the fact that Finnish has hundreds of direct loanwords (mostly from Swedish) and a great many translation loans, expressions that have been translated into Finnish equivalents.
　　　Examples of direct loans are the following (both Swedish and English equivalents are given): *ankka* 'anka, duck'; *kahvi* 'kaffe, coffee'; *kakku* 'kaka, cake'; *kallo* 'skalle, skull'; *keppi* 'käpp, cane'; *kirkko* 'kyrka, church'; *kruunu* 'krona, crown'; *pankki* 'bank, bank'; *penkki* 'bänk, bench'; *sohva* 'soffa, sofa'; *tulli* 'tull, customs'; *tuoli* 'stol, chair'; *viini* 'vin, wine'.
　　　Compound words which are direct loans include: *kirja/kauppa* 'bokhandel, bookshop'; *olut/pullo* 'ölflaska, bottle of beer'; *rauta/tie/asema* 'järnvägsstation, railway station'.

14

In §3 it was said that the inflection of Finnish words is easy in that the endings are often attached "mechanically" to the stem. However, this is not always true. The form of the stem often alters when certain endings are added to it. Compare e.g. the inflection of the noun *käsi* 'hand' in different cases.

kä**si**	hand	(hand)
kä**de**/ssä	in the hand	(hand/in)
kä**te**/en	into the hand	(hand/into)
kä**t**/tä	hand (partitive case)	(hand/partitive)
kä**s**/i/ssä	in the hands	(hand/s/in)
kä**si**/kin	the hand, too	(hand/too)
kä**te**/ni	my hand	(hand/my)

The basic form *käsi* takes different forms according to the following ending and its sound structure. These sound alternations are governed by rules that can sometimes be extremely complex. Here are a few more example pairs:

tunte/a	—	tunne/n	(to) know	—	I know
hyppää/n	—	hypä/tä	I jump	—	(to) jump
matto	—	mato/lla	mat	—	on the mat
maa	—	ma/i/ssa	country	—	in countries
tie	—	te/illä	road	—	on the roads
tietä/ä	—	ties/i	(to) know	—	(he) knew

case endings   Case endings are usually added to nouns, adjectives and other nominals, but they may also be added to verbs.

Minä lähden Jyväskylä/**än**.	I'm going to Jyväskylä.
Minä lähden kävele/mä/**än**.	I'm going "walking" (= for a walk).

The verb form *kävelemään* literally means 'into walking', just as *Jyväskylään* means 'into (the town of) J.'. Both forms contain the case ending -**än** meaning 'into'.

object   The object in Finnish is marked by a case ending. In the two following sentences the ending -**n** indicates "this word is the object of the sentence". The rules governing the use of this ending and the other possible object endings are fairly complex.

Minä ostan kirja/**n**.	I (shall) buy the book.
Kalle näki auto/**n**.	Kalle saw the car.

vowel and consonant length   The most difficult feature of the pronunciation of Finnish is the length (duration) of the sounds: differences of length serve very frequently to distinguish separate words. Compare pairs such as *kansa* 'people' — *kanssa* 'with', *tuli* 'fire' — *tulli* 'customs', *muta* 'mud' — *mutta* 'but', *muta* 'mud' — *muuta* 'other', *muta* 'mud' — *mutaa* 'mud' (partitive case), *tuulee* 'it is windy' — *tuullee* 'it is probably windy'.

2   Pronunciation and sound structure

Writing and pronunciation
Vowels and consonants
Short and long sounds
Diphthongs
Syllables
Stress and intonation
Vowel harmony

§5. *WRITING AND PRONUNCIATION*

letters

Finnish has 8 letters for vowels and 13 for consonants: **i e ä y ö u o a** and **p t k d g s h v j l r m n**. The following important one-to-one correspondence holds between letters and phonemes (phonemes are sounds thought of as types, irrespective of slight variations in the speech of the same person or between different people).

> EACH LETTER CORRESPONDS TO ONE AND THE SAME PHONEME, and EACH PHONEME CORRESPONDS TO ONE AND THE SAME LETTER

additional comments

1) The vowel corresponding to the letter **u** is a close rounded back vowel (cf. English b**oo**k, German g**u**t, Swedish g**o**d).

2) The vowel corresponding to the letter **o** is a half-close rounded back vowel (cf. English b**o**rn, German r**o**t, Swedish g**å**).

3) The vowel corresponding to the letter **ä** is an open unrounded front vowel (cf. English sh**a**ll, Swedish b**ä**ra).

4) The vowel corresponding to the letter **y** is a close rounded front vowel (cf. German F**ü**hrer, Swedish n**y**).

5) The vowel corresponding to the letter **ö** is a half-close rounded front vowel (cf. German G**ö**ring, Swedish d**ö**).

6) The combination of letters **ng** is pronounced as a long [ŋŋ] sound (cf. *rengas* 'ring' [reŋŋas]).

7) The letter **n** before a **k** is pronounced as a short [ŋ] sound (cf. *Helsinki* [helsiŋki]).

8) When length is used to differentiate meanings, short phonemes are written with one letter and long phonemes with two (e.g. t**u**li 'fire' — t**uu**li 'wind' — t**u**lli 'customs'; kansa 'people' — kanssa 'with'; mut**a** 'mud' — mut**aa** 'mud' (partitive)).

9) Words of foreign origin may contain other letters than those mentioned above, e.g. **b c f w x z**.

10) The pronunciation of the everyday spoken language differs in several respects from that of the standard spoken norm (see chapter 22).

§6. VOWELS AND CONSONANTS

Finnish has 8 vowel and 13 consonant phonemes: **i e ä y ö u o a** and **p t k d s h v j l r m n** η. All vowels and consonants (except **d v j h**) can occur as either short or long sounds. Special attention should be paid to the following details.

pronunciation of vowels

1) The long vowels **ii, yy, uu** are pronounced as pure long vowels, not as if they were diphthongs or as if they ended in **-j** or **-v**.

2) Long **aa** and short **a** have the same quality. Cf. *palassa* 'in a bit', *maa* 'country', *maalla* 'in the country', *vaara* 'danger'.

3) The quality of long **öö** is [ø:] and that of the short **ö** is [ø], also before **r**, cf. *sinäkö* 'you?', *pöllö* 'owl', *mörkö* 'goblin', *Närpiöön* 'to Närpiö'.

4) **ee** and **e**, and also **ää** and **ä**, are differentiated in all positions in a word, including before **r** and in unstressed syllables. Cf. *te* 'you' — *tee* 'tea', *meille* 'to us' — *meillä* ' "at" us' (= at our house), *teellä* 'with tea' — *täällä* 'here', *piste* 'point' — *pistä* 'sting!' *veneen* 'of the boat' — *nenään* 'into the nose', *lehti* 'leaf' — *lähti* '(he) left', *veri* 'blood' — *väri* 'colour', *veressä* 'in the blood' — *värissä* 'in the colour'; *perkele* 'devil', *merkki* 'mark', *Eero* (masculine name), *väärä* 'wrong'.

pronunciation of consonants

5) **p t k** are pronounced without aspiration, i.e. without a breathy "**h**" sound after them.

6) **s** is often pronounced as rather a dark, thick sound that can be close to **š**, especially in the environment of **u**. Cf. *pussi* 'bag', *luussa* 'in the bone', *sumu* 'fog', *myös* 'also'.

7) **h** may occur between vowels and is then pronounced weakly. **h** can also co-occur with consonants, and is then a stronger sound, particularly if the following consonant is **t** or **k**. Cf. *huono* 'bad', *miehen* 'of the man', *paha* 'evil', *ihminen* 'person', *varhain* 'early', *vanha* 'old', *vihko* 'notebook', *vihta* 'bunch of birch twigs', *sähkö* 'electricity', *tuhka* 'ash'.

8) **l** is pronounced as rather a thick sound when it occurs between the vowels **u** and **o**. Cf. *pullo* 'bottle', *hullu* 'mad', *kulta* 'gold', *pala* 'bit', *villi* 'wild'.

9) **r** is always trilled with the tip of the tongue, e.g. *pyörä* 'wheel', *Pori* (town), *Turku* (town), *virrassa* 'in the stream', *kierrän* 'I turn'.

10) *After* certain grammatical forms the initial consonant of the following word or particle *lengthens*. These forms are mainly nominals ending in -**e** like *perhe* 'family' (§19), the present indicative negative e.g. *en tule* 'I am not coming' (§29), the second person singular imperative e.g. *tule!* 'come!' (§66), and the first infinitive e.g. *tulla* '(to) come' (§74). Examples:

	WRITTEN	PRONOUNCED	MEANING
nominals in -**e**	vene tuli	[venettuli]	the boat came
	venekin	[venekkin]	the boat, too
	liikemies	[liikemmies]	businessman
pres. indic. negative	en tule Turkuun	[entuletturkuun]	I'm not coming to Turku
	emme tulekaan	[emmetulekkaan]	We're not coming after all
	en ole sairas	[enolessairas]	I am not ill
2nd. sing. imperative (-*e* -stems)	tule tänne	[tulettänne]	come here
	mene pois	[meneppois]	go away
	ole hiljaa	[olehhiljaa]	be quiet
1st infinitive	haluan olla täällä	[haluanollattäällä]	I want to be here
	haluan lähteä pois	[haluanlähteäppois]	I want to go away

17

§7. SHORT AND LONG SOUNDS

The difference between short and long sounds is used very widely in Finnish to distinguish different words. Long sounds can occur in almost any position in a word, and there are few restrictions on permissible combinations of long and short sounds. This is clear from the following examples.

Tule tänne	*Come* here.
Ulkona ei *tuule*.	Outside *it is not windy*.
Ulkona ei *tuulle*.	Outside *it is probably not windy*.
Ulkona *tuulee*.	Outside *it is windy*.
Pekka *tulee*.	Pekka *comes*.
Pekka *tullee*.	Pekka *will probably come*.
Ulkona *tuullee*.	Outside *it is probably windy*.

Almost all the possible combinations of short and long sounds occur: short-short-short, short-long-short, long-short-long, long-long-short, short-long-long, etc. Note in particular the following three points:

three
important
points

1) The difference between a short and a long vowel before a short and a long consonant, e.g. *tili* 'account' — *tiili* 'brick', *tuli* '(he) came' — *tuuli* 'wind', *vino* 'slanting' — *viini* 'wine', *takana* 'behind' — *taakka* 'burden', *muna* 'egg' — *muuna* 'other' (essive case) — *muunna* 'transform!', *viilin* 'of Finnish yoghurt' — *viillin* 'kind of knife', *takka* 'fireplace' — *taakka* 'burden' — *takkaa* 'fireplace' (partitive case) — *taakkaa* 'burden' (partitive case) — *taka* 'back' — *takaa* 'from behind'.

2) The difference between a short and a long consonant after a short consonant, e.g. *karta* 'avoid!' — *kartta* 'map', *korpi* 'wilderness' — *korppi* 'raven', *arki* 'weekday' — *arkki* 'ark', *Antila* (proper name) — *Anttila* (proper name), *kansa* 'people' — *kanssa* 'with', *pelko* 'fear' — *palkki* 'beam', *lampi* 'pond' — *lamppu* 'lamp', *valta* 'power' — *valtti* 'trump'.

3) The main stress is always on the first syllable of a word. Long vowels elsewhere than in the first syllable must be pronounced without main stress, cf. *táloon* 'into the house', *hýppään* 'I jump', *káappiin* 'into the cupboard', *rávintolaan* 'into the restaurant', *tálossaan* 'in his house'.

§8. DIPHTHONGS

Finnish has 16 common diphthongs, i.e. combinations of two vowels occurring in the same syllable. Diphthongs can be divided into four groups according to the final vowel.

final
vowel -i

1) **ei**   *ei* 'no', *leipä* 'bread', *Veikko* (masculine name)
    äi   *äiti* 'mother', *päivä* 'day', *väittää* '(to) claim'
    ui   *uin* 'I swim', *puissa* 'in the trees'
    ai   *kaikki* 'all', *aika* 'time', *vaikka* 'although'
    oi   *poika* 'boy', *voin* 'I can', *toinen* 'other'
    öi   *söin* 'I ate', *töissä* 'in the works'
    yi   *hyi* 'ugh!', *lyijy* 'lead'

18

final vowel -u	2)	**au**	*taulu* 'picture', *kaula* 'neck', *sauna* 'sauna'

		ou	*koulu* 'school', *noudan* 'I fetch', *krouvi* 'tavern'
		eu	*reuna* 'edge', *Keuruu* (place name), *seutu* 'region'
		iu	*viulu* 'violin', *kiusaan* 'I tease', *hius* 'hair'

final
vowel -y

3) **äy** *täynnä* 'full', *käyn* 'I go', *näytän* 'I show'
    öy *köyhä* 'poor', *löydän* 'I find', *löyly* 'steam'

ie, uo, yö

4) **ie** *tie* 'road', *vien* 'I take', *mies* 'man'
    yö *yö* 'night', *työ* 'work', *syön* 'I eat'
    uo *tuo* 'that', *Puola* 'Poland', *juon* 'I drink'

Note particularly the differences between the following pairs: **ei — äi, öi — öy, äy — öy, ei — eu** and **äy — eu**.

Finnish also has other kinds of vowel combinations, but these others do not form diphthongs. Between the vowels there is almost always a syllable boundary. Examples:

sanoa	(to) say	rupean	I begin
ainoa	only	tapahtua	(to) happen
vaikea	difficult	kireä	tense
sallia	(to) allow	etsiä	(to) look for

§9. *SYLLABLES*

Syllabification in Finnish is in most cases determined by the following basic rule.

**THERE IS A SYLLABLE BOUNDARY BEFORE EACH
COMBINATION OF CONSONANT + VOWEL**

In the following examples the syllable boundary is indicated by a dash (-): *ka-la* 'fish', *jo-kai-nen* 'every', *kaik-ki* 'all', *kui-ten-kin* 'however', *sit-ten* 'then', *suu-ri* 'big', *päi-vä* 'day', *al-kaa* '(to) begin', *purk-ki* 'jar', *pur-kis-sa* 'in the jar', *purk-kiin* 'into the jar', *Ant-ti* (masculine name), *An-tin* 'of Antti', *An-til-le* 'to Antti', *Hel-sin-ki* 'Helsinki', *Hel-sin-kiin* 'to Helsinki', *Hel-sin-gis-sä-kin* 'in Helsinki, too'.

There is also a syllable boundary between vowels that do not form a diphthong (§8), e.g. *no-pe-a* 'fast', *ai-no-a* 'only', *hert-tu-an* 'of the duke', *sal-li-a* '(to) allow'.

§10. *STRESS AND INTONATION*

Finnish word-stress follows this important rule:

stress rule

> **THE MAIN STRESS IS ALWAYS ON THE FIRST SYLLABLE OF A WORD**

Vowels elsewhere than in the first syllable therefore do not receive main stress. The main stress also falls on the first syllable in loanwords which may have been stressed differently in the original language. Cf. *Hélsinkiin* 'to Helsinki', *vápaa* 'free', *vóida* '(to) be able', *jókainen* 'every', *máalaan* 'I paint', *áatteellisuus* 'idealism'; *élefantti* 'elephant', *límonaati* 'lemonade', *psýkologi* 'psychologist', *psýkologia* 'psychology', *búlevardi* 'boulevard'.

intonation
Finnish sentence intonation is generally falling, but the first syllable of the final word of a sentence can nevertheless be pronounced with a rising intonation without the word being given a strong stress. In the following examples the intonation contour is shown above the sentence.

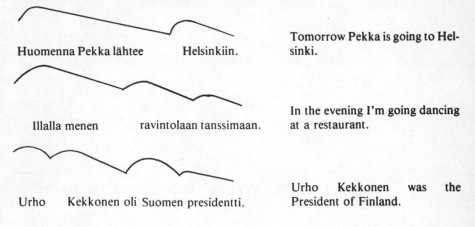

Huomenna Pekka lähtee   Helsinkiin.
Tomorrow Pekka is going to Helsinki.

Illalla menen   ravintolaan tanssimaan.
In the evening I'm going dancing at a restaurant.

Urho   Kekkonen oli Suomen presidentti.
Urho Kekkonen was the President of Finland.

strong stress
When a word needs to be given particularly strong emphasis this is done by means of intonation. In addition, such a word is often moved to the beginning of the sentence.

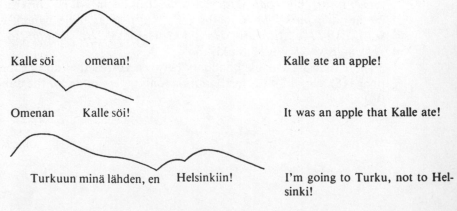

Kalle söi   omenan!
Kalle ate an apple!

Omenan   Kalle söi!
It was an apple that Kalle ate!

Turkuun minä lähden, en   Helsinkiin!
I'm going to Turku, not to Helsinki!

§11. *VOWEL HARMONY*

Many endings occur in two forms with alternative vowels, e.g. -**ssa** ∼ -**ssä** 'in', -**ko** ∼ -**kö** (interrogative), -**nut** ∼ -**nyt** (past participle). These vowel alternations form three pairs; each pair has one back vowel and one front vowel.

vowel pairs

BACK VOWEL	—	FRONT VOWEL	EXAMPLE
a	—	ä	-ssa ∼ -ssä
o	—	ö	-ko ∼ -kö
u	—	y	-nut ∼ -nyt

If a given ending contains one of these six vowels, there will also exist a parallel ending with the other vowel of the pair. If we have the ending -**han** 'emphasis', there will also be -**hän**; if -**koon** (3rd p. sing. imp.), then also -**köön**, etc. The vowels of the stem determine which ending of the pair is to be chosen.

ending vowels

> IF THE STEM CONTAINS ONE OR MORE OF THE VOWELS **u, o, a**, THE ENDING ALSO HAS TO HAVE A BACK VOWEL (**u, o, a**). IF THE STEM HAS NO BACK VOWELS, THE ENDING HAS TO HAVE A FRONT VOWEL (**y, ö, ä**).

In the following examples the back vowels of the stem, and also all the ending vowels which are governed by vowel harmony, are indicated in bold type.

ENDING WITH BACK VOWEL		ENDING WITH FRONT VOWEL	
talo/ssa	in the house	kylä/ssä	in the village
Turu/ssa	in Turku	käde/ssä	in the hand
Pori/ssa	in Pori	venee/ssä	in the boat
Porvoo/ssa	in Porvoo	Helsingi/ssä	in Helsinki
poja/lla	boy (adessive)	äidi/llä	mother (adessive)
auto/lla	by car	tä/llä	with this
kato/lla	on the roof	miehe/llä	man (adessive)
naise/lta	from the woman	Ville/ltä	from Ville
Kekkose/lta	from Kekkonen	tytö/ltä	from the girl
sisare/lta	from the sister	velje/ltä	from the brother
he tule/vat	they come	he syö/vät	they eat
he sano/vat	they say	he mene/vät	they go
on luke/nut	has read	on pitä/nyt	has kept
tuo/ko?	that?	tämä/kö?	this?
tuo/ssa/ko	in that?	tä/ssä/kö?	in this?
kirja/han	book (+emphasis)	kynä/hän	pen (+emphasis)
kirja/ ssa/han	in the book (+emphasis)	kynä/llä/hän	with a pen (+emphasis)
Turu/ sta/ko?	from Turku?	Kemi/ stä/kö?	from Kemi?
kahvi/la/ ssa/han	in the café (+emphasis)	kylpy/lä/ ssä/hän	at the bathing resort (+ emphasis)

3   A Survey of Word Structure

Nominals and their endings
Finite verb-forms and their endings
Non-finite verb-forms and their endings

§12. *NOMINALS AND THEIR ENDINGS*

nominals Nominals are nouns, adjectives, pronouns and numerals, i.e. words like the following:

NOUNS		ADJECTIVES		PRONOUNS		NUMERALS	
auto	car	*iso*	big	*minä*	I	*yksi*	one
katu	street	*kallis*	expensive	*he*	they	*kymmenen*	ten
nainen	woman	*pitkä*	long	*tämä*	this	*toinen*	second
hinta	price	*vanha*	old	*se*	it	*seitsemäs*	seventh

These four word-classes take the same endings, they are inflected in the same way. In addition to derivational suffixes, Finnish nominals can take four kinds of endings: number and case endings, possessive suffixes, and enclitic particles. The main features of all these will be introduced here, and they will be discussed in more detail in later chapters.

1) number The Finnish number system has two terms: singular and plural. The singular is never marked by an ending. The plural has two endings: **-t** in the nominative or basic form, and **-i-** in other cases.

SINGULAR		PLURAL	
auto	car	auto/**t**	cars
auto/ssa	in the car	auto/**i**/ssa	in the cars
auto/on	into the car	auto/**i**/hin	into the cars
pullo	bottle	pullo/**t**	bottles
pullo/sta	out of the botle	pullo/**i**/sta	out of the bottles
pullo/lla	with a bottle	pullo/**i**/lla	with the bottles

2) case Finnish has some 15 cases. The table below shows the grammatical names of the cases, their endings and basic meanings or functions. The principle of vowel harmony (§11) determines whether the ending variant contains a front or a back vowel.

CASE	ENDINGS	MEANINGS	EXAMPLE	MEANING[1]
nominative	— (pl. **-t**)	(basic form)	auto	car
genitive	**-n; -den, -tten**	possession	auto/n	of the car
accusative	**-n, -t, -**	object ending	häne/t	him, her
partitive	**-a ∼ -ä; -ta ∼ -tä;**	indefinite	maito/a	(some) milk
	-tta ∼ -ttä	quantity	vet/tä	(some) water
			perhe/ttä	(some) family
inessive	**-ssa ∼ -ssä**	inside	auto/ssa	in the car
elative	**-sta ∼ -stä**	out of	auto/sta	out of the car
illative	**-Vn, -hVn,**[2]	into	auto/on	into the car
	-seen, -siin		maa/han	into the country
			Porvoo/seen	to Porvoo

adessive	-lla ~ -llä	on; instrument	pöydä/llä	on the table
ablative	-lta ~ -ltä	off	pöydä/ltä	off the table
allative	-lle	onto	pöydä/lle	onto the table
essive	-na ~ -nä	state	opettaja/na	as a teacher
translative	-ksi	change of state	opettaja/ksi	(become) a teacher
comitative	-ine-	accompanying	vaimo/ine/ni	with my wife
instructive	-n	(idiomatic)	jala/n	on foot

3) possessor Listed below are the possessive suffixes; with the exception of the 3rd person, the endings are different for each person.

	SINGULAR		PLURAL	
1st PERSON	(minun) kirja/**ni**	my book	(meidän) kirja/**mme**	our book
2nd PERSON	(sinun) kirja/**si**	your book	(teidän) kirja/**nne**	your book
3rd PERSON	hänen kirja/**nsa**	his/her book	heidän kirja/**nsa**	their book

4) enclitic particles The fourth group of nominal suffixes is that of the enclitic particles; these occur also with finite and non-finite verb-forms. The most common particles are -**kin** 'also', -**ko** ~ -**kö** 'interrogative', -**han** ~ -**hän** 'emphasis', -**pa** ~ -**pä** 'emphasis'[3], and -**kaan** ~ -**kään** '(not...) either'. Examples:

Sinä/**kö** tulit?	Was it you that came?
Kekkonen/**ko** lähti Moskovaan?	Was it Kekkonen who went to Moscow?
Sinä/**hän** tulit.	It was you who came.
Sinä/**kin** tulit.	You came too.
Kekkonen/**kin** tuli.	Kekkonen came too.
Sinä/**kään** et tullut.	You didn't come either.
Kekkonen/**kaan** ei tullut.	Kekkonen didn't come either.

A Finnish nominal can have endings from all of the above four groups, but the order in which the endings occur is fixed: NUMBER + CASE + POSSESSIVE + PARTICLE. More examples are given in the diagram below. Each "ending box" also shows how many endings there are of that type. "Root" here means the basic form of the word, without any ending. Note that if a word contains derivational suffixes these occur between the root and the number ending.

---

[1] Translator's note: With the adessive and translative cases there is often no straightforward equivalent in English that can be used to gloss examples of isolated words. The meanings of these cases are explained in the relevant chapters below, but in the tables and short examples of the book the conventions adopted are as follows. The adessive ending is glossed 'on' where this could make sense ('on the table'), 'with' where an instrument interpretation would be more natural ('with a hammer'), 'at' or 'in' for places, and ' "at" ' for people etc. since in these latter contexts the adessive commonly marks the possessor (*minulla on* 'I have', glossed literally as ' "at" me is'). The translative is glossed 'to (become) + nominal' in order to indicate how it would be usually understood in context; thus e.g. *punaiseksi* would be glossed 'to (become) red', since the form would typically occur in such contexts as 'it became / turned / changed to red'. The essive is usually glossed 'as', although this might not be natural in all contexts. And the partitive is simply marked 'partitive', since it often corresponds to 'no article' in English.

[2] The sign -V- indicates a vowel which is the same as the nearest preceding vowel, e.g. Turku/**un** 'to Turku', Helsinki/**in** 'to Helsinki', maa/**han** 'into the country', tie/**hen** 'to the road'.

[3] Translator's note: Both -**han** and -**pa** are glossed 'emphasis' since an idiomatic translation in English would usually have to be structurally rather different. However, the two particles are not synonymous. -**han** often has the sense 'I assume you know' (*Mutta sehän on kallis* 'But it's expensive, isn't it?'), while -**pa** is closer to surprise or pure emphasis (*Onpa kallis!* 'That IS expensive!').

STRUCTURE OF NOMINALS

ROOT	NUMBER (2)	CASE (15)	POSSESSIVE (6)	PARTICLE (6)	EXAMPLE (written form)	MEANING
pullo					pullo	bottle
pullo	t				pullot	bottles
pullo		ssa			pullossa	in the bottle
pullo			ni		pulloni	my bottle
pullo				kin	pullokin	the bottle too
pullo	i	sta			pulloista	out of the bottles
pullo		sta	ni		pullostani	out of my bottle
pullo		ssa		han	pullossahan	in the bottle + emphasis
pullo	t			kin	pullotkin	the bottles too
pullo		ssa	si	ko	pullossasiko	in your bottle?
pullo	i	ssa	mme		pulloissamme	in our bottles
pullo	i	sta		kaan	pulloistakaan	(not) out of the bottles, either
pullo	i	ssa	nne	kin	pulloissannekin	in your bottles too
hylly		ssä			hyllyssä	in the shelf
hylly		llä			hyllyllä	on the shelf
hylly			si		hyllysi	your shelf
hylly		lle	si		hyllyllesi	onto your shelf
hylly		ltä		kö	hyllyltäkö	off the shelf?
hylly	t			kö	hyllytkö	shelves?
hylly		n		hän	hyllynhän	of the shelf + emphasis
talo		on			taloon	into the house
talo		na			talona	as a house
(hänen) talo			nsa	ko	(hänen) talonsako	his/her house?
(hänen) hylly			nsä		(hänen) hyllynsä	his/her shelf
hylly	i	llä	mme		hyllyillämme	on our shelves

finite
verb

A finite verb-form means a form with a personal ending, e.g. *(minä) tule/n* 'I come', *sinä tule/t* 'you come', *Maija tule/e* 'Maija comes'. In addition to person, Finnish finite verb-forms also inflect for tense, mood and the passive. The passive forms contain two endings: that of the passive itself, and also a personal ending -**Vn**. The enclitic particles can also be attached to finite verb-forms.

1) person

There are six personal endings, one for each grammatical person.

SINGULAR			PLURAL	
1st P	(minä) puhu/**n**	I speak	(me) puhu/**mme**	we speak
2nd P	(sinä) puhu/**t**	you (s.) speak	(te) puhu/**tte**	you (pl.) speak
3rd P	hän puhu/**u**	he/she speaks	he puhu/**vat**	they speak

2) tense

Finnish has two simple tenses: present, which indicates non-past time, and past, which indicates past time. There is no separate ending for the present, and the ending for the past tense is -**i**-. The personal endings occur after the tense ending.

PRESENT		PAST	
minä puhu/n	I speak	minä puhu/i/n	I spoke
me sano/mme	we say	me sano/i/mme	we said
he sano/vat	they say	he sano/i/vat	they said
te seiso/tte	you (pl.) stand	te seiso/i/tte	you (pl.) stood
sinä kysy/t	you (s.) ask	sinä kysy/i/t	you (s.) asked

3) mood

Finnish has four moods, which express e.g. the speaker's attitude to the content of the message.

INDICATIVE	Ø
CONDITIONAL	-isi-
POTENTIAL	-ne-
IMPERATIVE	see below

The indicative is the most common of the moods; it has no ending, and represents an action as a fact or as something that has happened. The conditional is mainly used in conditional clauses; cf. English *should*, Swedish *skulle* and the German subjunctive. The potential is a rare mood, presenting an action as possible.

   The personal ending is attached after the tense ending. The fourth mood, the imperative, is different in that its own ending often merges with the personal ending so that the two become indistinguishable.

	SINGULAR		PLURAL	
1st PERSON	—		sano/**kaamme**	let us say
2nd PERSON	sano	say!	sano/**kaa**	say!
3rd PERSON	sano/**koon**	may he say	sano/**koot**	may they say

The most common form is the 2nd person singular, which has no ending. Because of vowel harmony the endings for the other persons also have front-vowel variants: *vie/köön* 'may he take', *vie/käämme* 'let us take', *vie/kää* 'take!', *vie/kööt* 'may they take'. The 3rd person imperatives express a wish rather than a command, and these forms are rare.

4) passive The passive forms indicate that the performer of the action is an indefinite, unspecified person, cf. English *one* (can say that...) and German *man* (kann sagen dass...)[1]. The endings for the passive itself are **-tta ~ -ttä** and **-ta ~ -tä** depending on the structure of the preceding stem. Sometimes **a/ä** disappear.

These endings are attached directly to the root-form of the verb (or the derived stem). Possible tense and mood endings come after the passive ending, and after them comes the passive personal ending **-Vn**, where V again stands for a vowel which is the same as the nearest preceding vowel.

ACTIVE		PASSIVE	
sano/**n**	I say	sano/**ta**/**an**	one says, it is said
sano/isi/**n**	I would say	sano/**tta**/isi/**in**	one would say
sano/i/**n**	I said	sano/**tt**/i/**in**	one said

To conclude this section, the diagram below shows the order in which these endings occur (p. 27). The tense and mood endings are in the same box, since they are mutually exclusive (the same word-form may not contain both tense and mood endings). The imperative endings are between those for mood and person, since they have become merged. In final position there may be an enclitic particle.

§14. *NON-FINITE VERB-FORMS AND THEIR ENDINGS*

non-finite verb Non-finite verb-forms are those which, unlike finite verbs, do not contain personal endings. There are two kinds of non-finite forms: infinitives and participles. As regards the way they are used, infinitives can be compared to nouns and participles to adjectives.

Characteristic of non-finite verb-forms is a function ending which does not usually carry any real meaning but simply indicates that "this is a non-finite form". Some non-finite forms are inflected in the passive like finite verbs (participles, and the inessive case of the 2nd infinitive). Unlike finite verbs, but like nouns, non-finite forms often take a case ending and a possessive suffix. Participles are also inflected for number. Enclitic particles can be attached to all non-finite forms.

infinitives Finnish has three important infinitives. The main one is the 1st infinitive, which is the dictionary form of a verb. Each infinitive has its own function ending indicating which infinitive it is. Case inflection in the infinitives is very defective. The first infinitive occurs in only two cases (nominative and transla-

---

[1] Translator's note: the passive will usually be glossed with the impersonal 'one' in order to show the sense of the Finnish, but a corresponding English passive form will often sound more natural in context ('one says' — 'it is said').

26

STRUCTURE OF FINITE VERB-FORMS

ROOT	PASSIVE	TENSE, MOOD	PERSON	PARTICLE	EXAMPLE (written form)	MEANING
puhu			n		puhun	I speak
puhu			mme		puhumme	we speak
puhu		i	tte		puhuitte	you spoke
(he) puhu		isi	vat		(he) puhuisivat	they would speak
puhu			t	han	puhuthan	you will speak!
sano		i	n	ko	sanoinko?	did I say?
sano		isi	mme	ko	sanoisimmeko?	should we say?
sano	ta		an		sanotaan	one says, it is said
sano	tta	isi	in		sanottaisiin	one would say
sano	tt	i	in	han	sanottiinhan	one did say (+ emphasis)
sano	tta	ne	en		sanottaneen	one may say
sano			kaa		sanokaa	say!
sano			kaa	pa	sanokaapa	say! (+ emphasis)
sano			kaamme		sanokaamme	let us say
sano			koot		sanokoot	may they say
sano	tta		koon		sanottakoon	may, let one say
saa			n	ko	saanko?	do I get?
sa		isi	n	ko	saisinko?	might I get?
sa		i	t	han	saithan	you did get
syö	t	i	in		syötiin	one ate
syö	tä	isi	in		syötäisiin	one would eat
syö	tä	isi	in	kö	syötäisiinkö?	might one eat?
syö	t	i	in	kin	syötiinkin	one also ate

tive), the 2nd also in only two (inessive and instructive), and the 3rd in six (inessive, elative, illative, adessive, abessive and instructive). Infinitives do not appear in the plural. With some cases infinitives may also take a possessive suffix.

INFINITIVES

	FUNCTION ENDING	EXAMPLE	MEANING
1st	-a ~ -ä	sano/**a**	(to) say
	-da ~ -dä	syö/**dä**	(to) eat
	-ta ~ -tä	juos/**ta**	(to) run
2nd	-e-	sano/**e**/ssa/ni	while I say
	-de-	syö/**de**/ssä/mme	while we eat
	-te-	juos/**te**/n	running
3rd	-ma- ~ -mä-	sano/**ma**/lla	by saying
		sano/**ma**/tta	without saying
		sano/**ma**/an	(in order) to say
		syö/**mä**/llä	by eating

participles   Finnish has two participles, the present and the past, which have almost the same function as ordinary adjectives; they also occur in the compound forms of verbs. Participles also have passive forms. Being similar to adjectives, participles take all cases and are also inflected for number. They can sometimes take possessive suffixes. The active participles are given below.

ACTIVE PARTICIPLES

	FUNCTION ENDING	EXAMPLE	MEANING
PRESENT	-va ~ -vä	juo/**va**	drinking
		syö/**vä**	eating
PAST	-nut ~ -nyt	juo/**nut**	drunk
		syö/**nyt**	eaten

The following diagram (p. 29) shows the structure of the non-finite verb-forms, and the order of occurrence of the endings.

STRUCTURE OF NON-FINITE VERB-FORMS

ROOT	PASSIVE	NON-FIN. ENDING	NUMBER	CASE	POSSESS. SUFFIX	PARTICLE	EXAMPLE (written form)	MEANING
puhu		a					puhua	(to) speak
puhu		a		kse	si		puhuaksesi	*in order for* you to speak
puhu		ma		lla			puhumalla	by speaking
syö		dä					syödä	(to) eat
syö		dä		kse	mme		syödäksemme	in order for us to eat
puhu		va				kin	puhuvakin	(the) speaking (one) too
puhu		va		ssa		kin	puhuvassakin	in the speaking (one) too
puhu		v	i	ssa		kin	puhuvissakin	in the speaking (ones) too
puhu		va	t				puhuvat	(the) speaking (ones)
(on) puhu		nut					(on) puhunut	(has) spoken
(ovat) puhu		nee	t				(ovat) puhuneet	(have) spoken
syö		mä		än			syömään	*(in order)* to eat
juo		ma		an			juomaan	*(in order)* to drink
juo		ma		an		ko	juomaanko?	*(in order)* to drink?
syö		mä		ttä			syömättä	without eating
juo		ma		tta		han	juomattahan	without drinking + emph.
juo	ta	va					juotava	that can be drunk
(on) sano	ttu						(on) sanottu	(one has) said
sano	tu			sta			sanotusta	out of the said (thing)
sano	tta	va					sanottava	(the) to-be-said (thing)
sano	tta	va		lla			sanottavalla	by the to-be-said (thing)
sano	tta	v	i	lla			sanottavilla	by the to-be-said (things)
sano	tta	v	i	ssa		ko	sanottavissako?	in the to-be-said (things)?
syö	tä	e		ssä			syötäessä	while one eats
vetä		mä		llä		hän	vetämällähän	by pulling + emph.
vetä		e		ssä	si		vetäessäsi	while you pull
syö	ty	vä		ä	mme		syötyämme	we having eaten
(...Kallen) syö		vä		n			(Kallen) syövän	(Kallen) eating

4 Two Important Sound Alternations

Consonant gradation (p, t, k)
Vowel changes before -i- endings

§15. *CONSONANT GRADATION (p, t, k)*

It would be easy to form Finnish words if all the endings were attached mechanically one after the other according to the patterns given above for nominals and finite and non-finite verb-forms. But the adding of endings is in fact a more complex matter, since endings are often accompanied by sound alternations (changes) in the stem (to the left of the ending).

The most important of these changes is that known as consonant gradation, which affects the stops **p**, **t** and **k** in both long and short forms. Section 15.1 below outlines the various types of alternation. Section 15.2 deals with the conditions determining the changes, and also presents some important rules. Sections 15.3—5 contain a great many examples to show how the rules are applied, and section 15.6 gives some special cases. The form to which the rules of consonant gradation are applied is called the "strong grade", and the resulting alternative form is called the "weak grade".

§15.1. *The types of consonant gradation*

The *long* consonants alternate with the corresponding short consonants.

	ALTERNATION				EXAMPLE		
	1)	pp	—	p	kaappi	cupboard	kaapi/ssa	in the cupboard
pp, tt, kk	2)	tt	—	t	matto	mat	mato/lla	on the mat
	3)	kk	—	k	kukka	flower	kuka/n	of the flower

The *short* consonants generally alternate with other consonants; however, **k** may sometimes be dropped altogether. The most important alternations of this type are (4—7).

ALTERNATION				EXAMPLE		
4)	p	—	v	tupa	hut	tuva/ssa	in the hut
5)	Vt	—	Vd	katu	street	kadu/lla	on the street
6)	ht	—	hd	lähte-	leave	lähde/n	I leave
7)	k	—	—	jalka	foot	jala/n	of the foot

30

t changes to **d** both after a vowel, **V**, and after **h**. A different type of alternation takes place in the following five cases, where either **p, t, k** occur after a nasal consonant (**m, n,** η), or **t** occurs after **l** or **r**.

p, t, k
after nasals

	ALTERNATION			EXAMPLE		
8)	mp — mm	ampu-	shoot	ammu/mme	we shoot
9)	nt — nn	ranta	shore	ranna/lla	on the shore
10)	nk — ng [$\eta\eta$]	kenkä	shoe	kengä/n	of the shoe
11)	lt — ll	kulta	gold	kulla/n	of the gold
12)	rt — rr	parta	beard	parra/ssa	in the beard

t after
l and r

Alternations (4—7), therefore, operate when the stops are not preceded by a nasal consonant or **l** or **r**: in such cases alternations (8—12) apply. In addition to these there are also four fairly rare alternations applying to **k**.

special
cases
with k

	ALTERNATION			EXAMPLE		
13)	lke — lje	polke-	trample	polje/n	I trample
14)	rke — rje	särke-	break	särje/n	I break
15)	hke — hje	rohkene/t	you dare	rohjet/a	(to) dare
16)	k — v	puku	dress	puvu/n	of the dress

Alternations (13—15) are very similar: in each of these **k** changes to **j** before **e**. Type (16) is rare, and occurs only in a few nominals, when **k** is preceded and followed by **u/y**.

§15.2. *The rules of consonant gradation*

All the alternations (1—16) are determined by the same set of conditions. Stops change in the stem of words with two or more syllables when certain endings are added. The change is determined partly by the vowels between the stop and the ending (alternation occurs only if the vowels are short; there is no alternation if this position is taken by a long vowel or a consonant), and partly by the following ending (alternation is caused only by certain types of case and personal ending). The following basic rule **A** applies to all words, nominals as well as verbs.

basic
rule

A

> IN POLYSYLLABIC STEMS **p, t, k** ARE SUBJECT TO CONSONANT GRADATION IF THEY ARE FOLLOWED BY AN ENDING WHICH
>
> a) CONSISTS OF ONLY ONE CONSONANT or
> b) BEGINS WITH TWO CONSONANTS,
> and also on condition that
> c) BETWEEN **p, t, k** AND THE ENDING THERE IS ONLY A SHORT VOWEL OR A DIPHTHONG (not consonants or a syllable boundary)

additional specifications for rule **A**	d) THE ENDING CAUSING CONSONANT GRADATION IS USUALLY THE CASE ENDING IN NOMINALS AND THE PERSONAL ENDING IN VERBS e) BETWEEN THIS ENDING AND THE CONSONANTS **p, t, k** THERE CAN BE AN **i**-ENDING (plural or past tense) f) ALTERNATION NEVER OCCURS BEFORE A LONG VOWEL g) THERE IS NO ALTERNATION IN MONOSYLLABIC STEMS

In addition to the basic rule **A** there is a second rule **B**, which governs consonant gradation in verbs only.

B special alternations in verbs	**p, t, k** IN VERBS ARE ALWAYS SUBJECT TO CONSONANT GRADATION BEFORE A SHORT VOWEL IF THEY OCCUR a) BEFORE THE PASSIVE ENDING (e.g. -tta- ~ -ttä-, -ta- ~ -tä-) b) IN THE 2nd PERSON SINGULAR IMPERATIVE c) IN THE PRESENT INDICATIVE NEGATIVE

Cases (**B**:b, c) are in fact equivalent, since these verb-forms are always the same, e.g. *kerro*! 'tell!' ~ *en kerro* 'I do not tell'; *anna*! 'give' ~ *en anna* 'I do not give'.

The examples below illustrate the way in which the basic rule **A** is applied to the noun *katto* 'roof', where there is alternation between **tt** and **t**. It is the structure of the following case ending (**A**:b) that primarily determines whether the alternation occurs or not; the reason is given on the right.

katto	roof	NO	no ending
kato/**n**	of the roof	YES	ending consists of one consonant
kato/**lla**	on the roof	YES	ending begins with two consonants
katto/na	as a roof	NO	ending does not consist of one consonant or begin with two
kato/**lta**	from the roof	YES	ending begins with two consonants
katto/on	into the roof	NO	no alternation before a long vowel
kato/**lle**	onto the roof	YES	ending begins with two consonants
kato/**t**	roofs	YES	ending consists of one consonant
kato/i/**lla**	on the roofs	YES	ending begins with two consonants; in between there can be an ending consisting of **i**
katto/i/na	as roof	NO	see katto/na
kato/**ksi**	to (become) a roof	YES	ending begins with two consonants
katto/mme	our roof	NO	no alternation before a possessive suffix

katto/kin	a roof, too	NO	ending does not consist of one consonant or begin with two
kato/i/**lle**	onto the roofs	YES	ending begins with two consonants; in between there can be an ending consisting of **i**
katto/i/hin	into the roofs	NO	ending does not consist of one consonant or begin with two
kato/i/**lta**	from the roofs	YES	ending begins with two consonants; in between there can be an ending consisting of **i**
katto/nne	your roof	NO	no alternation before a possessive suffix
katto/a	roof (partitive)	NO	ending does not consist of one consonant or begin with two
katto/j/en	of the roofs	NO	same as above; **j** = the plural **i**

The two following sections contain further examples of the application of rules **A** and **B**, in both nominals and verbs.

§15.3. *Applying the basic rule to nominals*

The table below (p. 34) shows how consonant gradation applies to the word *katu* 'street', where the alternation is of type (5); **t** changes to **d**. The examples are given in the form of the familiar box diagram; the actual word-form is written on the right, followed by the reason for the occurrence or non-occurrence of the alternation.

The nominative plural ending -**t** also causes consonant gradation. This form shows both number and case. In accordance with the basic rule, alternation occurs only before *short* vowels. The vowels of diphthongs are short, and therefore there is usually alternation before a diphthong: kato/**lla** 'on the roof' ~ kato/i/**lla** 'on the roofs'. The latter form has the diphthong **oi**, before which consonant gradation occurs. (However, the type *renka/i/ssa* 'in the rings' is an exception to this diphthong rule: see below.)

no alternation before long vowels Before *long* vowels the rules of consonant gradation do not apply, even if the case ending does consist of one consonant or begin with two. Nominals with an inflectional stem ending in a long vowel (§§19, 20.3) are unaffected by consonant gradation in almost all singular and plural case forms, including those where the otherwise long stem vowel shortens before the plural ending **i** (§16). The examples below illustrate what happens in the inflection of *rengas : renkaa-* 'ring'.

NOTE plural forms

SINGULAR		PLURAL	
re**nk**aa/n	of the ring	re**nk**aa/t	rings
re**nk**aa/ssa	in the ring	re**nk**a/i/ssa	in the rings
re**nk**aa/sta	out of the ring	re**nk**a/i/sta	out of the rings
re**nk**aa/lla	with the ring	re**nk**a/i/lla	with the rings
re**nk**aa/na	as a ring	re**nk**a/i/na	as rings
re**nk**aa/seen	into the ring	re**nk**a/i/siin	into the rings
re**nk**aa/lta	from the ring	re**nk**a/i/lta	from the rings

ROOT	NUMBER	CASE	POSS. SUFFIX	PARTICLE	WRITTEN FORM	MEANING	CONSONANT GRADATION?	REASON
katu		n			kadun	of the street	YES	case ending of 1 cons.
katu			nne		katunne	your street	NO	no case ending
katu				kin	katukin	the street, too	NO	no case ending
katu		lla			kadulla	on the street	YES	case ending begins 2 cons.
katu		na			katuna	as a street	NO	case ending is 1 cons. + vowel
katu		lle			kadulle	onto the street	YES	case ending begins 2 cons.
katu		a			katua	street (part.)	NO	case ending is vowel
katu	i	lla			kaduilla	on the streets	YES	case ending begins 2 cons.
katu			mme	ko	katummeko?	our street?	NO	no case ending
katu	t				kadut	streets	YES	case ending of 1 cons.
katu				han	katuhan	street + emph.	NO	no case ending
katu	j	a			katuja	streets (part.)	NO	case ending is vowel
katu	i	ssa			kaduissa	in the streets	YES	case ending begins 2 cons.
katu		n		pa	kadunpa	of the street + emph.	YES	case ending of 1 cons.
katu		lta	nne		kadultanne	from your street	YES	case ending begins 2 cons.
katu	i	na			katuina	as streets	NO	case ending of cons. + vowel
katu	t			han	kaduthan	streets + emph.	YES	case ending of 1 cons.
katu		un			katuun	into the street	NO	long vowel

In these words the vowel preceding the plural **i** counts as long because it is long in almost all the corresponding singular forms.

In words of the *rengas : renkaa-* type consonant gradation does apply, however, in two case forms: the nominative singular, which ends either in a short vowel + **s** (§20.3) or in **-e** (§19), and the partitive singular; occasionally also the genitive plural. Cf. ren**gas** 'ring' (nom. sing.) : ren**gas**/ta (part. sing.) : ren**gas**/ten (gen. pl.). Further examples of this type:

	ALTERNATION		STEM	BASIC FORM (nom. sing.)	MEANING
(1)	pp	— p	saappaa-	saapas	boot
(2)	tt	— t	rattaa-	ratas	wheel
(3)	kk	— k	rakkaa-	rakas	dear
(4)	p	— v	varpaa-	varvas	toe
(5)	t	— d	hitaa-	hidas	slow
(6)	ht	— hd	tehtaa-	tehdas	factory
(8)	mp	— mm	lampaa-	lammas	lamb
(9)	nt	— nn	kintaa-	kinnas	mitten
(10)	nk	— ng	kuninkaa-	kuningas	king
(11)	lt	— ll	altaa-	allas	basin
(12)	rt	— rr	portaa-	porras	step
(13)	lke	— lje	hylkee-	hylje	seal
(15)	hke	— hje	pohkee-	pohje	calf (of leg)

We thus have saa**pas** 'boot' (nom. sing.) and saa**pas**/ta (part. sing.) but saa**ppaa**/n (gen. sing.), saa**ppaa**/ssa (iness. sing.), saa**ppaa**/na (ess. sing.), saa**ppaa**/t (nom. pl.), saa**ppa**/i/ssa (iness. pl.), saa**ppa**/i/ta (part. pl.), etc.

the type
keittiö
In three-syllable nominals like *keittiö* 'kitchen', *lapio* 'spade', *herttua* 'duke', where there is a syllable boundary between the two final vowels in the basic form (§9), there is no consonant gradation (A:c). They are thus inflected keittiö/n (gen. sing.), keittiö/ssä (iness. sing.), keittiö/tä (part. sing.), keittiö/i/ssä (iness. pl.), etc.

§15.4. *Applying the rules to verbs*

rules
A and B
In verbs the personal ending generally determines whether or not consonant gradation occurs (A:d). In addition to the basic rule verbs are also governed by rule **B**: the rules of consonant gradation are always applied before the passive ending, and also in the 2nd person singular imperative and the present indicative negative.

Let us take the verb *kerto-* '(to) tell' as an example (see p. 37): **rt** alternates with **rr** (type 12). On the right of the table there is an indication of whether or not consonant gradation has occurred, and a brief explanation.

Note condition (A:e): there may be the past tense ending -**i**- between an alternating **p**, **t** or **k** and the personal ending. But the rules of consonant gradation cannot be applied if this mid-position contains the conditional -**isi**- or the potential -**ne**- ending. We therefore have ke**rro**/i/n 'I told' but ke**rto**/isi/n 'I would tell' and ke**rto**/ne/n 'I may tell'.

As with nominals, consonant gradation does not occur before long vowels in verbs either (A:c). In the following important class of verbs, known as contracted verbs (§23.2), there is thus no consonant gradation in the present, nor in the past either although the vowel is shortened (§60).

	PRESENT			PAST	
	hyppää/n	I jump		hyppä/si/n	I jumped
	hyppää/t	you (sing.) jump		hyppä/si/t	you (sing.) jumped
(hän)	hyppää	he/she jumps	(hän)	hyppä/si	he/she jumped
	hyppää/mme	we jump		hyppä/si/mme	we jumped
	hyppää/tte	you (pl.) jump.		hyppä/si/tte	you (pl.) jumped
(he)	hyppää/vät	they jump	(he)	hyppä/si/vät	they jumped

In addition, contracted verbs are not affected by consonant gradation in the 2nd person singular imperative, nor in the present indicative negative: hyppää! 'jump' ∿ en hyppää 'I do not jump'. But these verbs do have a few inflected forms where the otherwise long stem vowel is shortened, the second vowel being replaced by a linking consonant t comparable to the case and personal endings that do cause consonant gradation (A:a), e.g. hyppää/n 'I jump' : hypät/ä '(to) jump'. The following forms are based on a stem containing the linking consonant, and consonant gradation therefore applies.

NB:	1st INFINITIVE	hypät/ä	(to) jump
consonant	2nd INFINITIVE	hypät/e/n	jumping
gradation	PASSIVE	hypät/t/i/in	one jumped
	IMPERATIVE	hypät/kää	jump! (plural; not 2nd person sing.)
	PAST PARTICIPLE	hypän/nyt	jumped (NOTE: t has changed to n)

Almost all types of consonant gradation may occur with contracted verbs:

	ALTERNATION			LONG VOWEL STEM	BASIC FORM	MEANING
(1)	pp	—	p	sieppaa-	siepat/a	snatch
(2)	tt	—	t	konttaa-	kontat/a	crawl
(3)	kk	—	k	hakkaa-	hakat/a	hew
(4)	p	—	v	kelpaa-	kelvat/a	be good enough
(5)	Vt	—	Vd	hautaa-	haudat/a	bury
(6)	ht	—	hd	rahtaa-	rahdat/a	freight
(7)	k	—	—	makaa-	maat/a	lie
(8)	mp	—	mm	kampaa-	kammat/a	comb
(9)	nt	—	nn	ryntää-	rynnät/ä	rush
(10)	nk	—	ng	hankaa-	hangat/a	rub
(11)	lt	—	ll	valtaa-	vallat/a	conquer
(12)	rt	—	rr	virtaa-	virrat/a	flow

For further discussion see §23.2. The section below (p. 38) includes more examples of consonant gradation in both nominals and verbs.

ROOT	PASSIVE	TENSE/-MOOD	PERSON	PARTICLE	WRITTEN FORM	MEANING	CONSONANT	REASON
kerto			n		kerron	I tell	YES	personal ending of 1 cons.
kerto			mme		kerromme	we tell	YES	pers. ending begins 2 cons.
kerto		isi	mme		kertoisimme	we would tell	NO	conditional mood -isi-
kerto	ta	i	an		kerrotaan	one tells	YES	passive
kerto		i	tte		kerroitte	you (pl.) told	YES	pers. ending begins 2 cons.
kerto			vat		kertovat	they tell	NO	pers. ending begins cons. + vowel
kerto		i	vat		kertoivat	they told	NO	pers. ending begins cons. + vowel
(ei) kerto		—			ei kerro	does not tell	YES	pres. indic. neg.
kerto	tt	i	in		kerrottiin	one told	YES	passive
kerto		—	o		kertoo	tells	NO	pers. ending of a vowel
kerto					kerro!	tell! (sing.)	YES	2nd pers. sing. imp.
kerto		kaa			kertokaa	tell! (pl.)	NO	ending of cons. + vowel
kerto			t		kerrot	you (sing.) tell	YES	pers. ending of 1 cons.
kerto		i	t		kerroit	you (sing.) told	YES	pers. ending of 1 cons.
kerto		ne	tte		kertonette	you (pl.) may tell	NO	potential mood -ne-
kerto		—		pa	kerropa!	tell! + emph.	YES	2nd pers. sing. imp.
kerto			tte	han	kerrottehan	you (pl.) tell + emph.	YES	pers. ending begins 2 cons.
kerto			t	ko	kerrotko?	do you (sing.) tell?	YES	pers. ending of 1 cons.
kerto		isi	vat	ko	kertoisivatko?	would they tell?	NO	conditional mood -isi-

§15.5. *More examples of types of consonant gradation*

(1)	pp	—	p	kauppa	shop	kaupassa	in the shop
				lamppu	lamp	lamput	lamps
				tappa-	kill	tapan	I kill
(2)	tt	—	t	katto	roof	katolla	on the roof
				käyttä-	use	käytämme	we use
				otta-	take	otan	I take
(3)	kk	—	k	takki	coat	takissani	in my coat
				kaikke-	everything	kaikessa	in everything
				nukku-	sleep	nukuimme	we slept
(4)	p	—	v	kylpe-	bathe	kylven	I bathe
				kipu	pain	kivussa	in pain
				korpe-	wilderness	korvesta	out of the wilderness
(5)	t	—	d	tietä-	know	tiedätkö?	do you know?
				vetä-	pull	vedä!	pull! (2nd. pers. sing.)
				äiti	mother	äidille	to mother
(6)	ht	—	hd	vihta	whisk	vihdalla	with a whisk
				vaihta-	change	vaihdatteko?	do you change?
				lehte-	newspaper	lehdessä	in the newspaper
(7)	k	—	—	joke-	river	joesta	out of the river
				jaka-	divide	jaamme	we divide
				poika	boy	pojalle	to the boy
				aika	time	ajassa	in time
(8)	mp	—	mm	ampu-	shoot	ammutaan	one shoots
				kampa	comb	kammalla	with a comb
(9)	nt	—	nn	tunte-	feel	ei tunne	does not feel
				anta-	give	annamme	we give
				ranta	shore	rannalla	on the shore
(10)	nk	—	ng	kenkä	shoe	kengästä	out of the shoe
				tunke-	shove	älä tunge!	dont shove! (2nd pers. sing.)
				tinki-	bargain	tingitkö?	do you bargain?
(11)	lt	—	ll	ilta	evening	illalla	in the evening
				kulta	gold	kullaksi	to (become) gold
				viheltä-	whistle	vihellän	I whistle
(12)	rt	—	rr	kiertä-	turn	kierrä!	turn! (2nd pers. sing.)
				kerta	time	kerran	once
				kerto-	tell	kerronko?	do I tell?
(13)	lke	—	lje	sulke-	close	suljemme	we close
				jälke-	trace	jäljet	traces
				kulke-	go	kuljet	you go
(14)	rke	—	rje	särke-	break	särjetkö?	do you break?
				arke-	everyday	arjen	of everyday
(15)	hke	—	hje	rohkene	dare	rohjeta	(to) dare
(16)	k	—	v	suku	family	suvussa	in the family
				puku	dress	puvut	dresses
				luku	number	luvuksi	to (become) a number

Type (13) and particularly types (14—16) are rare.

§15.6. *Additional comments*

Besides the case and personal endings dealt with above there are also certain other endings which cause consonant gradation, in particular the ending -**sti** on adjectives (which forms adverbs from them), the comparative ending -**mpi** (§85), and the superlative ending -**in** (§86). Note also the semantically negative derivational suffix -**ton** ~ -**tön**: ko**t**i 'home' : ko**d**i/ton 'homeless'; pal**kk**a 'salary' : pal**k**a/ton 'unsalaried'.

BASIC FORM	ADVERBS	COMPARATIVE	SUPERLATIVE
kil**tt**i	kil**t**i/sti	kil**t**i/mpi	kil**t**e/in
nice	nicely	nicer	nicest
tar**kk**a	tar**k**a/sti	tar**k**e/mpi	tar**k**/in
accurate	accurately	more accurate	most accurate
hel**pp**o	hel**p**o/sti	hel**p**o/mpi	hel**p**o/in
easy	easily	easier	easiest

p, t, k do not undergo consonant gradation when they occur next to **s** or **t**. **k** in the combination **hk** alternates occasionally.

sk	tasku	pocket	taskusta	out of the pocket
	laske-	count	lasket	you count
sp	piispa	bishop	piispat	bishops
st	pistä-	sting	pistän	I sting
	piste	point	pisteet	points
tk	matka	journey	matkalla	on the journey
	potki-	kick	potkimme	we kick
hk	keuhko	lung	keuhkot	lungs
	vihki-	marry	vihkitte	you marry
NOTE:	vihko	notebook	vihot	notebooks
NOTE:	nahka	leather	nahasta	out of leather

Many loanwords and proper names do not have consonant gradation. This is particularly true of alternation types (4—16).

loanwords, proper names	auto	car	autolla	by car
	Malta	Malta	Maltan	of Malta
	Kauko	(masculine name)	Kaukolle	to Kauko
	Arto	(masculine name)	Artolta	from Arto

§16. *VOWEL CHANGES BEFORE -I- ENDINGS*

The second important group of sound alternations is the set of vowel changes which often occur before certain endings beginning with -**i**. These endings are:

IN NOMINALS	IN VERBS
the plural -**i**- (sometimes -**j**-: see §26)	the past -**i**-
the superlative -**in** (of adjectives)	the conditional -**isi**-

The vowel changes are often the same for all these endings, but there are also some differences. Eight rules are given below.

---

1) THE SHORT VOWELS -o, -ö, -u, -y (i.e. rounded vowels) DO NOT CHANGE BEFORE -i- ENDINGS

	BASIC FORM	PLURAL		BASIC FORM	SUPERLATIVE	
	talo	taloissa	in the houses	helppo	helpoin	easiest
	pöllö	pöllöille	to the owls	jörö	jöröin	crossest
	katu	kaduilla	on the streets	hullu	hulluin	craziest
	hylly	hyllyissä	in the shelves	pidetty	pidetyin	most liked

	BASIC FORM	PAST			CONDITIONAL	
1) no change if -o, -ö, -u, -y	sano-	sanoi	said		sanoisi	would say
	löhö-	löhöi	lounged		löhöisi	would lounge
	puhu-	puhui	spoke		puhuisi	would speak
	pysähty-	pysähtyi	stopped		pysähtyisi	would stop

---

2) A LONG VOWEL SHORTENS

	BASIC FORM	PLURAL		BASIC FORM	SUPERLATIVE	
	puu	puita	trees (part.)	vapaa	vapain	most free
2) a long vowel shortens	maa	maissa	in the countries	vakaa	vakain	firmest
	syy	syiden	of the reasons	tervee-	tervein	healthiest
	venee-	veneistä	out of the boats			
	perhee-	perheissä	in the families			

	BASIC FORM	PAST			CONDITIONAL	
	saa-	sai	got		saisi	would get
	jää-	jäi	remained		jäisi	would remain
	avaa-	avasi	opened		avaisi	would open
	makaa-	makasi	lay (cf. §60)		makaisi	would lie

---

3) THE FIRST VOWEL OF THE DIPHTHONGS ie, uo, yö IS DROPPED

		PLURAL		(there are no adjectives)
3) ie, uo, yö, → e, o, ö	tie	teillä	on the roads	
	tuo	noissa	in those	
	yö	öitä	nights (part.)	
	suo	soista	out of the marshes	
	työ	töiden	of the works	

		PAST			CONDITIONAL	
	vie-	vei	took		veisi	would take
	juo-	joi	drank		joisi	would drink
	syö-	söi	ate		söisi	would open
	tuo-	toi	brought		toisi	would bring
	lyö-	löi	hit		löisi	would hit

4) i IS DROPPED IN DIPHTHONGS ENDING IN -i

4) -i is dropped in diphthongs

	PLURAL		(there are no adjectives)
hai	ha/i/ssa	in the sharks	
koi	ko/i/ta	moths (part.)	
täi	tä/i/den	of the lice	

	PAST			CONDITIONAL	
voi-	vo/i	could		vo/isi	would be able
ui-	u/i	swam		u/isi	would swim
nai-	na/i	married		na/isi	would marry

5) SHORT e IS ALWAYS DROPPED

5) -e is always dropped

	PLURAL			SUPERLATIVE	
tuule-	tuulia	winds (part.)	nuore-	nuorin	youngest
tule-	tulia	fires (part.)	suure-	suurin	greatest
lapse-	lapsilla	"at" the children	uute-	uusin	newest
kiele-	kielinä	as languages			
naise-	naisille	to the women			

	PAST			CONDITIONAL	
tule-	tuli	came		tulisi	would come
mene-	meni	went		menisi	would go
ole-	oli	was		olisi	would be
hymyile-	hymyili	smiled		hymyilisi	would smile
teke-	teki	did		tekisi	would do
näke-	näki	saw		näkisi	would see

6) SHORT i CHANGES TO e BEFORE THE PLURAL AND THE SUPERLATIVE, BUT IS DROPPED BEFORE THE PAST AND THE CONDITIONAL

6a) -i → e

	PLURAL			SUPERLATIVE	
lasi	laseissa	in the glasses	kiltti	kiltein	nicest
tuoli	tuoleilla	on the chairs	nätti	nätein	prettiest
väri	väreinä	as colours			
tunti	tunneilla	in the lessons			

6b) -i is dropped

	PAST			CONDITIONAL	
salli-	sall/i	allowed		sall/isi	would allow
etsi-	ets/i	looked for		ets/isi	would look for
oppi-	opp/i	learned		opp/isi	would learn
vaati-	vaat/i	demanded		vaat/isi	would demand

7) ä IS DROPPED EXCEPT IN THE CONDITIONAL

7) -ä is dropped

	PLURAL			SUPERLATIVE	
päivä	päiviä	days (part.)	syvä	syvin	deepest
ystävä	ystävillä	"at" the friends	ikävä	ikävin	dullest
			kylmä	kylmin	coldest
seinä	seinien	of the walls	märkä	märin	wettest
kylä	kyliin	into the villages	hämärä	hämärin	dimmest
hedelmä	hedelmiä	fruit (part.)			

NB : not in the conditional

	PAST			CONDITIONAL	
vetä-	veti	pulled		vetäisi	would pull
kestä-	kesti	lasted		kestäisi	would last
kiittä-	kiitti	thanked		kiittäisi	would thank
viettä-	vietti	spent		viettäisi	would spend
tietä-	tiesi	knew		tietäisi	would know

Contrary to this rule, in some three-syllable *nouns* -ä changes in the plural to -ö, e.g. when the only vowel of the preceding syllable is i: kynttilä : kynttilö/i/tä 'candles (part.)', tekijä : tekijö/i/tä 'makers (part.)', päärynä : päärynö/i/ssä 'in the pears'.

---

8) a REMAINS UNCHANGED IN THE CONDITIONAL AND IS DROPPED IN THE PAST. IN THE PLURAL AND PAST TENSE OF TWO-SYLLABLE WORDS a CHANGES TO o IF THE FIRST VOWEL OF THE WORD IS a, e OR i, BUT IS DROPPED IF THE FIRST VOWEL IS u OR o

8a) -a remains

	CONDITIONAL	
anta-	antaisi	would give
otta-	ottaisi	would take
sata-	sataisi	would rain
muista-	muistaisi	would remember
alka-	alkaisi	would begin

8b) -a is dropped

	SUPERLATIVE	
kova	kovin	hardest
vahva	vahvin	strongest
tarkka	tarkin	most accurate
vanha	vanhin	oldest
matala	matalin	lowest

8c) -a changes to -o after i, e and a...

	PLURAL			PAST	
matka	matkoilla	on the journeys	alka-	alkoi	began
kirja	kirjoissa	in the books	anta-	antoi	gave
sana	sanoilla	with words	sata-	satoi	rained
piha	pihoilla	in the yards	kaata-	kaatoi	fell
herra	herrojen	of the masters	raata-	raatoi	toiled

42

8d) ...but is dropped after **u** and **o**	PLURAL			PAST		
	koira	koirien	of the dogs	otta-	otti	took
	poika	poikien	of the boys	muista-	muisti	remembered
	muna	munia	eggs (part.)	osta-	osti	bought
	kuuma	kuumissa	in the hot	huuta-	huusi	shouted

polysyllabic nouns

In *nouns* with three or more syllables -**a** either changes to -**o** or is dropped; sometimes both changes may be possible. The change to -**o** occurs in particular when a) the only vowel of the preceding syllable is **i**; b) -**a** is preceded by a short **l**, **n** or **r**; or c) -**a** is preceded by two consonants.

-**a** → **o** after **i**	a) lukija	lukijoiden	of the readers
	apina	apinoilla	"at" the monkeys
	pakina	pakinoissa	in the columns
	vakoilija	vakoilijoille	to the spies
after **l, n, r**	b) omena	omenoita	apples (part.)
	ikkuna	ikkunoissa	in the windows
	tavara	tavaroita	things (part.)
	kampela	kampeloita	flounders (part.)
after two consonants	c) kirsikka	kirsikoihin	into the cherries
	vasikka	vasikoille	to the calves
	sanonta	sanontojen	of the expressions
	jalusta	jalustoilla	on the pedestals

In the plural forms of other nouns of three or more syllables, and of nearly all adjectives, and also in the past tense of verbs with three or more syllables, -**a** is dropped.

-**a** is dropped	kanava	kanavissa	in the canals
	korkea	korkeiden	of the high
	sanoma	sanomia	messages (part.)
	ainoa	ainoissa	in the only
	vaikea	vaikeita	difficult (part.)
	ihana	ihania	lovely (part.)
	kamala	kamalia	frightful (part.)
	matkusta-	matkusti	travelled
	pohjusta-	pohjusti	founded

5 The Declension of Nominals

§17. GENERAL

Both nominals and verb-forms are built up by the addition of endings to stems. For nominals, in general the basic form itself functions as the stem, and in many declension types the basic form remains unchanged when endings are added: e.g. *auto/n, auto/ssa, auto/on, auto/ni, auto/kin.* However, sound alternations may sometimes occur with certain endings; **p**, **t**, and **k** in the stem are subject to consonant gradation (§15), and the final vowel may change or disappear when an **i**-ending is added (§16).

stems   A word may sometimes have different stems according to what kind of ending follows. The different stems are formed via sound alternations. Often the basic form (nom. sing.), or the basic form and the partitive singular have their own stems, and all other case, number and possessive endings are **inflectional** attached to a second or third stem. This is called the inflectional stem. **stem**

Nominals where the basic form differs from the inflectional stem can be divided into three groups. The first consists of nominals with a basic form ending in -**i** and a corresponding inflectional stem in -**e**, e.g. kiel**i** 'language' : kiel**e**/n. The second group comprises nominals with a basic form ending in -**e** and an inflectional stem in -**ee**, e.g. perh**e** 'family' : perh**ee**/n. And in the third group the basic form ends in a consonant which alternates with other sounds in the inflectional stem, e.g. kysym**ys** 'question' : kysym**ykse**/n.

In the following sections these groups are presented in turn. The inflectional stem is represented by the genitive form, e.g. *kiele/n, perhee/n, kysymykse/n.* **genitive** Almost all the other forms can be made by replacing the genitive ending -**n** by **gives the** other endings: *kiele/n : kiele/ssä, kiele/stä, kiele/llä, kiele/ni, kiele/mme,* **inflectional** etc. The following rule is therefore an important one: **stem**

> ALL CASE, NUMBER AND POSSESSIVE FORMS ARE FORMED FROM THE INFLECTIONAL STEM (although the partitive singular sometimes has a separate stem)

The rules of consonant gradation and vowel change affect both basic form stems and inflectional stems.

Some examples now follow of how the inflectional stem *kiele-* is combined with various nominal endings marking case, number and possession.

BASIC FORM		INFLECTIONAL STEM + CASE	
kieli	language	kiele/n	of the language
		kiele/t	languages
		kiele/ssä	in the language
		kiele/stä	out of the language
		kiele/en	into the language
		kiele/llä	with the language
		kiele/lle	to the language
		kiele/nä	as the language
		kiel/tä	language (part.)
			etc.

NOTE:
-e is
dropped in
part. sing.

INFLECTIONAL STEM + PLURAL		INFLECTIONAL STEM + POSSESSIVE	
kiel/i/ssä	in languages	kiele/ni	my language
kiel/i/stä	out of languages	kiele/si	your language
kiel/i/in	into languages	kiele/nsä	his/her/their language
kiel/i/llä	with languages	kiele/mme	our language
kiel/i/nä	as languages	kiele/nne	your language
kiel/i/lle	to languages		
	etc.		

Enclitic particles are attached directly to the inflected or uninflected form.

kieli/*kin*	the language too
kiele/n/*hän*	of the language + emph.
kiele/ssä/*hän*	in the language + emph.
kiel/tä/*kö*?	language? (part.)
kiel/i/ssä/*hän*	in languages + emph.
kiele/ni/*pä*	my language + emph.

§18. *NOMINALS WITH A BASIC FORM IN* -i

§18.1. Most nominals with a basic form ending in -i do not have a separate inflectional stem, but endings are attached directly to the basic form itself (and consonant gradation and vowel change rule consequently apply, §§15, 16). These nominals of the type **tunti** 'hour, lesson' include the following. The plus sign indicates that the form has undergone consonant gradation.

tunti-
nominals

45

| | BASIC FORM | | INFLECTIONAL STEM FOLLOWED BY | | |
			CASE	PLURAL	POSSESSIVE SUFFIX
-i → e **in plural**	tunti	hour	+tunni/n	+tunne/i/ssa	tunti/mme
	merkki	mark	+merki/n	+merke/i/ssä	merkki/mme
	väri	colour	väri/n	väre/i/ssä	väri/mme
	laki	law	+lai/n	+lae/i/ssa	laki/mme
	risti	cross	risti/n	riste/i/ssä	risti/mme
	sali	hall	sali/n	sale/i/ssa	sali/mme

kivi-nominals

§18.2. There are three kinds of nominals with a basic form ending in -i, all with an inflectional stem in -e. The first group, words like **kivi** 'stone', also form the partitive singular from this inflectional stem.

| | BASIC FORM | | INFLECTIONAL STEM FOLLOWED BY | | |
			CASE	PLURAL	POSSESSIVE SUFFIX
-e is **dropped** **in plural**	kivi	stone	kive/n	kiv/i/ssä	kive/mme
	Suomi	Finland	Suome/n		Suome/mme
	kaikki	all	+kaike/n	+kaik/i/ssa	kaikke/mme
	lehti	newspaper	+lehde/n	+lehd/i/ssä	lehte/mme
	hetki	moment	hetke/n	hetk/i/ssä	hetke/mme
	talvi	winter	talve/n	talv/i/ssa	talve/mme
	järvi	lake	järve/n	järv/i/ssä	järve/mme
	lahti	bay	+lahde/n	+lahd/i/ssa	lahte/mme
	jälki	trace	+jälje/n	+jälj/i/ssä	jälke/mme
	joki	river	+joe/n	+jo/i/ssa	joke/mme
	nimi	name	nime/n	nim/i/ssä	nime/mme
	ovi	door	ove/n	ov/i/ssa	ove/mme

Words like **kivi** thus form their partitive singular from an inflectional stem in -e, and differ in precisely this respect from words of the **kieli**-type (§18.3) and the **vesi**-type (§18.4).

NOTE:
part. sing.
-e/a,
-e/ä

BASIC FORM		INFLECTIONAL STEM FOLLOWED BY PARTITIVE
kaikki	all	kaikke/a
Suomi	Finland	Suome/a
kivi	stone	kive/ä
lehti	newspaper	lehte/ä
hetki	moment	hetke/ä
ovi	door	ove/a

A comparison of the **tunti** and **kivi** types shows that it is not possible to derive a rule from the basic form which would determine which nominals have an inflectional stem in -e and which do not. However, it is possible to state a rule operating in the opposite direction.

basic form -i

> NOMINALS WITH AN INFLECTIONAL STEM ENDING IN SHORT -e HAVE A BASIC FORM ENDING IN SHORT -i

This rule always allows us to derive the basic form from the inflectional stem. The rule does not cover nominals with an inflectional stem in long -ee, such as perhe 'family' : perhee/n (§19). There are a few exceptions: kolme 'three' : kolme/n, itse 'self' : itse/n, nalle 'teddy' : nalle/n, nukke 'doll' : nuken.

kieli-
nominals

§18.3. **Kieli**-type nominals only differ from the **kivi**-type in the partitive singular, where the -e- of the inflectional stem is dropped. Compare §18.2 and note the partitive singular.

	BASIC FORM		INFLECTIONAL STEM FOLLOWED BY		
			CASE	PLURAL	POSSESSIVE SUFFIX
-e- is	kieli	language	kiele/n	kiel/i/ssä	kiele/ni
dropped	veri	blood	vere/n	ver/i/ssä	vere/ni
in plural	meri	sea	mere/n	mer/i/ssä	mere/ni
	tuli	fire	tule/n	tul/i/ssa	tule/ni
	tuuli	wind	tuule/n	tuul/i/ssa	tuule/ni
	ääni	sound	ääne/n	ään/i/ssä	ääne/ni
	lumi	snow	lume/n	lum/i/ssa	lume/ni
	uni	dream	une/n	un/i/ssa	une/ni
	nuori	young	nuore/n	nuor/i/ssa	
	suuri	great	suure/n	suur/i/ssa	
	pieni	small	piene/n	pien/i/ssä	
	lapsi	child	lapse/n	laps/i/ssa	lapse/ni

	BASIC FORM		INFLECTIONAL STEM FOLLOWED BY	
			CASE (except partitive)	PARTITIVE
NB:	kieli	language	kiele/n	kiel/tä
part. sing.	veri	blood	vere/n	ver/ta
	meri	sea	mere/n	mer/ta
	tuli	fire	tule/n	tul/ta
	tuuli	wind	tuule/n	tuulta
	ääni	sound	ääne/n	ään/tä
	lumi	snow	lume/n	lun/ta	(NOTE: m→n)
	pieni	small	piene/n	pien/tä

The -e of the inflectional stem is dropped before the partitive singular ending only when it is preceded by certain consonants.

deletion
rule for
-e

> -e- IS DROPPED IN THE PARTITIVE SINGULAR IF THE PRE-CEDING CONSONANT IS **l**, **r**, OR **n**, OR **t** OCCURRING AFTER THESE OR AFTER A VOWEL

vesi-
nominals

§18.4. The rule given above also covers **vesi**-nominals. These are a group of words with a basic form in -**si** and an inflectional stem in -**te**-.

> IN **vesi**-NOMINALS -**si** ALTERNATES WITH -**te**-; BEFORE THE PLURAL -**i**-, -**te**- CHANGES TO -**s**-; -**t(e)**- IS SUBJECT TO CONSONANT GRADATION (§15)

To illustrate the inflectional stem not subject to consonant gradation let us take the illative singular, e.g. **vete/en** 'into the water'.

	BASIC FORM		INFLECTIONAL STEM FOLLOWED BY			
			CASE (except partitive)	PARTITIVE	PLURAL	POSSESSIVE SUFFIX
NB: plural!	vesi	water	vete/en	vet/tä	ves/i/ssä	vete/ni
	käsi	hand	käte/en	kät/tä	käs/i/ssä	käte/ni
	uusi	new	uute/en	uut/ta	uus/i/ssa	
	viisi	five	viite/en	viit/tä	viis/i/ssä	
	tosi	true	tote/en	tot/ta	tos/i/ssa	
	kansi	cover	kante/en	kant/ta	kans/i/ssa	kante/ni
	varsi	handle	varte/en	vart/ta	vars/i/ssa	varte/ni

	NO ALTERNATION		ALTERNATION	
consonant gradation	vete/nä	as water	+ vede/n	of the water
	vete/en	into the water	+ vede/t	waters
	vete/mme	our water	+ vede/ssä	in the water
	vete/nne	your water	+ vede/stä	out of the water
	vete/ni	my water	+ vede/llä	with water

§19. NOMINALS WITH A BASIC FORM IN -e

-e : -ee-

The second group of nominals with a special inflectional stem is (almost all) nominals with a basic form ending in -e. The other inflected forms are made from a stem ending in a long -ee. The following points should also be noted.

> 1) THE PARTITIVE SINGULAR IS FORMED BY ADDING THE ENDING -tta ~ -ttä DIRECTLY TO THE BASIC FORM
> 2) THE RULES OF CONSONANT GRADATION APPLY TO THE BASIC FORM AND TO THE PARTITIVE SINGULAR, NOT TO THE INFLECTIONAL STEM, WHICH HAS A LONG VOWEL (§15.3)
> 3) THE -ee- OF THE INFLECTIONAL STEM SHORTENS BEFORE THE PLURAL -i- (§16.2)

BASIC FORM		PARTITIVE SINGULAR	INFLECTIONAL STEM FOLLOWED BY		
			CASE (except. part. sing.)	PLURAL	POSSESSIVE SUFFIX
perhe	family	perhe/ttä	perhee/n	perhe/i/ssä	perhee/ni
vene	boat	vene/ttä	venee/n	vene/i/ssä	venee/ni
joukkue	team	joukkue/tta	joukkuee/n	joukkue/i/ssa	joukkuee/ni
+ liike	shop	+ liike/ttä	liikkee/n	liikke/i/ssä	liikkee/ni
+ suhde	relation	+ suhde/tta	suhtee/n	suhte/i/ssä	suhtee/ni
kone	machine	kone/tta	konee/n	kone/i/ssa	konee/ni
+ tarve	need	+ tarve/tta	tarpee/n	tarpe/i/ssa	tarpee/ni
+ sade	rain	+ sade/tta	satee/n	sate/i/ssa	satee/ni
+ ote	grasp	+ ote/tta	ottee/n	otte/i/ssa	ottee/ni
+ liikenne	traffic	+ liikenne/ttä	liikentee/n	liikente/i/ssä	liikentee/ni

	NO ALTERNATION		ALTERNATION	
NB:	liikkee/n	of the movement	+ liike	movement
consonant	liikkee/t	movements		(nom. sing.)
gradation!	liikkee/ssä	in the movement	+ liike/ttä	movement
	liikke/i/ssä	in the movements		(part. sing.)
	liikkee/stä	out of the movement		
	liikke/i/stä	out of the movements		
	liikkee/mme	our movement		
	liikkee/nne	your movement.		
		etc.		

Almost all nominals with a basic form in -e are declined in this way. For exceptions, see the end of §18.2.

§20. *NOMINALS WITH A BASIC FORM ENDING IN A CONSONANT*

The third nominal stem type consists of nominals with a basic form ending in a consonant. Several sub-groups need to be distinguished (§§20.1—8), but they all have the following features in common.

---

1) THE INFLECTIONAL STEM OFTEN ENDS IN THE VOWEL -e, AND THE FINAL CONSONANT OF THE BASIC FORM ALTERNATES WITH OTHER SOUNDS
2) THE PARTITIVE SINGULAR IS GENERALLY FORMED WITH THE ENDING -ta ~ -tä, WHICH IS ATTACHED DIRECTLY TO THE BASIC FORM (cf. §19)
3) CONSONANT GRADATION AFFECTS THE BASIC FORM AND THE PARTITIVE SINGULAR
4) THE FINAL VOWEL OF THE INFLECTIONAL STEM (usually -e) CHANGES BEFORE THE PLURAL -i-

---

ihminen-nominals

§20.1. The most important sub-group of these nominals is those ending in -**nen**, the type **ihminen** 'person'.

IN **ihminen**-NOMINALS -**nen** CHANGES TO -**se**- IN THE INFLECTIONAL STEM; THE PARTITIVE SINGULAR IS FORMED FROM THE INFLECTIONAL STEM WITH THE FINAL -e DROPPED

	BASIC FORM		CASE (except part. sing.)	PARTITIVE	PLURAL	POSSESSIVE SUFFIX
			INFLECTIONAL STEM FOLLOWED BY			
-e- is dropped in plural	ihminen	person	ihmise/n	ihmis/tä	ihmis/i/ssä	ihmise/ni
	nainen	woman	naise/n	nais/ta	nais/i/ssa	naise/ni
	yleinen	general	yleise/n	yleis/tä	yleis/i/ssä	
	hevonen	horse	hevose/n	hevos/ta	hevos/i/ssa	hevose/ni
	punainen	red	punaise/n	punais/ta	punais/i/ssa	
	toinen	another	toise/n	tois/ta	tois/i/ssa	
	jokainen	every	jokaise/n	jokais/ta		

§20.2. There are two groups of nominals with a basic form ending in a short vowel + s. The most common of these is the type **ajatus** 'thought' (cf. §20.3.).

ajatus-nominals

IN **ajatus**-NOMINALS **-s** CHANGES TO **-kse-** IN THE INFLECTIONAL STEM; THE PARTITIVE SINGULAR IS FORMED DIRECTLY FROM THE BASIC FORM

	BASIC FORM		PARTITIVE SINGULAR	CASE (except part. sing.)	PLURAL	POSSESSIVE SUFFIX
				INFLECTIONAL STEM FOLLOWED BY		
-e- is dropped in plural	ajatus	thought	ajatus/ta	ajatukse/n	ajatuks/i/ssa	ajatukse/ni
	kysymys	question	kysymys/tä	kysymykse/n	kysymyks/i/ssä	kysymykse/ni
	vastaus	answer	vastaus/ta	vstaukse/n	vastauks/i/ssa	vastaukse/ni
	teos	work	teos/ta	teokse/n	teoks/i/ssa	teokse/ni
	rakennus	building	rakennus/ta	rakennukse/n	rakennuks/i/ssa	rakennukse/ni
	hallitus	government	hallitus/ta	hallitukse/n	hallituks/i/ssa	hallitukse/ni
	päätös	decision	päätös/tä	päätökse/n	päätöks/i/ssä	päätökse/ni

taivas-nominals

§20.3. In nominals like **taivas** 'heaven' the -s of the basic form alternates with a vowel identical with the preceding vowel.

IN **taivas**-NOMINALS **-s** CHANGES IN THE INFLECTIONAL STEM TO A VOWEL IDENTICAL WITH THE PRECEDING VOWEL; THE PARTITIVE SINGULAR IS FORMED DIRECTLY FROM THE BASIC FORM

	BASIC FORM		PARTITIVE SINGULAR	CASE (except part. sing.)	PLURAL	POSSESSIVE SUFFIX
				INFLECTIONAL STEM FOLLOWED BY		
vowel shortens in plural	taivas	heaven	taivas/ta	taivaa/n	taiva/i/ssa	taivaa/ni
	valmis	ready	valmis/ta	valmii/n	valmi/i/ssa	
	+rikas	rich	+rikas/ta	rikkaa/n	rikka/i/ssa	
	oppilas	pupil	oppilas/ta	oppilaa/n	oppila/i/ssa	oppilaa/ni
	+tehdas	factory	+tehdas/ta	tehtaa/n	tehta/i/ssa	tehtaa/ni
	+porras	step	+porras/ta	portaa/n	porta/i/ssa	portaa/ni
	+kirkas	bright	+kirkas/ta	kirkkaa/n	kirkka/i/ssa	

	NO ALTERNATION		ALTERNATION	
NB: consonant gradation!	tehtaa/n	of the factory	+ tehdas	factory (nom. sing.)
	tehtaa/t	factories	+ tehdas/ta	factory (part. sing.)
	tehtaa/ssa	in the factory		
	tehta/i/ssa	in the factories		
	tehta/sta	out of the factory		
	tehta/i/sta	out of the factories		
	tehtaa/mme	our factory		
	tehtaa/nne	your factory		

hyvyys-nominals

§20.4. The third group of nominals with a basic form ending in -s is the type **hyvyys** 'goodness'. This includes all nouns with a final -s preceded by a long vowel, and many nouns with two different vowels preceding the final -s. All the words in this group are derived forms, cf. *hyvä* 'good' — *hyv/yys* 'goodness', *kaunis* 'beautiful' — *kaune/us* 'beauty', *osa* 'part' — *os/uus* 'share'. They have several special sound alternations.

> IN **hyvyys**-NOMINALS -s CHANGES TO -te- IN THE INFLECTIONAL STEM OF THE SINGULAR; BEFORE THE PLURAL -i, -s CHANGES TO -ks-; THE PARTITIVE SINGULAR IS FORMED FROM THE INFLECTIONAL STEM AND -e- IS DROPPED

BASIC FORM		INFLECTIONAL STEM FOLLOWED BY			
		PARTITIVE SINGULAR	CASE (except part. sing.)	PLURAL	POSSESSIVE SUFFIX
hyvyys	goodness	hyvyyt/tä	+ hyvyyde/n	hyvyyks/i/ssä	hyvyyte/ni
korkeus	height	korkeut/ta	+ korkeude/n	korkeuks/i/ssa	korkeute/ni
rakkaus	love	rakkaut/ta	+ rakkaude/n	rakkauks/i/ssa	rakkaute/ni
totuus	truth	totuut/ta	+ totuude/n	totuuks/i/ssa	totuute/ni
yhteys	connection	yhteyt/tä	+ yhteyde/n	yhteyks/i/ssä	yhteyte/ni

	NO ALTERNATION		ALTERNATION	
NB: consonant gradation!	totuutee/n	into truth	+ totuude/n	of truth
	totuute/na	as truth	+ totuude/ssa	in truth
	totuute/mme	our truth	+ totuude/sta	out of truth
			+ totuude/lla	with truth

avain-nominals

§20.5. There are not many nonderived nominals of the type **avain** 'key'. The stem alternates between -in- and -ime-, and the partitive singular is made from the basic form.

BASIC FORM		INFLECTIONAL STEM FOLLOWED BY			
		PARTITIVE SINGULAR	CASE (except part. sing.)	PLURAL	POSSESSIVE SUFFIX
avain	key	avain/ta	avaime/n	avaim/i/ssa	avaime/ni
puhelin	telephone	puhelin/ta	puhelime/n	puhelim/i/ssa	puhelime/ni
kirjain	letter	kirjain/ta	kirjaime/n	kirjaim/i/ssa	kirjaime/ni

§20.6. Derived nominals of the type **työ/tön** 'unemployed' are very common. The partitive singular is made from the basic form. The other inflected forms are based on a stem where **-ton ~ -tön** has changed to **-ttoma- ~ -ttömä-**. In the plural **-a-/-ä-** is dropped (§16.7—8).

			INFLECTIONAL STEM FOLLOWED BY	
BASIC FORM		PARTITIVE SINGULAR	CASE (except part. sing.)	PLURAL
työ/**tön**	unemployed	työ/**tön**/tä	työ/**ttömä**/n	työ/**ttöm**/i/ssä
onne/**ton**	unhappy	onne/**ton**/ta	onne/**ttoma**/n	onne/**ttom**/i/ssa
tie/**tön**	without roads	tie/**tön**/tä	tie/**ttömä**/n	tie/**ttöm**/i/ssä

§20.7. There are a few dozen nominals ending in a consonant which form another small sub-group. The two final sounds of the basic form are generally **-el** or **-en**. The partitive singular is made from the basic form. The inflectional stem adds an **-e-** (which is dropped before the plural **-i-**).

			INFLECTIONAL STEM FOLLOWED BY		
BASIC FORM		PARTITIVE SINGULAR	CASE (except. part. sing.)	PLURAL	POSSESSIVE SUFFIX
aske**l**	step	aske**l**/ta	aske**le**/n	aske**l**/i/ssa	aske**le**/ni
säve**l**	tune	säve**l**/tä	säve**le**/n	säve**l**/i/ssä	säve**le**/ni
jäse**n**	member	jäse**n**/tä	jäse**ne**/n	jäse**n**/i/ssä	jäse**ne**/ni

§20.8. There are a few nominals ending in **-ut, -yt**, where in the inflectional stem the **-t** changes to **-e-**, which is then dropped before the plural **-i-**. The group includes *kevyt* 'light', *lyhyt* 'short', *ohut* 'thin', *olut* 'beer'. The nouns *mies* 'man' and *kevät* 'spring' also have unusual declensions.

			INFLECTIONAL STEM FOLLOWED BY		
BASIC FORM		PARTITIVE SINGULAR	CASE (except part. sing.)	PLURAL	POSSESSIVE SUFFIX
lyhyt	short	lyhyt/tä	lyhye/n	lyhy/i/ssä	
olut	beer	olut/ta	olue/n	olu(e)/i/ssa	olue/ni
mies	man	mies/tä	miehe/n	mieh/i/ssä	miehe/ni
kevät	spring	kevät/tä	kevää/n	kevä/i/ssä	kevää/ni

New loanwords ending in a final consonant form their inflectional stem by adding the vowel **-i-**, which changes to **-e-** before the plural **-i-** (§16.6). Cf. stadion 'stadium': stadioni/n : stadioni/a : stadione/i/ta. Loanwords with a final **-s**, however, generally decline like **ajatus**-nominals (§20.2), e.g. anis 'aniseed' : ani**kse**/n : ani**kse**/ssa : anis/ta (part. sing.)

6 The Conjugation of Verbs

General
Infinitive endings
Inflectional stems

§21. *GENERAL*

Verb-forms are built up like nominals by adding endings to stems. Verbs differ from nominals in that they do not have an independent basic form as such to which inflectional endings could be attached, as is the case with nominals: cf. the basic form *auto* 'car' and the inflected forms *auto/n, auto/ssa, auto/i/hin*.

The dictionary form of Finnish verbs, i.e. the shorter form of the 1st infinitive, already has an ending, e.g. *osta/a* '(to) buy', *vastat/a* '(to) answer', *juo/da* '(to) drink'. Before other verb-forms can be made one must first take off the infinitive ending from the stem, to which other endings are then added, cf. *osta/a* '(to) buy' : *osta/isi/n* 'I would buy' : *osta/nut* 'bought'.

Some verbs have more than one stem, in which case one is formed from the other, e.g. vastat/a '(to) answer' : vastaa/n 'I answer' and tul/la '(to) come' : tule/n 'I come'. Consonant gradation (§15) and vowel changes before -i- (§16) affect verbs in much the same way as nominals, e.g. anta/a '(to) give' : anna/n 'I give' (consonant gradation); anta/a : anno/i/n 'I gave' (vowel change).

NB: consonant gradation and vowel change!

The stems needed for the conjugation of verbs are the *infinitive stem*, which is arrived at after the infinitive endings are detached according to the rules given in §22, and the *inflectional stem*, which can be formed from the infinitive stem and to which e.g. the personal endings are added (§23). The rules for the formation of the inflectional stem are given in §23.

The following examples illustrate the use of the 1 st infinitive (cf. also §74).

Haluan juo/**da** olutta.	I want to drink some beer.
Tahtoisitko syö/**dä**?	Would you like to eat?
Yritän sano/**a** asiat selvästi.	I try to say the things clearly.
Minun täytyy lähte/**ä**.	I must leave.
Saako täällä laula/**a**?	Can one sing here?
Nyt sinun pitää lopetta/**a**.	Now you must stop.
Tässä on mukava istu/**a**.	It is nice to sit here.
Olisi kiva men/**nä** ulos.	It would be nice to go out.

§22. *INFINITIVE ENDINGS*

The 1st infinitive has four endings, 1) -a ~ -ä, 2) -da ~ -dä, 3) -ta ~ -tä and 4) -la ~ -lä, -ra ~ -rä, -na ~ -nä. The most common one is -a ~ -ä. All the infinitive endings are preceded by the infinitive stem.

53

1) anta/a-verbs

> -a ~ -ä OCCURS WHEN THE INFINITIVE STEM ENDS IN A SHORT VOWEL

Examples:

anta/a	give	kysy/ä	ask
alka/a	begin	lähte/ä	leave
katso/a	look	pitä/ä	hold
puhu/a	talk	tietä/ä	know

2) huomat/a-verbs

> -a ~ -ä ALSO OCCURS WHEN THE INFINITIVE STEM ENDS IN A SHORT VOWEL + t (usually -at/a, -ät/ä)

Examples:

huomat/a	notice	herät/ä	awake
halut/a	want	hypät/ä	jump
korjat/a	repair	määrät/ä	order
vastat/a	answer	kerät/ä	collect

3) saa/da-verbs

> -da ~ -dä OCCURS WHEN THE INFINITIVE STEM ENDS IN A LONG VOWEL OR A DIPHTHONG

Examples:

saa/da	get	jää/dä	remain
tuo/da	bring	vie/dä	take
voi/da	be able	syö/dä	eat
luennoi/da	lecture	pysäköi/dä	park

4) nous/ta-verbs

> -ta ~ -tä OCCURS WHEN THE INFINITIVE STEM ENDS IN -s

Examples:

nous/ta	rise	pääs/tä	be allowed
juos/ta	run	tönäis/tä	shove
mumis/ta	mumble	pes/tä	wash
valais/ta	light	vilis/tä	swarm

> -la ∼ -lä, -na ∼ -nä, -ra ∼ -rä OCCUR WHEN THE INFINITIVE
> STEM ENDS IN AN IDENTICAL CONSONANT (-l, -n, -r)

Examples:

tul/**la**	come	vietel/**lä**	entice
ol/**la**	be	niel/**lä**	swallow
ajatel/**la**	think	hymyil/**lä**	smile
pan/**na**	put	men/**nä**	go
pur/**ra**	bite		

The most important types are those exemplified by **anta/a** and **huomat/a**.
Saa/da-verbs also also important. There are not many verbs with infinitives
ending in -**na** ∼ -**nä** and -**ra** ∼ -**rä**.

In **anta/a** and **saa/da**-verbs all inflected forms are based on the infinitive
stem. But also in the other verb-groups at least some forms are based on this
stem. The following rule states which inflected forms of *all* verbs are made
from the infinitive stem.

> WITH ALL VERBS THE INFINITIVE STEM IS USED TO FORM
> 1) THE PAST PARTICIPLE (§61)
> 2) MOST IMPERATIVE FORMS (§66)
> 3) POTENTIAL FORMS (§67)
> 4) PASSIVE FORMS (§§69—72)
> 5) THE SECOND INFINITIVE (§76)

§23. *INFLECTIONAL STEMS*

This section shows how the five groups of verbs introduced above form their
inflectional stems (§23.1—4); it concludes with a few special cases (§23.5—6).
All forms except those mentioned in the above rule are made from the
inflectional stem. For each verb, two examples of the inflectional stem are
given in order to illustrate the effect of consonant gradation (e.g. **anta/a** '(to)
give' : **anna/n** 'I give').

§23.1. Anta/a-verbs, where the infinitive ending occurs after a short vowel,
do not have a separate inflectional stem; other endings are added directly to
the infinitive stem. The plus sign indicates consonant gradation.

anta/a VERBS HAVE ONLY AN INFINITIVE STEM

INFINITIVE		1ST P. SING.		3RD P. SING.	
osta/a	buy	osta/n	I buy	osta/a	he buys
alka/a	begin	+ala/n	etc.	alka/a	etc.
ymmärtä/ä	understand	+ymmärrä/n		ymmärtä/ä	
etsi/ä	look for	etsi/n		etsi/i	
luke/a	read	+lue/n		luke/e	
neuvo/a	advise	neuvo/n		neuvo/o	
unohta/a	forget	+unohda/n		unohta/a	
herättä/ä	wake	+herätä/n		herättä/ä	
kysy/ä	ask	kysy/n		kysy/y	

huomat/a-verbs

§23.2 Huomat/a-verbs, which generally end in *-at/a, -ät/ä,* are a very important group ("contracted verbs"). The relation here between the infinitive stem and the inflectional stem is a complex one. The -t- of the infinitive alternates with -a-/-ä- and consonant gradation applies to the infinitive, whereas there is no alternation in the inflectional stem (§15.4).

NB: important rule!

IN **huomat/a** VERBS THE -t- OF THE INFINITIVE STEM CHANGES TO -a- or -ä- ACCORDING TO VOWEL HARMONY; CONSONANT GRADATION AFFECTS THE INFINITIVE STEM

NB: consonant gradation (§15.4)!

INFINITIVE		1ST P. SING.		3RD P. SING.	
huomat/a	notice	huomaa/n	I notice	huomaa	he notices
osat/a	know how	osaa/n	etc.	osaa	etc.
+hypät/ä	jump	hyppää/n		hyppää	
seurat/a	follow	seuraa/n		seuraa	
tarjot/a	offer	tarjoa/n		tarjoa/a	
halut/a	want	halua/n		halua/a	
+pelät/ä	fear	pelkää/n		pelkää	
määrät/ä	order	määrää/n		määrää	
+veikat/a	bet	veikkaa/n		veikkaa	
+hakat/a	hew	hakkaa/n		hakkaa	
+maat/a	lie	makaa/n		makaa	
+tavat/a	meet	tapaa/n		tapaa	
+kadot/a	disappear	katoa/n		katoa/a	
varat/a	reserve	varaa/n		varaa	

saa/da-verbs

§23.3. The third group, **saa/da**-verbs, where the infinitive ending occurs after a long vowel or a diphthong, is similar to the **anta/a** group in that these verbs too have only an infinitive stem.

saa/da VERBS HAVE ONLY AN INFINITIVE STEM

INFINITIVE		1ST P. SING.		3RD P. SING.	
saa/da	get	saa/n	I get	saa	he gets
myy/dä	sell	myy/n	etc.	myy	etc.

juo/da	drink	juo/n		juo	
voi/da	be able	voi/n		voi	
luennoi/da	lecture	luennoi/n		luennoi	
kanavoi/da	canalize	kanavoi/n		kanavoi	
pysäköi/dä	park	pysäköi/n		pysäköi	
teh/dä	do	+ **tee/n**		**teke/e**	
näh/dä	see	+ **näe/n**		**näke/e**	

<table>
<tr><td>NB:
teh/dä,
näh/dä</td><td>The common verbs teh/dä 'do' and näh/dä 'see' are exceptional, since they have an inflectional stem ending in -ke-, with -k alternating with the -h- of the infinitive stem.</td></tr>
</table>

nous/ta and tul/la-verbs

§23.4. These two groups form their inflectional stem by adding -e- to the infinitive.

> THE INFLECTIONAL STEM OF **nous/ta** and **tul/la**-VERBS IS FORMED BY ADDING -e- TO THE INFINITIVE STEM

NB: consonant gradation!

INFINITIVE		1ST P. SING.		3RD P. SING.	
nous/ta	rise	nouse/n	I rise	nouse/e	he rises
pes/tä	wash	pese/n	etc.	pese/e	etc.
tul/la	come	tule/n		tule/e	
men/nä	go	mene/n		mene/e	
hymyil/lä	smile	hymyile/n		hymyile/e	
+ ajatel/la	think	ajattele/n		ajattele/e	
kiistel/lä	dispute	kiistele/n		kiistele/e	
+ työskennel/lä	work	työskentele/n		työskentele/e	
julkais/ta	publish	julkaise/n		julkaise/e	

In these verbs too, consonant gradation occurs in the infinitive stem (§15.4), e.g. ajatel/la '(to) think' : ajattele/n 'I think'.

tarvit/a-verbs

§23.5. Verbs in -it/a, -it/ä, e.g. **tarvit/a** 'need', are similar to **huomat/a** verbs (§23.2), but their inflectional stem is formed differently:

> THE INFLECTIONAL STEM OF **tarvit/a**-VERBS IS FORMED BY ADDING -se- TO THE INFINITIVE STEM

INFINITIVE		1ST P. SING.		3RD P. SING.	
tarvit/a	need	tarvitse/n	I need	tarvitse/e	he needs
ansait/a	earn	ansaitse/n	etc.	ansaitse/e	etc.
hallit/a	rule	hallitse/n		hallitse/e	
harkit/a	consider	harkitse/n		harkitse/e	
häirit/ä	disturb	häiritse/n		häiritse/e	

57

lämmet/ä-verbs

§23.6. Verbs in *-et/a*, *-et/ä* like **lämmet/ä** 'get warm' also form their inflectional stem in a different way (cf. §23.2).

IN **lämmet/ä**-VERBS THE -t- OF THE INFINITIVE STEM CHANGES TO -ne- IN THE INFLECTIONAL STEM

INFINITIVE		1ST P. SING.		3RD P. SING.	
+ lämmet/ä	get warm	lämpene/n	I get warm	lämpene/e	he gets warm
vanhet/a	grow old	vanhene/n	etc.	vanhene/e	etc.
+ paet/a	flee	pakene/n		pakene/e	
+ kalvet/a	turn pale	kalpene/n		kalpene/e	
laajet/a	grow wider	laajene/n		laajene/e	

NB: consonant gradation!

|| just memorise these -- the pattern is too confusing ||

58

7   **Basic Sentence Structure**

Present tense personal endings
The nominative (basic form of nominals)
Singular and plural
The verb olla *'(to) be'*
'To have' in Finnish
Negative sentences
Questions and answers
Concord of attributes

§24. *PRESENT TENSE PERSONAL ENDINGS*

Finnish has six grammatical persons. They correspond to the following pronouns.

personal pronouns				
minä	I		**me**	we
sinä	you (sing.)		**te**	you (pl.)
hän; se	he, she; it		**he, ne**	they

The six grammatical persons correspond to these pronouns; the 3rd person singular covers all singular nominals except the pronouns *minä* and *sinä*, and the 3rd person plural covers all plural nominals except the pronouns *me* and *te*. Finite verb-forms (§13) show concord of person with the grammatical subject. The persons have their own endings, which are added to the verb stem (the 3rd person singular often has no ending).

personal endings of verbs		SINGULAR	PLURAL
	1ST PERSON	**-n**	**-mme**
	2ND PERSON	**-t**	**-tte**
	3RD PERSON	(cf. Delow)	**-vat ~ -vät**

These endings are attached to the inflectional stem (§23) after any tense and mood endings (§13). In the 3rd person singular of the present indicative the final vowel of the stem is lengthened.

IN THE 3RD PERSON SINGULAR OF THE PRESENT INDICA-
TIVE THE SHORT VOWEL FOLLOWING THE FINAL CONSO-
NANT OR SYLLABLE BOUNDARY OF THE INFLECTIONAL
STEM IS LENGTHENED

	SINGULAR		PLURAL	
1ST PERSON	(minä) osta/**n**	I buy	(me) osta/**mme**	we buy
	(minä) sano/**n**	I say	(me) sano/**mme**	we say
	(minä) saa/**n**	I get	(me) saa/**mme**	we get
	(minä) syö/**n**	I eat	(me) syö/**mme**	we eat
	(minä) tule/**n**	I come	(me) tule/**mme**	we come
2ND PERSON	(sinä) osta/**t**	you buy	(te) osta/**tte**	you buy
	(sinä) sano/**t**	you say	(te) sano/**tte**	you say
	(sinä) saa/**t**	you get	(te) saa/**tte**	you get
	(sinä) syö/**t**	you eat	(te) syö/**tte**	you eat
	(sinä) tule/**t**	you come	(te) tule/**tte**	you come
3RD PERSON	hän osta/**a**	he/she buys	he osta/**vat**	they buy
	Pekka sano/**o**	Pekka says	he sano/**vat**	they say
	tyttö saa	the girl gets	tytöt saa/**vat**	the girls get
	mies syö	the man eats	miehet syö/**vät**	the men eat
	auto tule/**e**	the car comes	autot tule/**vat**	the cars come

NB: 3rd
p. sing.!

A long vowel, and the second vowel of a diphthong, are not lengthened in the 3rd person singular, cf. Kalle *saa* 'Kalle gets'; Kalle *syö* 'Kalle eats'. Note words such as *halua/a* 'wants', *kohoa/a* 'rises', where vowel lengthening occurs after a syllable boundary (cf. § 9). The independent subject words of the 3rd person cannot usually be omitted, but subject pronouns in the 1st and 2nd persons often are, in which case the personal ending of the verb is all that indicates the person (shown in brackets above).

> **1ST AND 2ND PERSON SUBJECT PRONOUNS (*minä, sinä, me, te*) ARE OFTEN OMITTED**

the polite
2nd person

The 2nd person plural ending -**tte** is also used as a polite form addressed to a single person. The form **osta/tte** can thus mean 'you (pl.) buy' or 'you (sing., polite) buy'.

Consonant gradation applies in the 1st and 2nd persons of many verbs on condition that the ending is not preceded by a long vowel (§§15.2, 15.4). Examples follow of **anta/a** 'give', **otta/a** 'take' and **vetä/ä** 'pull'.

	SINGULAR	PLURAL
1ST PERSON	a**nn**a/n	a**nn**a/mme
	o**t**a/n	o**t**a/mme
	ve**d**ä/n	ve**d**ä/mme
2ND PERSON	a**nn**a/t	a**nn**a/tte
	o**t**a/t	o**t**a/tte
	ve**d**ä/t	ve**d**ä/tte
3RD PERSON	a**nt**a/a	a**nt**a/vat
	o**tt**a/a	o**tt**a/vat
	ve**t**ä/ä	ve**t**ä/vät

consonant
gradation

In these forms there is no consonant gradation in **huomat/a**-verbs on account of the long vowel, cf. hy**pp**ää/n 'I jump', hy**pp**ää/t 'you jump', hän hy**pp**ää 'he/she jumps'. The following examples illustrate the personal endings of the most important verb types (cf. §23).

60

etsi/ä	look for	**luke/a**	read	**lentä/ä**	fly
etsi/n	etsi/mme	lue/n	lue/mme	lennä/n	lennä/mme
etsi/t	etsi/tte	lue/t	lue/tte	lennä/t	lennä/tte
etsi/i	etsi/vät	luke/e	luke/vat	lentä/ä	lentä/vät
osat/a	know how	**maat/a**	lie	**halut/a**	want
osaa/n	osaa/mme	makaa/n	makaa/mme	halua/n	halua/mme
osaa/t	osaa/tte	makaa/t	makaa/tte	halua/t	halua/tte
osaa	osaa/vat	makaa	makaa/vat	halua/a	halua/vat
saa/da	get	**juo/da**	drink	**myy/dä**	sell
saa/n	saa/mme	juo/n	juo/mme	myy/n	myy/mme
saa/t	saa/tte	juo/t	juo/tte	myy/t	myy/tte
saa	saa/vat	juo	juo/vat	myy	myy/vät
nous/ta	rise	**tul/la**	come	**men/nä**	go
nouse/n	nouse/mme	tule/n	tule/mme	mene/n	mene/mme
nouse/t	nouse/tte	tule/t	tule/tte	mene/t	mene/tte
nouse/e	nouse/vat	tule/e	tule/vat	mene/e	mene/vät
tarvit/a	need	**ansait/a**	earn	**häirit/ä**	disturb
tarvitse/n	tarvitse/mme	ansaitse/n	ansaitse/mme	häiritse/n	häiritse/mme
tarvitse/t	tarvitse/tte	ansaitse/t	ansaitse/tte	häiritse/t	häiritse/tte
tarvitse/e	tarvitse/vat	ansaitse/e	ansaise/vat	häiritse/e	häiritse/vät

§25. THE NOMINATIVE (BASIC FORM OF NOMINALS)

The nominative is the basis upon which the Finnish case system is built. The nominative is the primary form of nominals in dictionaries, and it is also the most common case. The functions of the nominative are seen most clearly when it is compared with the partitive, the second basic case in the system. The partitive often expresses an indefinite, non-limited quantity of something, allowing the possibility that there may exist more of it. The nominative, on the other hand, expresses either a concrete or abstract *whole or a definite, limited, total quantity.*

§25.1. *Nominative endings*

> THE NOMINATIVE HAS
> 1) NO ENDING IN THE SINGULAR
> 2) THE ENDING -t IN THE PLURAL

NOMINATIVE SINGULAR		NOMINATIVE PLURAL	
auto	car	auto/t	the cars
maa	country	maa/t	the countries
talo	house	talo/t	the houses
hylly	shelf	hylly/t	the shelves
nainen	woman	naise/t	the women (cf. §20.1)
kivi	stone	kive/t	the stones (cf. §18.2)
käsi	hand	käde/t	the hands (cf. §18.4)

no articles There are no articles in Finnish corresponding to the way the difference between definite and indefinite meaning is expressed e.g. in English (*the car* : *a car*). Whether the Finnish expression *auto* is to be interpreted as definite or indefinite is often indicated by the word order of the sentence in question (§25.3). The nominative plural, e.g. auto/**t**, almost always has the meaning 'definite'.

§25.2. *Non-divisible and divisible nouns*

In order to explain the use of the nominative we also need to make a distinction with respect to the partitive. A noun is **non-divisible** (countable) if it refers to a more or less concrete entity that cannot be divided into smaller parts in such a way that the parts share the quality of the whole. Non-divisible nouns can be counted (one x, two x's etc.). Examples: *auto* 'car', *talo* 'house', *hylly* 'shelf', *nainen* 'woman', *käsi* 'hand', *ajatus* 'thought', *sielu* 'soul'. (In English these nouns would be classified as singular count nouns.)

A noun is **divisible** non-comfable if it refers to a concrete mass or an abstract entity that can be divided into parts in such a way that the arts share the quality of the whole. Examples: *kahvi* 'coffee', *maito* 'milk', *rauta* 'iron', *kulta* 'gold', *olut* 'beer', *vesi* 'water', *vahvuus* 'strength', *rakkaus* 'love'. Divisible nouns cannot normally be counted.

§25.3. *Use of the nominative*

The use of the nominative depends on three factors: whether the noun is divisible or non-divisible, whether a divisible word is definite or indefinite, and sometimes whether the noun is singular or plural. Four rules follow below.

---

1) SINGULAR, NON-DIVISIBLE SUBJECT NOUNS APPEAR IN THE NOMINATIVE AND EXPRESS
   a) DEFINITE MEANING AT THE BEGINNING OF THE SENTENCE
   b) INDEFINITE MEANING AT THE END OF THE SENTENCE

Auto on kadulla.　　　　*The car* is in the street.
Kadulla on *auto*.　　　　There is *a car* in the street.

Nainen on talossa.　　　*The woman* is in the house.
Talossa on *nainen*.　　　There is *a woman* in the house.

Kirja ilmestyi.　　　　　*The book* was published.
Ilmestyi *kirja*.　　　　　*A book* was published.

Pullo on kaapissa.　　　*The bottle* is in the cupboard.
Kaapissa on *pullo*.　　　There is *a bottle* in the cupboard.

62

Nouns at the beginning of a sentence are generally interpreted as definite, i.e. to be known in the sense that the hearer (reader) knows what they refer to.

Sentences where both subject and object are non-divisible are often ambiguous as regards definiteness:

Mies osti *kirjan.*	A/The man bought a/the book.
Nainen hankki *auton.*	A/The woman got a/the car.

If the word order is inverted, with the object at the beginning and the subject at the end, the object is interpreted as definite (known) and the subject as indefinite (new):

Kirjan osti *mies.*	A man bought the book / The book was bought by a man.

Singular non-divisible predicate nouns (complements) are always in the *nominative*.

predicate
noun

Pekka on *mies.*	Pekka is *a man.*
Tuula on *nainen.*	Tuula is *a woman.*
Tämä on *pöytä.*	This is *a table.*
Tuo on *auto.*	That is *a car.*
Auto tuo on!	That's *a CAR!*
Paavo on *opettaja.*	Paavo is *a teacher.*

Singular predicative adjectives are also in the nominative if the subject is a non-divisible word.

predicative
adjective

Auto on *sininen.*	The car is *blue.*
Tuo vene on *kallis.*	That boat is *expensive.*
Kalle on *pitkä.*	Kalle is *tall.*
Ajatuksesi oli *hyvä.*	Your idea was *good.*
Kone on *likainen.*	The machine is *dirty.*

---

2) NON-DIVISIBLE PLURAL NOUNS WITH DEFINITE MEANING TAKE THE ENDING -t

---

Auto/t ovat kadulla.	*The cars* are in the street.
Kadulla ovat auto/t.	In the street are *the cars!*
Miehe/t tulivat kotiin.	*The men* came home.
Kirja/t maksavat 10 mk.	*The books* cost 10 marks.
Ministeri/t lähtivät lomalle.	*The ministers* went on holiday.
Pekka osti kirja/t.	Pekka bought *the books.*
Leena näki laiva/t.	Leena saw *the ships.*
Syön nämä omena/t.	I'll eat these *apples.*

Ruoka maistuu hyvältä.	*(The) food* tastes good.
Kahvi on kupissa.	*The coffee* is in the cup.
Liha maksaa paljon.	*(The) meat* is expensive.
Aika loppuu.	*(The) time* is up.
Osta *olut*! (cf. §§37, 38)	Buy *the beer*!
Kahvi juotiin. (cf. §§37, 38)	*The coffee* was drunk.
Tämä on Pekan *maito*.	This is Pekka's *milk*.
Maito on valkoista.	*(The) milk* is white.
Ilma on kirkas.	*The air* is clear.
Musiikki rentouttaa.	*(The) music* relaxes.

a) *Poika* potkii palloa.	*A/The boy* kicks a/the ball.
a) *Pojat* potkivat palloa.	*(The) boys* kick a/the ball.
b) *Kahvi* on hyvää.	*(The) coffee* is good.
b) *Mikään* ei ole mahdotonta.	*Nothing* is impossible.

§26. *SINGULAR AND PLURAL*

-t and
-i-

Nominals inflect for singular and plural. The singular always has no ending. The plural has two endings, -t and -i-. -t occurs only in the nominative and accusative (§§37, 38), and -i- in all other cases.

SINGULAR			PLURAL	
Nominative	talo	house	talo/t	the houses
Genitive	talo/n	of the house	talo/j/en	of the houses
Partitive	talo/a	house	talo/j/a	houses
Inessive	talo/ssa	in the house	talo/i/ssa	in the houses
Elative	talo/sta	out of the house	talo/i/sta	out of the houses
Illative	talo/on	into the house	talo/i/hin	into the houses
Adessive	talo/lla	on the house	talo/i/lla	on the houses
Ablative	talo/lta	off the house	talo/i/lta	off the houses
Allative	talo/lle	onto the house	talo/i/lle	onto the houses
Essive	talo/na	as a house	talo/i/na	as houses
Translative	talo/ksi	to (become) a house	talo/i/ksi	to (become) houses

THE PLURAL -i- CHANGES TO -j- BETWEEN TWO VOWELS

This rule concerns the genitive plural and the partitive plural: hylly/j/en 'of the shelves', hylly/j/ä 'shelves', pullo/j/en 'of the bottles', pullo/j/a 'bottles', tyttö/j/en 'of the girls', tyttö/j/ä 'girls'.

All plural forms are made from the inflectional stem (§§18—20), and before the plural -i- the vowel changes apply (§16). The table below illustrates the formation of the plural.

NOMINATIVE SINGULAR		INFLECTIONAL STEM	(cf. §)	NOMINATIVE PLURAL	INESSIVE PLURAL	VOWEL CHANGE (cf. §)
pullo	bottle	pullo/n	—	pullo/t	pullo/i/ssa	—
katu	street	kadu/n	—	kadu/t	kadu/i/ssa	—
maa	country	maa/n	—	maa/t	ma/i/ssa	16.2
risti	cross	risti/n	18.1	risti/t	riste/i/ssä	16.6
kivi	stone	kive/n	18.2	kive/t	kiv/i/ssä	16.5
lehti	newspaper	lehde/n	18.2	lehde/t	lehd/i/ssä	16.5
meri	sea	mere/n	18.3	mere/t	mer/i/ssä	16.5
vesi	water	vede/n	18.4	vede/t	ves/i/ssä	16.5; s: 18.4
kone	machine	konee/n	19	konee/t	kone/i/ssa	16.2
liike	movement	liikkee/n	19	liikkee/t	liikke/i/ssä	16.2
työ	work	työ/n	—	työ/t	tö/i/ssä	16.3
hai	shark	hai/n	—	hai/t	ha/i/ssa	16.4
seinä	wall	seinä/n	—	seinä/t	sein/i/ssä	16.7
vanha	old	vanha/n	—	vanha/t	vanho/i/ssa	16.8
tavara	thing	tavara/n	—	tavara/t	tavaro/i/ssa	16.8
koira	dog	koira/n	—	koira/t	koir/i/ssa	16.8
ihminen	person	ihmise/n	20.1	ihmise/t	ihmis/i/ssä	16.5
vanhus	old person	vanhukse/n	20.2	vanhukse/t	vanhuks/i/ssa	16.5
taivas	heaven	taivaa/n	20.3	taivaa/t	taiva/i/ssa	16.2
rikas	rich	rikkaa/n	20.3	rikkaa/t	rikka/i/ssa	16.2
totuus	truth	totuude/n	20.4	totuude/t	totuuks/i/ssa	16.5; ks: 20.4
avain	key	avaime/n	20.5	avaime/t	avaim/i/ssä	16.5
työtön	unemployed	työttömä/n	20.6	työttömä/t	työttöm/i/ssä	16.7
jäsen	member	jäsene/n	20.7	jäsene/t	jäsen/i/ssä	16.5
mies	man	miehe/n	20.8	miehe/t	mieh/i/ssä	16.5

There are many nouns which appear only in the plural even though they refer to a singular concept. Plural words of this kind include:

	NOMINATIVE PLURAL		INESSIVE PLURAL
invariable plurals	kasvot	face	kasvoissa
	housut	trousers	housuissa
	sakset	scissors	saksissa
	kärryt	cart	kärryissä
	häät	wedding	häissä
	markkinat	fair	markkinoissa
	tanssit	dance	tansseissa
	arpajaiset	lottery	arpajaisissa

§27. *THE VERB* OLLA *'(TO) BE'*

The conjugation of the verb **olla** is exceptional in the third person. The inflectional stem is formed by adding -e- (§23.4).

(minä) **ole/n**	I am	(me) **ole/mme**	we are
(sinä) **ole/t**	you are	(te) **ole/tte**	you are
hän **on**	he/she is	he **o/vat**	they are

-e- is dropped before the past tense ending -i- and also before the conditional **-isi-** (§16.5).

(minä) **ol/i/n**	I was	(me) **ol/i/mme**	we were
(sinä) **ol/i/t**	you were	(te) **ol/i/tte**	you were
hän **ol/i**	he/she was	he **ol/i/vat**	they were
(minä) **ol/isi/n**	I would be	(me) **ol/isi/mme**	we would be
(sinä) **ol/isi/t**	you would be	(te) **ol/isi/tte**	you would be
hän **ol/isi**	he/she would be	he **ol/isi/vat**	they would be

§28. *'TO HAVE' IN FINNISH*

In the Finnish possessive structure the possessor appears in the adessive case **-lla ~ -llä**; the form **on** of the verb **olla** follows, and then the person or thing possessed.

possessive structure

> **POSSESSOR + -lla ~ -llä + on + PERSON OR THING POSSESSED**

Paavo/lla on uusi pyörä.	Paavo *has* a new bicycle (''at'' Paavo is...).
Isä/llä on kaksi autoa.	Father *has* two cars.
Suome/lla on hyvät mahdollisuudet.	Finland *has* good chances.
Äidi/llä on silmälasit.	Mother *has* glasses.

The adessive forms of the personal pronouns are very common.

minu/lla on	I have	**mei/llä on**	we have
sinu/lla on	you have	**tei/llä on**	you have
häne/llä on	he/she has	**hei/llä on**	they have

inalienable possession

For inalienable possession or ''intimate connection'' the inessive **-ssa ~ -ssä** is used instead of the adessive.

Maa/ssa on uusi hallitus.	The country *has* a new government.
Venee/ssä on pitkä masto.	The boat *has* a tall mast.
Puu/ssa on vihreät lehdet.	The tree *has* green leaves.
Auto/ssa on neljä pyörää.	The car *has* four wheels.

§29. NEGATIVE SENTENCES

There is no invariable negation word in Finnish negative sentences. Negation is expressed by an inflected verb, which shows concord of grammatical person with the subject of the sentence like any other finite verb.

		SINGULAR	PLURAL
negation verb	1ST PERSON	en	emme
	2ND PERSON	et	ette
	3RD PERSON	ei	eivät

The negative forms of the present indicative are based on this negation verb, which is followed by the inflectional stem (§23) of the main verb, without any personal ending and in the weak grade (§15) except before a long vowel.

present indicative negative

NEGATION VERB + PERSONAL ENDING	+	INFLECTIONAL STEM OF MAIN VERB IN WEAK GRADE (unless before long vowel)

The changes caused by consonant gradation are important: cf. **anta**/a '(to) give' : hän **anta**/a 'he/she gives' : **anna**/n 'I give' : **anna**/tte 'you (pl.) give'. Further examples follow of the present indicative negative. The form of the main verb can always be derived by detaching the 1st or 2nd person ending from the present affirmative.

AFFIRMATIVE				NEGATIVE	
	tulet	you come		**et** tule	you do not come
	luemme	we read		**emme** lue	we do not read
he	lukevat	they read	he	**eivät** lue	they do not read
hän	lukee	he/she reads	hän	**ei** lue	he/she does not read
	hyppään	I jump		**en** hyppää	I do not jump
	hyppäätte	you (pl.) jump		**ette** hyppää	you (pl.) do not jump
se	vetää	it pulls	se	**ei** vedä	it does not pull
	vedän	I pull		**en** vedä	I do not pull
he	vetävät	they pull	he	**eivät** vedä	they do not pull
	vedämme	we pull		**emme** vedä	we do not pull
hän	tarvitsee	he/she needs	hän	**ei** tarvitse	he/she does not need

The negative forms of **olla** all contain the stem **ole-**.

en ole	I am not	**emme ole**	we are not
et ole	you are not	**ette ole**	you are not
ei ole	(he/she) is not	**eivät ole**	(they) are not

The negative forms of other tenses will be presented later together with the tenses themselves (§63). The following rule concerning negative sentences is an important one.

partitive
rule

> IN NEGATIVE SENTENCES THE FOLLOWING CONSTITUENTS
> ARE IN THE PARTITIVE:
> 1) THE OBJECT
> 2) THAT WHICH IS POSSESSED
> 3) THAT WHICH DOES NOT EXIST

1) Emme juo olut/**ta**. — We do not drink *beer*.
   Ettekö näe auto/**a**? — Don't you see *the car*?
   En tunne hän/**tä**. — I don't know *him/her*.
   He eivät omista vene/**ttä**. — They do not own *a boat*.

2) Minulla ei ole auto/**a**. — I don't have *a car*.
   Meillä ei ole punaviini/**ä**. — We don't have any *red wine*.
   Eikö teillä ole lämmin/**tä** ruoka/**a**? — Don't you have any *warm food*?
   Maassa ei ole hallitus/**ta**. — The country has no *government*.

3) Kadulla ei ole auto/**a**. — There is no *car* in the street.
   Kotona ei ole isä/**ä**. — There is no *father* at home.
   Jääkaapissa ei ole maito/**a**. — There is no *milk* in the fridge.
   Komerossa ei ole vaatte/i/**ta**. — There are no *clothes* in the cupboard.

§30. *QUESTIONS AND ANSWERS*

§30.1. *Questions with -ko ~ -kö (Yes/No questions)*

formation
of
questions

Direct questions that can be answered by "yes" or "no" are formed by moving the word being questioned to the beginning of the sentence and adding to it the enclitic particle **-ko ~ -kö**, which is almost always the last ending of the word. The word questioned is most commonly the verb. If we take the sentence *Pekka saapui Turkuun aamulla* 'Pekka arrived at Turku in the morning', we can form the following questions:

NB:
word
order!

Saapu/i/**ko** Pekka Turkuun aamulla? — Did Pekka arrive at Turku in the morning?

Pekka/**ko** saapui Turkuun aamulla? — Was it Pekka who arrived at Turku in the morning?

Turku/un/**ko** Pekka saapui aamulla? — Was it at Turku that Pekka arrived in the morning?

Aamu/lla/**ko** Pekka saapui Turkuun? — Was it in the morning that Pekka arrived at Turku?

Here are some more examples of the formation of these direct questions.

Mene/t/**kö** ulos? — Are you going out?
Ole/t/**ko** sairas? — Are you ill?
Sa/isi/n/**ko** oluen? — Could I have a beer?
Pitä/ä/**kö** Jussi Marjasta? — Does Jussi like Marja?
Tietä/vät/**kö** he, että tulen? — Do they know that I am coming?
Puu/**ko** tämä on? — Is this a TREE?
Ruotsi/ssa/**ko** Kalle on? — Is Kalle in SWEDEN?
Häne/t/**kö** sinä tapasit? — Was it him/her that you met?
Presidenti/ksi/**kö** Koivisto valittiin? — Was Koivisto elected PRESIDENT?

affirmative answers

There are many ways of answering such questions in the affirmative. The word being questioned is often repeated (in the right person, if it is a verb, and without the ending -ko ~ -kö). If the word questioned is a verb one can also answer **kyllä** 'yes', and if it is some other word one can answer **niin** (literally: 'so'). Both **kyllä** and **niin** can be used with a repetition of the word questioned. The word **joo** 'yes, yeah' are used mostly in the spoken language.

QUESTION	VARIOUS AFFIRMATIVE ANSWERS
Tul/i/**ko** Pekka Turkuun? Did Pekka come to Turku?	— Tuli. — Kyllä tuli. — Kyllä.
Ole/t/**ko** sairas? Are you ill?	— Olen. — Kyllä olen. — Kyllä.
Mene/tte/**kö** tanssimaan? Are you going dancing?	— Menemme. — Kyllä menemme. — Kyllä.
O/vat/**ko** lapset ulkona? Are the children outside?	— Ovat. — Kyllä ovat. — Kyllä.
Auto/n/**ko** ostitte? Was it a car that you bought?	— Niin. — Niin, auton. — Auton.
Tamminieme/ssä/**kö** presidentti asuu? Is it at Tamminiemi that the president lives?	— Niin. — Niin, Tamminiemessä. — Tamminiemessä.

negative answer

Negative answers to direct questions are formed from the negation verb (§28), which must be in the right person and may be followed by the inflectional stem of the main verb with no personal ending.

QUESTION	NEGATIVE ANSWER
Mene/e/**kö** Tauno Kotkaan? Is Tauno going to Kotka?	— Ei (mene).
Ole/t/**ko** kovin sairas? Are you very ill?	— En (ole).
Syö/tte/**kö** hernekeittoa? Do you eat pea-soup?	— Emme (syö). — En (syö).
O/vat/**ko** kirjat laukussa? Are the books in the bag?	— Eivät (ole).
Viljo/**ko** siellä on? Is that Viljo there?	— Ei (vaan Auli). No (it's Auli).
Juna/lla/**ko** tulitte? Did you come by train?	— Emme (vaan linja-autolla). No (by bus).

A question can be made especially polite by using the conditional ending -isi- and/or the particle -**han** ~ -**hän**.

polite question

Sa/**isi**/n/**ko** pullon punaviiniä? Sa/**isi**/n/**ko**/**han** kylmän oluen? On/**ko**/**han** Viljo Kohonen tavattavissa? Ol/**isi**/**ko**/**han** teillä nailonsukkia?	Could I have a bottle of red wine? Might I have a cold beer? I wonder if Viljo Kohonen is in? I wonder if you might have any nylon stockings?

69

The ending -ko ~ -kö is also used in indirect questions.

indirect questions	En tiedä, men/i/kö Auli kotiin.	I don't know if Auli went home.
	Kysy, on/ko heillä lämmintä ruokaa.	Ask if they have warm food.
	Ole/t/ko varma, saa/ko sinne mennä?	Are you sure that (lit.: whether) one can go there?
	Kerro, maistu/i/ko ruoka hyvältä.	Say whether the food tasted good.

§30.2. *Question-word questions (Wh-questions)*

The second main class of questions is question-word questions, which are answered more precisely (not just "yes" or "no"). The most important question words in Finnish are the following (cf. §56):

important question-words	mikä	what, which (more concrete, definite meaning)
	mitä	what, which (more abstract, indefinite meaning; partitive of mikä)
	missä	where
	mistä	from where, whence
	mihin	where to, whither (more precise)
	minne	where to, whither (less precise)
	miten	how, in what way
	millainen	what kind of
	koska	when
	milloin	when
	kuka	who
	kuinka	how
	kumpi	which of two

Mikä, kuka and **millainen** decline in different cases like ordinary nominals. In fact, **mitä, missä, mistä** and **mihin** are inflected forms of the pronoun **mikä**. **Kenen** 'whose' is the genitive of the pronoun **kuka**.

QUESTION	ANSWER
Mikä tämä on?	(Se on) kynä.
What is this?	(It is) a pen.
Mitä tämä on?	(Se on) olutta.
What is this?	(It is) beer.
Missä Auli on?	(Auli on) luennolla.
Where is Auli?	(Auli is) at the lecture.
Mistä tulet?	(Tulen) Oslosta.
Where do you come **from**?	(I come) from Oslo.
Mihin panen vaatteeni?	(Pane ne) sohvalle.
Where shall I put my clothes?	(Put them) on the sofa.
Millainen mies hän on?	(Hän on) mukava (mies).
What kind of a man is he?	(He is a) nice (man).
Koska John tuli Suomeen?	(Hän tuli Suomeen) viime vuonna.
When did John come to Finland?	(He came to Finland) last year.
Kuka tuo pitkä punatukkainen nainen on?	(Hän on) Tyyne Nyrkiö.
Who is that tall red-haired woman?	(She is) Tyyne Nyrkiö.
Kuinka paljon pullo olutta maksaa?	(Se maksaa) kolme markkaa.
How much does a bottle of beer cost?	(It costs) three marks.

Kenen lasi tämä on?	(Se on) Jorman.
Whose glass is this?	(It is) Jorma's.
Kenellä pallo on?	(Pallo on) minulla.
Who has got the ball?	I have. (Lit.: (The ball is) "at" me.)
(Lit.: "at" whom is...)	

§31. CONCORD OF ATTRIBUTES

Attributes are modifiers of nouns. There are two kinds of attributes occurring before the noun: pronoun attributes (*tämä* auto 'this car') and adjective attributes (*sininen* auto 'a blue car'). Both agree with the headword in case and number.

concord rule

> ATTRIBUTES AGREE WITH THE HEADWORD IN CASE AND NUMBER

iso auto	a big car
iso/*t* auto/*t*	the big cars
iso/**ssa** auto/**ssa**	in the big car
iso/*i*/**ssa** auto/*i*/**ssa**	in the big cars
sininen kukka	a blue flower
sinise/*t* kuka/*t*	the blue flowers
sinise/**ssä** kuka/**ssa**	in the blue flower
sinis/*i*/**ssä** kuk/*i*/**ssa**	in the blue flowers

pronouns, cf. §55

tuo punainen kukka	that red flower
tuo/**n** punaise/**n** kuka/**n**	of that red flower
tuo/**ssa** punaise/**ssa** kuka/**ssa**	in that red flower
nuo punaise/*t* kuka/*t*	those red flowers
no/*i*/**lla** punais/*i*/**lla** kuk/*i*/**lla**	with those red flowers
tämä vanha kahvi	this old coffee
tä/**tä** vanha/**a** kahvi/**a**	this old coffee (part.)
tä/**stä** vanha/**sta** kahvi/**sta**	out of this old coffee
tä/**llä** vanha/**lla** kahvi/**lla**	with this old coffee

Attributes occurring before plural headwords (§26) are always in the plural. But such expressions may refer to either singular or plural concepts.

invariable plurals

kaunii/*t* kasvo/*t*	a beautiful face / the beautiful faces
nämä kasvo/*t*	this face / these faces
terävä/*t* sakse/*t*	sharp scissors (one pair or several)
harma/*i*/**ssa** housu/*i*/**ssa**	in grey trousers
yhde/*t* sakse/*t*	one pair of scissors
kahde/*t* kasvo/*t*	two faces

exceptions There are a few adjectives or adjective-like words which are exceptions to the concord rule and do not agree with the headword. The most common ones are: *ensi* 'first', *eri* 'different', *joka* 'every', *koko* 'whole', *pikku* 'little', *viime* 'last', cf. *ensi kerra/lla* 'next time'; *viime talve/na* 'last winter'; *koko kaupungi/ssa* 'in the whole town'; *joka ihmise/lle* 'to every person'; *eri sängy/ssä* 'in a different bed'.

8 The Partitive

After the nominative, the most important case in Finnish is the partitive. In many instances the nominative and the partitive are in opposition to each other. Both may appear as the case of the subject, object and complement (for the object, see also §37).

basic
meaning

The nominative expresses a concrete or abstract whole or a definite quantity (§25). The partitive often expresses an indefinite, non-limited quantity of something, allowing the possibility that more of it may exist.

§32. *FORMATION OF THE PARTITIVE*

§32.1. *Partitive singular*

In the singular the partitive has three endings: -a ~ -ä, -ta ~ -tä, -tta ~ -ttä. The first two also appear in the plural.

1)
-a ~ -ä

> THE ENDING -a ~ -ä OCCURS WHEN THE INFLECTIONAL STEM ENDS IN A CONSONANT FOLLOWED BY A SHORT VOWEL (which is not an -e- that may be dropped)

BASIC FORM		INFLECTIONAL STEM (gen. sing.)	Cf. §	PARTITIVE SINGULAR
oma	own	oma/n		oma/a
päivä	day	päivä/n		päivä/ä
vanha	old	vanha/n		vanha/a
elämä	life	elämä/n		elämä/ä
talo	house	talo/n		talo/a
tuoli	chair	tuoli/n		tuoli/a
hetki	moment	hetke/n	18.2	hetke/ä
katu	street	kadu/n		katu/a
käsky	order	käsky/n		käsky/ä
Suomi	Finland	Suome/n	18.2	Suome/a
koti	home	kodi/n		koti/a
kaupunki	town	kaupungi/n		kaupunki/a
kivi	stone	kive/n	18.2	kive/ä
presidentti	president	presidenti/n		presidentti/ä
Helsinki	Helsinki	Helsingi/n		Helsinki/ä
kaikki	all	kaike/n	18.2	kaikke/a
onni	luck	onne/n	18.2	onne/a
asia	matter	asia/n		asia/a

72

ainoa	only	ainoa/n	ainoa/**a**
tärkeä	important	tärkeä/n	tärkeä/**ä**
vaikea	difficult	vaikea/n	vaikea/**a**

Words ending in **-ea**, **-eä** in particular may also take the longer ending **-ta** ~ **-tä**, e.g. korkea/**a** ~ korkea/**ta** 'high', pehmeä/**ä** ~ pehmeä/**tä** 'soft'.

2) **-ta** ~ **-tä**

> THE ENDING **-ta** ~ **-tä** OCCURS AFTER
> a) A BASIC FORM ENDING IN A LONG VOWEL OR A DIPH-THONG
> b) AN INFLECTIONAL STEM ENDING IN A CONSONANT + AN -e- WHICH HAS THEN BEEN DROPPED
> c) A BASIC FORM ENDING IN A CONSONANT
> d) A MONOSYLLABIC PRONOUN STEM

BASIC FORM		INFLECTIONAL STEM (gen. sing.)	Cf. §	PARTITIVE SINGULAR
a) maa	country	maa/n		maa/**ta**
syy	reason	syy/n		syy/**tä**
tie	road	tie/n		tie/**tä**
Porvoo	(place name)	Porvoo/n		Porvoo/**ta**
työ	work	työ/n		työ/**tä**
pää	head	pää/n		pää/**tä**
yö	night	yö/n		yö/**tä**
kuu	moon	kuu/n		kuu/**ta**
b) kieli	language	kiele/n	18.3	kiel/**tä**
pieni	small	piene/n	18.3	pien/**tä**
lumi	snow	lume/n	18.3	lun/**ta** (NB:m→n)
ääni	sound	ääne/n	18.3.	ään/**tä**
meri	sea	mere/n	18.3	mer/**ta** (NB:-ta)
vesi	water	vede/n	18.4	vet/**tä**
uusi	new	uude/n	18.4	uut/**ta**
kansi	cover	kanne/n	18.4	kant/**ta**
ihminen	person	ihmise/n	20.1	ihmis/**tä**
Virtanen	(surname)	Virtase/n	20.1	Virtas/**ta**
tavallinen	ordinary	tavallise/n	20.1	tavallis/**ta**
hyvyys	goodness	hyvyyde/n	20.4	hyvyyt/**tä**
likaisuus	dirtiness	likaisuude/n	20.4	likaisuut/**ta**
c) ajatus	thought	ajatukse/n	20.2	ajatus/**ta**
kysymys	question	kysymykse/n	20.2	kysymys/**tä**
kiitos	thanks	kiitokse/n	20.2	kiitos/**ta**
taivas	heaven	taivaa/n	20.3	taivas/**ta**
kirves	axe	kirvee/n	20.3	kirves/**tä**
puhelin	telephone	puhelime/n	20.6	puhelin/**ta**
arvoton	valueless	arvottoma/n	20.6	arvoton/**ta**
askel	pace	askele/n	20.7	askel/**ta**
mies	man	miehe/n	20.8	mies/**tä**
olut	beer	olue/n	20.8	olut/**ta**
d) tuo	that	tuo/n		tuo/**ta**
tämä	this	tämä/n		tä/**tä**
se	it	se/n		si/**tä**
joka	which (relative)	jonka		jo/**ta**
mikä	which	minkä		mi/**tä**
kuka	who	kene/n		ke/**tä**

NB: -e- is dropped

<table>
<tr><td>words in
-io, -iö</td><td>The partitive ending for words ending in -io, -iö is -ta ~ -tä, e.g. valtio/ta 'state', radio/ta 'radio', keittiö/tä 'kitchen', yhtiö/tä 'company.</td></tr>
</table>

3)
-tta ~ -ttä

> **THE ENDING -tta ~ -ttä IS ATTACHED TO BASIC FORMS ENDING IN -e- (§19)**

BASIC FORM		INFLECTIONAL STEM (gen. sing.)	PARTITIVE SINGULAR
perhe	family	perhee/n	perhe/ttä
suhde	relation	suhtee/n	suhde/tta
liikenne	traffic	liikentee/n	liikenne/ttä
kone	machine	konee/n	kone/tta
tunne	feeling	tuntee/n	tunne/tta
kirje	letter	kirjee/n	kirje/ttä
virhe	mistake	virhee/n	virhe/ttä

exceptions However, the words *itse* 'self', *kolme* 'three', and *nukke* 'doll', and proper names like *Kalle, Raahe, Ville,* take the ending -a ~ -ä.

§32.2. *Partitive plural*

In the plural the partitive has two endings, -a ~ -ä and -ta ~ -tä, which are added to the inflectional stem after the plural -i- (§26). The plural -i- causes vowel changes in the stem (§16), and between vowels -i- changes to -j- (§26). Consonant gradation is rare in the partitive plural, since the endings do not fulfil the basic conditions for alternation (§15.2).

1) -a ~ -ä

> **THE ENDING -a ~ -ä IS ALWAYS USED WHEN THE INFLECTIONAL STEM OF THE SINGULAR ENDS IN A SHORT VOWEL**

BASIC FORM		INFLECTIONAL STEM	§	PARTITIVE SINGULAR	PARTITIVE PLURAL
talo	house	talo/n		talo/a	talo/j/a
katu	street	kadu/n		katu/a	katu/j/a
tunti	hour	tunni/n		tunti/a	tunte/j/a
lasi	glass	lasi/n		lasi/a	lase/j/a
kivi	stone	kive/n	18.2	kive/ä	kiv/i/ä
lehti	newspaper	lehde/n	18.2	lehte/ä	leht/i/ä
tuuli	wind	tuule/n	18.3	tuul/ta	tuul/i/a
pieni	small	piene/n	18.3	pien/tä	pien/i/ä
käsi	hand	käde/n	18.4	kät/tä	käs/i/ä
kansi	cover	kanne/n	18.4	kant/ta	kans/i/a
päivä	day	päivä/n		päivä/ä	päiv/i/ä
sama	same	sama/n		sama/a	samo/j/a
poika	boy	poja/n		poika/a	poik/i/a
kirja	book	kirja/n		kirja/a	kirjo/j/a
nainen	woman	naise/n	20.1	nais/ta	nais/i/a

for vowel changes see §16						
	yleinen	general	yleise/n	20.1	yleis/tä	yleis/i/a
	sormus	ring	sormukse/n	20.2	sormus/ta	sormuks/i/a
	nuoruus	youth	nuoruude/n	20.4	nuoruut/ta	nuoruuks/i/a
	avain	key	avaime/n	20.5	avain/ta	avaim/i/a
	koditon	homeless	kodittoma/n	20.6	koditon/ta	kodittom/i/a
	jäsen	member	jäsene/n	20.7	jäsen/tä	jäsen/i/ä
	mies	man	miehe/n	20.8	mies/tä	mieh/i/ä

In words of three or more syllables such as *kanava* 'canal', *aurinko* 'sun', *ammatti* 'profession', the ending -a ~ -ä occurs when the last vowel of the stem is dropped, and otherwise when the penultimate syllable of the word ends in a consonant (pääl.lik.kö 'chief', au.rin.ko 'sun') or in two vowels (rat. kai.su 'decision').

	BASIC FORM		INFLECTIONAL STEM	PARTITIVE SINGULAR	PARTITIVE PLURAL
NB:	aurinko	sun	auringo/n	aurinko/a	aurinko/j/a
polysyl-	ammatti	profession	ammati/n	ammatti/a	ammatte/j/a
labic	hedelmä	fruit	hedelmä/n	hedelmä/ä	hedelm/i/ä
words	ystävä	friend	ystävä/n	ystävä/ä	ystäv/i/ä
	metalli	metal	metalli/n	metalli/a	metalle/j/a
	kysely	inquiry	kysely/n	kysely/ä	kysely/j/ä
	päällikkö	chief	päällikö/n	päällikkö/ä	päällikkö/j/ä
	ratkaisu	decision	ratkaisu/n	ratkaisu/a	ratkaisu/j/a
	omena	apple	omena/n	omena/a	omen/i/a

2) -ta ~ -tä

> THE ENDING -ta ~ -tä IS USED WHEN THE INFLECTIONAL STEM OF THE SINGULAR ENDS IN TWO VOWELS

	BASIC FORM		INFLECTIONAL STEM	§	PARTITIVE SINGULAR	PARTITIVE PLURAL
	maa	country	maa/n		maa/ta	ma/i/ta
	kuu	moon	kuu/n		kuu/ta	ku/i/ta
	syy	reason	syy/n		syy/tä	sy/i/tä
	vapaa	free	vapaa/n		vapaa/ta	vapa/i/ta
NOTE	perhe	family	perhee/n	19	perhe/ttä	perhe/i/tä
perhe-	lääke	medicine	lääkkee/n	19	lääke/ttä	lääkke/i/tä
words	aine	substance	ainee/n	19	aine/tta	aine/i/ta
	tie	road	tie/n		tie/tä	te/i/tä
	tuo	that	tuo/n		tuo/ta	no/i/ta
	työ	work	työ/n		työ/tä	tö/i/tä
	rikas	rich	rikkaa/n	20.3	rikas/ta	rikka/i/ta
	hammas	tooth	hampaa/n	20.3	hammas/ta	hampa/i/ta
	kallis	expensive	kallii/n	20.3	kallis/ta	kalli/i/ta
	ohut	thin	ohue/n	20.8	ohut/ta	ohu/i/ta
	lyhyt	short	lyhye/n	20.8	lyhyt/tä	lyhy/i/tä
	asia	matter	asia/n		asia/a	asio/i/ta
	tärkeä	important	tärkeä/n		tärkeä/ä	tärke/i/tä
	ainoa	only	ainoa/n		ainoa/a	aino/i/ta
	komea	fine	komea/n		komea/a	kome/i/ta

75

Many *nouns* of three or more syllables, with a penultimate syllable ending in short vowel, take the partitive plural ending -ta ∼ -tä. This also applies to nouns ending in -kka,-kkä and -la, -lä.

BASIC FORM		PARTITIVE SINGULAR	PARTITIVE PLURAL	
lukija	reader	lukija/a	lukijo/i/**ta**	
kulkija	wanderer	kulkija/a	kulkijo/i/**ta**	
lusikka	spoon	lusikka/a	lusiko/i/**ta**	(NB: consonant
kahvila	café	kahvila/a	kahvilo/i/**ta**	gradation!)
käymälä	toilet	käymälä/ä	käymälö/i/**tä**	
omena	apple	omena/a	omeno/i/**ta**	
päärynä	pear	päärynä/ä	päärynö/i/**tä**	
peruna	potato	peruna/a	peruno/i/**ta**	
tavara	thing	tavara/a	tavaro/i/**ta**	
ankkuri	anchor	ankkuri/a	ankkure/i/**ta**	
arvelu	supposition	arvelu/a	arvelu/i/**ta**	

In many words of this type both -ta ∼ -tä and -a ∼ -ä are possible, but consonant gradation then affects the stem differently depending on the form chosen. E.g. *päällikkö/j/ä* (: *päällikö/i/tä*) 'chiefs', *lusiko/i/ta* (: *lusikko/j/a*) 'spoons', *sairaalo/i/ta* (: *sairaalo/j/a*) 'hospitals', *omen/i/a* (: *omeno/i/ta)* 'apples'.

Adjectives of three or more syllables form their partitive plural in the normal way by adding the ending -a ∼ -ä (cf. §16).

BASIC FORM		PARTITIVE SINGULAR	PARTITIVE PLURAL
ahkera	hard-working	ahkera/a	ahker/i/**a**
ankara	severe	ankara/a	ankar/i/**a**
hämärä	dim	hämärä/ä	hämär/i/**ä**
vikkelä	quick	vikkelä/ä	vikkel/i/**ä**

The following pronoun forms are important:

BASIC FORM		PARTITIVE SINGULAR	PARTITIVE PLURAL
minä	I	minu/**a**	
sinä	you (sing.)	sinu/**a**	
hän	he, she	hän/**tä**	
me	we		me/i/**tä**
te	you (pl.)		te/i/**tä**
he	they		he/i/**tä**
se	it	si/**tä**	ni/i/**tä**
tämä	this	tä/**tä**	nä/i/**tä**
tuo	that	tuo/**ta**	no/i/**tä**

§33. *USE OF THE PARTITIVE*

§33.1. *Partitive subject*

It is helpful to compare the use of the partitive with that of the nominative (§25.3): these two cases are semantically complementary to each other. The following rule concerns the use of the partitive as a subject and object case.

> **WITH DIVISIBLE WORDS THE PARTITIVE EXPRESSES AN INDEFINITE, NON-LIMITED QUANTITY**

Typical uses of the partitive are thus e.g. *vet/tä* 'water', *valo/a* 'light', *rakkaut/ta* 'love', *tuole/j/a* 'chairs', *auto/j/a* 'cars'. The following rule concerns the partitive subject.

> **IN SENTENCES WITH A PARTITIVE SUBJECT**
> 1) **THE SUBJECT IS GENERALLY AT THE END OF THE SENTENCE**
> 2) **THE FINITE VERB IS ALWAYS IN THE 3RD PERSON SINGULAR**

The examples below are divided into two groups: divisible indefinite singular words (indefinite mass nouns), and divisible indefinite plural forms of words that are non-divisible in the singular (i.e. indefinite plural count forms).

> **1) DIVISIBLE SUBJECTS EXPRESSING AN INDEFINITE QUANTITY ARE IN THE PARTITIVE SINGULAR (mass, abstract and collective words)**

partitive
singular

Purkissa on leipä/**ä**.	There is (*some*) *bread* in the tin.
Pullossa on maito/**a**.	There is (*some*) *milk* in the bottle.
Torille tuli kansa/**a**.	*People* came to the market-place.
Huoneessa on valo/**a**.	There is (*some*) *light* in the room.
Kellariinkin valui vet/**tä**.	(*Some*) *water* leaked into the cellar, too.
Suomessa on vielä puhdas/**ta** ilma/**a**.	Finland still has *clean air*.
Täällä tapahtuu kaikenlais/**ta**.	"Here there happens everything possible." (i.e. "All kinds of things happen here.")
Kaikenlais/**ta** täällä tapahtuu.	"Everything possible happens here." ("All kinds...")
Jääkaapissa on olut/**ta**.	In the fridge there is (*some*) *beer*.
Olut/**ta** on jääkaapissa.	There is (*some*) *beer* in the fridge.
Olut/**ta** jääkaapissa on!	There is (*some*) *BEER* in the fridge!

The sentences above should be compared with the following ones, where the subject expresses a definite (total) amount. These subjects are normally at the beginning of the sentence.

compare
the
nominative

Leipä on purkissa.	*The bread* is in the tin.
Maito on pullossa.	*The milk* is in the bottle.
Kansa tuli torille.	*The people* came to the market-place.
Vesi valui kellariin.	*The water* leaked into the cellar.
Kulta löytyi Outokummusta.	*The gold* was found at Outokumpu.

2) PLURAL SUBJECT NOUNS (NON-DIVISIBLE IN THE SINGULAR) EXPRESSING AN INDEFINITE QUANTITY APPEAR IN THE PARTITIVE PLURAL

partitive plural	Kadulla on auto/j/a.	There are *cars* in the street.
	Liikkui huhu/j/a.	There were (lit.: ''moved'') *rumours* around.
	Täällä on pien/i/ä laps/i/a.	There are *small children* here.
	Ihmis/i/ä kuolee joka päivä.	(*Some*) *people* die every day.
	Syntyi vaikeuks/i/a.	*Difficulties* arose.
	Minulla on mon/i/a ystäv/i/ä.	I have *many friends*.
	Onko Kallella laps/i/a?	Does Kalle have *any children*?
	Sellais/i/a virhe/i/tä esiintyy usein.	*Such mistakes* occur often.

The corresponding ''total'' subjects (usually, but not always, definite in English) are in the nominative plural, and the finite verb then shows concord of person with the subject.

definite (total) subject in nominative plural	Auto/t ovat kadulla.	*The cars* are in the street.
	Lapse/t ovat täällä.	*The children* are here.
	Ihmise/t kuolevat.	*People* die (i.e. *all* people).
	Laiva/t tulevat satamaan.	*The ships* come to the harbour.
	Vaikeude/t eivät tule yksin.	*Difficulties* do not come singly (*all*, not just some).

3) THE PARTITIVE IS USED IF THE EXISTENCE OF THE ENTITY REFERRED TO BY THE SUBJECT WORD IS COMPLETELY DENIED (i.e. in most negative sentences)

partitive subject in negative sentences	Kadulla ei ole auto/a.	There is no *car* in the street.
	Maassa ei ole hallitus/ta.	The country has no *government*.
	Minulla ei ole tieto/a siitä.	I have no *knowledge* of it.
	Koti/a ei enää ollut.	*Home* was no longer.
	Täällä ei ole yhtään tuttu/a.	There is not a single *person* I know here.
	Juna/a ei vielä näy.	*The train* is not yet in sight (lit.: ''is not seen'').

However, if the actual existence of something is not completely denied but only e.g. its being in a particular place, the nominative is used.

Auto ei ole kadulla.	*The car* is not in the street.
Hallitus ei ole Turussa.	*The government* is not in Turku.
Juna ei ole asemalla.	*The train* is not in the station.

The partitive can sometimes also be the subject case of non-divisible words, in interrogative sentences expecting a negative answer.

Onko teillä tä/tä kirja/a?	Do you have *this book*?
Tuleeko hänestä lääkäri/ä?	Will he really become *a doctor*? (lit.: ''will out of him come a doctor'')

§33.2. *Partitive object*

The cases of the object are partitive and accusative, as the cases of the subject are nominative and partitive. The accusative object in some ways corresponds to the nominative subject (for the different accusative endings see §38: the most common is -**n**).

ACCUSATIVE OBJECT

Minä ostan auto/**n**.	I('ll) buy *a/the car*.
Silja joi maido/**n**.	Silja drank (up) *the milk*.
Osta auto.	Buy *a/the car*.
Auto/**t** hankittiin halvalla.	*The cars* were obtained cheaply (lit.: "one obtained...").
Ostamme auto/**t**.	We('ll) buy *the cars*.

Like the nominative subject, the accusative object expresses a whole or a definite quantity. The partitive usually expresses an indefinite quantity (rule 3 below), but as one of the object cases it also has other functions (rules 1 and 2).

---

1) THE OBJECT OF A NEGATIVE SENTENCE IS IN THE PARTITIVE

---

1) partitive object in negative sentences

En osta auto/**a**.	I don't/won't buy *a/the car*.
Pekka ei nähnyt Leena/**a**.	Pekka did not see *Leena*.
Silja ei juo maito/**a**.	Silja does not drink (*the*) *milk*.
En tunne Kekkos/**ta**.	I do not know *Kekkonen*.
Paavo ei syö puuro/**a**.	Paavo does not eat (*the*) *porridge*.
Etkö opiskele suome/**a**?	Don't you study *Finnish*?
He eivät ymmärrä tä/**tä**.	They don't understand *this*.
En ole koskaan tavannut hän/**tä**.	I have never met *him/her*.
Si/**tä** emme vielä tiedä.	*That* we don't know yet.
Janne ei lue sanomaleht/i/**ä**.	Janne does not read (*the*) *newspapers*.
En tunne no/i/**ta** mieh/i/**ä**.	I don't know *those men*.
Ettekö ole lukeneet nä/i/**tä** kirjo/j/**a**?	Haven't you read *these books*?

This rule always applies. It makes no difference whether the meaning of the object is definite or indefinite. The same negative sentence thus corresponds to two different affirmative sentences.

AFFIRMATIVE

Silja joi maido/**n**.
Silja drank *the milk*.

Silja joi maito/**a**.
Silja drank (*some*) *milk*.

NEGATIVE

Silja ei juonut maito/**a**.
Silja didn't drink *the/any milk*.

79

In English this use of the partitive often corresponds to the progressive form of the verb (*be* + *-ing*); see the translation of the examples below. The accusative, on the other hand, expresses that the action expressed by the verb *has* led to an important result (is resultative).

2) irresultative partitive object

IRRESULTATIVE (partitive object)	RESULTATIVE (accusative object)
Tyttö luki läksy/**ä**. The girl *was doing* her homework (i.e. had not yet finished).	Tyttö luki läksy/**n**. The girl *did* (i.e. finished) her homework.
Väinö rakensi talo/**a**. Väinö *was building* a/the house.	Väinö rakensi talo/**n**. Väinö *built* a/the house.
Väinö rakentaa talo/**a**. Väinö *is building* a/the house.	Väinö rakentaa talo/**n**. Väinö *will build* a/the house.
Hän ajaa auto/**a**. He/she *is driving* a/the car.	Hän ajaa auto/**n** talliin. He/she *drives* the car *into the garage*.
Presidentti ampui lintu/**a**. The president *shot at* (or: *shot and wounded*) a/the bird.	Presidentti ampui linnu/**n**. The president *shot* (*and killed*) a/the bird.
Kalle lämmittää sauna/**a**. Kalle *is warming up* the sauna.	Kalle lämmittää sauna/**n**. Kalle *will warm up* the sauna.

Many verbs are intrinsically irresultative, and their objects are thus generally in the partitive. One important group of such verbs is those expressing an emotion or state of mind.

verbs of emotion

rakasta/a	love	vihat/a	hate
pelät/ä	fear	kaivat/a	miss, long for
kunnioitta/a	honour	sur/ra	grieve
arvosta/a	value	valitta/a	complain
katu/a	regret	sääli/ä	pity
kiittä/ä	thank	harrasta/a	be interested in
kiinnosta/a	interest	huvitta/a	amuse
miellyttä/ä	please	moitti/a	blame
arvostel/la	criticise	haukku/a	scold
loukat/a	insult	syyttä/ä	accuse
uhat/a	threaten	kiusat/a	annoy

Minä rakastan sinu/**a**!	I love *you*!
Rakastan tuo/**ta** nais/**ta**.	I love *that woman*.
Suomi kiinnostaa minu/**a**.	Finland interests *me*.

Pelkäätkö koir/i/a?	Are you afraid of *dogs*?
Kekkonen kiitti hallitus/ta.	Kekkonen thanked *the government*.
Säälin hän/tä.	I pity *him/her*.
Tauno kaipaa jo/ta/kin uut/ta.	Tauno longs for *something new*.

There are also other verbs which have an irresultative meaning and therefore very often take the partitive object.

jatka/a	continue	*puolusta/a*	defend
verrat/a	compare	*seurat/a*	follow
ehdotta/a	suggest	*tarkoitta/a*	mean
vastusta/a	oppose	*vaikeutta/a*	make difficult
edusta/a	represent	*korosta/a*	emphasize
ajatel/la	think	*heikentä/ä*	weaken

Ajattelen sinu/a.	I think of *you*.
Keihänen jatkoi toiminta/a.	Keihänen continued *his business*.
Joku seuraa minu/a.	Someone is following *me*.
Voiko suome/a verrata ruotsiin?	Can one compare *Finnish* to Swedish?
Mi/tä sinä tarkoitat?	*What* do you mean?
Sorsa edustaa sosialidemokraatte/j/a.	Sorsa represents *the Social Democrats*.

3) indefinite quantity

> ## 3) THE OBJECT IS IN THE PARTITIVE WHEN IT EXPRESSES AN INDEFINITE, NON-LIMITED QUANTITY (divisible words and plural words)

PARTITIVE OBJECT (indefinite quantity)	ACCUSATIVE OBJECT (definite quantity)
Ostan jäätelö/ä.	Ostan jäätelö/n.
I('ll) buy *some ice-cream*.	I('ll) buy *an/the ice-cream*.
Pekka juo olut/ta.	Pekka juo olue/n.
Pekka drinks *beer* / is drinking (*some*) *beer*.	Pekka (will) drink *a/the beer*.
Opitko suome/a?	Opin suomen kiele/n.
Are you learning (*some*) *Finnish*? (Also: did you learn...)	I learned *the Finnish language*.
Näen ihmis/i/ä.	Näen ihmise/t.
I see (*some*) *people*.	I see *the people*.
Tuula tapaa viera/i/ta.	Tuula tapaa vieraa/t.
Tuula meets / is meeting *some guests*.	Tuula meets *the guests*.
Nieminen myy metsä/ä.	Nieminen myy metsä/n.
Nieminen sells / is selling *some forest*.	Nieminen sells / will sell *the forest*.

§33.3. *Partitive complement*

A complement is a constituent occurring after the verb *olla*, expressing some characteristic of the subject, e.g. *nainen* and *mukava* in the sentences *Marketta on nainen* 'Marketta is a woman' and *Marketta on mukava* 'Marketta is nice'. The cases of the complement are nominative and partitive, and occasionally also genitive (e.g. *Auto on minu/n* 'The car is mine'). When the complement is an adjective the following rules hold.

A SINGULAR ADJECTIVE COMPLEMENT (i.e. a predicative adjective) IS IN THE PARTITIVE WHEN THE SUBJECT IS DIVISIBLE

---

1) singular adjective complement

Maito on valkois/**ta**.	(The) milk is *white*.
Rauta on kova/**a**.	(The) iron is *hard*.
Kahvi on kuuma/**a**.	(The) coffee is *hot*.
Tämä on merkillis/**tä**.	This is *peculios*.
Musiikki on kaunis/**ta**.	(The) music is *beautiful*.
Rehellisyys on harvinais/**ta**.	Honesty is *rare*.
Uiminen on hauska/**a**.	Swimming is *nice*.

When the subject is non-divisible, the adjective complement is normally in the nominative.

nominative complement

Heidän koiransa on *valkoinen*.	Their dog is *white*.
Tämä pala on *kova*.	This bit is *hard*.
Kuppi on *kuuma*.	The cup is *hot*.
Hän on *merkillinen*.	He/she is *funny*.
Autoni ei ole *kaunis*.	My car is not *beautiful*.

An adjective complement is also in the partitive when the subject is an infinitive or a subordinate clause, or when there is no subject.

infinitives and clauses

On ilmeis/**tä**, että...	It is *clear* that...
On paras/**ta** lähteä.	It is *best* to leave.
Luennolla oli hauska/**a**.	It was *nice* at the lecture (lit.: "at the lecture was nice").

With some adjectives both nominative and partitive are equally possible as complement cases; often the nominative is better.

Minun on *vaikea(a)* tulla.	It is *difficult* for me to come.
Oli *hauska(a)* tutustua.	It was *nice* to meet (you).
Ei ole *helppo(a)* päättää.	It is not *easy* to decide.

If the subject is plural, the adjective complement must also be in the plural (concord), and is usually in the partitive plural. But the nominative plural is often equally possible; this form is obligatory if the subject is a plural invariable word (§26) or if the concept referred to by the subject is clearly of limited scope.

2)
plural
adjective
comple-
ment

Oletteko ilois/i/a?	Are you (pl.) *glad*?
Omenat ovat tanskalais/i/a.	The apples are *Danish*.
Nämä kirjat ovat kalli/i/ta.	These books are *expensive*.
Tulppaanit ovat punais/i/a.	The tulips are *red*.
He ovat miellyttäv/i/ä.	They are *pleasant*.
Voileivät ovat hyv/i/ä.	The sandwiches are *good*.

In sentences like the above the nominative is also possible: *Nämä kirjat ovat
kallii/t*; *Tulppaanit ovat punaise/t*; *Voileivät ovat hyvä/t*. In the following
examples, however, the nominative is obligatory; the subject is either an
invariable plural or word referring to a part of the body.

Jalat ovat likaise/t.	The feet are *dirty*.
Saappaat ovat pitkä/t.	The boots are *tall*.
Kasvot olivat valkoise/t.	The face was *white*.
Sakset ovat terävä/t.	The scissors are *sharp*.
Housut ovat harmaa/t.	The trousers are *grey*.

Noun complements can also be either nominative or partitive.

3) noun
comple-
ment

Oletteko ruotsalais/i/a?	Are you (pl.) *Swedish*?
Olemme suomalais/i/a.	We are *Finnish*.
He ovat nais/i/a.	They are *women*.
Tuoli on puu/ta.	The chair is (made) *of wood*.
Paitani on villa/a.	My shirt is (made) *of wool*.
Aika on raha/a.	Time is *money*.
Tämä on punaviini/ä.	This is *red wine*.

The noun complement is otherwise in the nominative when it is a non-divisible
word and refers to a definite quantity.

Keijo on *mies*.	Keijo is *a man*.
Tämä on *auto*.	This is *a car*.
Olavi Järvinen on *lääkäri*.	Olavi Järvinen is *a doctor*.
Tässä on *viini*!	This (lit.: "here") is *(the) wine*!

§33.4. *The partitive in expressions of quantity*

The partitive is used in expressions of quantity, i.e. after numerals and words
like *monta* 'many', *paljon* 'much', *vähän* '(a) little, few' (except when the
numeral is inflected, see §52.2).

yksi +	yksi tyttö	one girl
nom.	kaksi tyttö/ä	two girls
	viisi tyttö/ä	five girls
kaksi,	neljä maa/ta	four countries
kolme,	yhdeksän vene/ttä	nine boats
neljä...	kaksikymmentä kirja/a	twenty books
+ part.	sata mies/tä	a hundred men
	monta nais/ta	many women

vähän maito/a	(a) little milk
vähän auto/j/a	few cars
paljon olut/ta	much beer
puoli tunti/a	half an hour
kuppi kuuma/a kahvi/a	a cup of hot coffee
kaksi kuppi/a kylmä/ä tee/tä	two cups of cold tea
lasi punaviini/ä	a glass of red wine
kilo omeno/i/ta	a kilo of apples
kaksi kilo/a appelsiine/j/a	two kilos of oranges
joukko ihmis/i/ä	a crowd of people
pari kenk/i/ä	a pair of shoes
pala leipä/ä	a bit of bread
pussi sokeri/a	a bag of sugar

If the numeral expression is the subject of the sentence, the finite verb is then in the 3rd person singular.

3rd person singular	Kaksi miestä kulke/e kadulla.	Two men walk / are walking in the street.
	(Compare: Miehet kulke/vat kadulla.	The men walk / are walking in the street.)
	Neljä pääministeriä kokoontu/u Helsinkiin.	Four prime ministers meet / are meeting in Helsinki.
	(Compare: Pääministerit kokoontu/vat Helsinkiin.	The prime ministers meet / are meeting in Helsinki.)

If the numeral is in a case other than the nominative, the whole phrase of which the numeral is a part must be in the same case (concord, §52.2).

concord	Ajamme Helsinkiin kahde/lla auto/lla.	We drive / are driving to Helsinki in two cars.
	Minulla ei ole kolme/a velje/ä.	I don't have three brothers.
	Kirjoitin kirjan kuude/ssa viiko/ssa.	I wrote a/the book in six weeks.

§33.5. *The partitive with pre- and postpositions*

There are several prepositions and a few postpositions which require the partitive for the word they modify, e.g. the prepositions *lähellä* 'near', *ilman* 'without', *ennen* 'before', *pitkin* 'along', *kohti* 'towards', *vasten* 'against', and the postpositions *kohtaan* 'towards', *varten* 'for'.

Tuletko kotiin *ennen* joulu/a?

Are you coming home *before Christmas*?

Pertti selviää *ilman* auto/a.
He kävelivät *pitkin* silta/a.
Tunnen sääliä sinu/a *kohtaan*.
Tä/tä *varten* olemme tulleet.

Pertti manages *without a car*.
They walked *along the bridge*.
I feel pity *for* (lit.: "towards") *you*.
This is what we have come *for* (lit.: "for this we have come").

9 The Genitive, Possessive Suffixes and the Accusative

Formation of the genitive
Use of the genitive
Possessive suffixes
What is the accusative?
The accusative endings
Quantity adverbs taking an object case

This chapter deals with two cases, the genitive and the accusative, and also the possessive suffixes, which are a class of endings distinct from case forms. The accusative is not really a case form proper but a collective name for certain cases used for the object (nominative, genitive and -t accusative) which are in opposition to the partitive. The genitive and the possessive suffixes are related since they both often express possession.

§34. *FORMATION OF THE GENITIVE*

§34.1. *Genitive singular*

-n

The genitive singular ending is always -**n**, which is added to the inflectional stem. As the genitive ending consists of only one consonant, it usually causes consonant gradation (weak grade) in the inflectional stem (§15). This does not apply to nominals ending in -**e** (§19), nor to some ending in a consonant (§20), where the basic form and the partitive singular take the weak grade and other cases the strong grade.

> THE GENITIVE SINGULAR ENDING IS -**n**, WHICH IS ADDED TO THE INFLECTIONAL STEM

NB:
formation
of the
inflectional
stem!

BASIC FORM		GENITIVE	Cf.§
Rauno	(masculine name)	Rauno/**n**	
puu	tree, wood	puu/**n**	
Suvikki	(feminine name)	Suviki/**n**	
Kaisu	(feminine name)	Kaisu/**n**	
teltta	tent	telta/**n**	
tunti	hour	tunni/**n**	
onni	luck	onne/**n**	18.2
Suomi	Finland	Suome/**n**	18.2
saari	island	saare/**n**	18.3

86

tuli	fire	tule/**n**	18.3
käsi	hand	käde/**n**	18.4
varsi	handle	varre/**n**	18.4
laite	appliance	laittee/**n**	19
kone	machine	konee/**n**	19
Järvinen	(surname)	Järvise/**n**	20.1
toinen	other	toise/**n**	20.1
teos	work	teokse/**n**	20.2
tehdas	factory	tehtaa/**n**	20.3
taivas	heaven, sky	taivaa/**n**	20.3
rakkaus	love	rakkaude/**n**	20.4
puhelin	telephone	puhelime/**n**	20.5
isätön	fatherless	isättömä/**n**	20.6
sävel	tune	sävele/**n**	20.7
mies	man	miehe/**n**	20.8
kevät	spring	kevää/**n**	20.8

If the genitive singular of nominals is known, the inflectional stem can always be found by removing the **-n** ending. Most other case forms are formed by adding the necessary number and case endings to this stem.

§34.2. *Genitive plural*

The genitive plural is the most complex of the Finnish case forms. The most common endings are **-den** (which can always be changed to **-tten**) and **-en**, which are normally added after the **-i-** of the plural stem (§§16, 26). In some declension types the ending **-ten** is also used, added to the consonant stem of the singular (especially in **ihminen**-words, §20.1). It is usually worth comparing the formation of the genitive plural with that of the partitive plural.

1) **-den**

> THE GENITIVE PLURAL ENDING IS **-den** IF THE PARTITIVE PLURAL ENDING IS **-ta ~ -tä** (i.e. if the inflectional stem ends in two vowels, and also in some monosyllabic words, §32.2)

BASIC FORM		INFLECTIONAL STEM (gen. sing.) §		PARTITIVE PLURAL	GENITIVE PLURAL
maa	country	maa/n		ma/i/ta	ma/i/**den**
puu	tree, wood	puu/n		pu/i/ta	pu/i/**den**
vapaa	free	vapaa/n		vapa/i/ta	vapa/i/**den**
este	obstacle	estee/n	19	este/i/tä	este/i/**den**
peite	cover	peittee/n	19	peitte/i/tä	peitte/i/**den**
hammas	tooth	hampaa/n	20.3	hampa/i/ta	hampa/i/**den**
hidas	slow	hitaa/n	20.3	hita/i/ta	hita/i/**den**
korkea	high	korkea/n		korke/i/ta	korke/i/**den**
tärkeä	important	tärkeä/n		tärke/i/tä	tärke/i/**den**
asia	matter	asia/n		asio/i/ta	asio/i/**den**
lukija	reader	lukija/n		lukijo/i/ta	lukijo/i/**den**
tavara	thing	tavara/n		tavaro/i/ta	tavaro/i/**den**
peruna	potato	peruna/n		peruno/i/ta	peruno/i/**den**
ankkuri	anchor	ankkuri/n		ankkure/i/ta	ankkure/i/**den** (or: ankkuri/**en**)
kukkula	hill	kukkula/n		kukkulo/i/ta	kukkulo/i/**den**

> THE ENDING -den CAN ALWAYS BE REPLACED BY THE
> ENDING -tten

Compare ma/i/**den** ∼ ma/i/**tten**, este/i/**den** ∼ este/i/**tten**, korke/i/**den** ∼
korke/i/**tten** etc.

2) -en

> THE GENITIVE PLURAL ENDING IS -**en** IF THE PARTITIVE
> PLURAL ENDING IS -**a** ∼ -**ä** (i.e. if the inflectional stem ends in a con-
> sonant followed by a short vowel, and also in some polysyllabic words,
> §32.2)

BASIC FORM		INFLECTIONAL STEM (gen. sing.) §		PARTITIVE PLURAL	GENITIVE PLURAL
katto	roof	kato/n		katto/j/a	katto/j/**en**
karhu	bear	karhu/n		karhu/j/a	karhu/j/**en**
kala	fish	kala/n		kalo/j/a	kalo/j/**en**
muna	egg	muna/n		mun/i/a	mun/i/**en**
isä	father	isä/n		is/i/ä	is/i/**en**
tunti	hour	tunni/n		tunte/j/a	tunti/**en**
lasi	glass	lasi/n		lase/j/a	lasi/**en**
ovi	door	ove/n	18.2	ov/i/a	ov/i/**en**
kaikki	all	kaike/n	18.2	kaikk/i/a	kaikk/i/**en**
kieli	language	kiele/n	18.3	kiel/i/ä	kiel/i/**en**
sieni	mushroom	siene/n	18.3	sien/i/ä	sien/i/**en**
käsi	hand	käde/n	18.4	käs/i/ä	käs/i/**en**
viisi	five	viide/n	18.4	viis/i/ä	viis/i/**en**
hevonen	horse	hevose/n	20.1	hevos/i/a	hevos/i/**en**
nainen	woman	naise/n	20.1	nais/i/a	nais/i/**en**
kokous	meeting	kokoukse/n	20.2	kokouks/i/a	kokouks/i/**en**
sormus	ring	sormukse/n	20.2	sormuks/i/a	sormuks/i/**en**
totuus	truth	totuude/n	20.4	totuuks/i/a	totuuks/i/**en**
vaikeus	difficulty	vaikeude/n	20.4	vaikeuks/i/a	vaikeuks/i/**en**
avain	key	avaime/n	20.5	avaim/i/a	avaim/i/**en**
työtön	unemployed	työttömä/n	20.6	työttöm/i/ä	työttöm/i/**en**
askel	pace	askele/n	20.7	askel/i/a	askel/i/**en**
mies	man	miehe/n	20.8	mieh/i/ä	mieh/i/**en**
hedelmä	fruit	hedelmä/n		hedelm/i/ä	hedelm/i/**en**
sopiva	suitable	sopiva/n		sopiv/i/a	sopiv/i/**en**
hämärä	dim	hämärä/n		hämär/i/ä	hämär/i/**en**
asema	station	asema/n		asem/i/a	asem/i/**en**
opettaja	teacher	opettaja/n		opettaj/i/a	opettaj/i/**en**
aurinko	sun	auringo/n		aurinko/j/a	aurinko/j/**en**
ammatti	profession	ammati/n		ammatte/j/a	ammatti/**en**
päällikkö	chief	päällikö/n		päällikkö/j/ä	päällikkö/j/**en**

NOTE
tunti-
words

NOTE
polysyl-
labic
words

In many words of three or more syllables both -**den** and -**en** are possible, but
in some words the effect of consonant gradation must then be noted: päälli-
kö/i/**den** ∼ päällikkö/j/**en**, ammate/i/**den** ∼ ammatti/**en**, ankkure/i/**den** ∼
ankkuri/**en**.

   Sometimes the genitive plural can also be formed using the ending -**ten**,
which is added to a basic form ending in a consonant (§32.1, group c), or to a
consonant stem formed after the final vowel has been dropped (§32.1, group
b). This ending is particularly common with **ihminen**-words (§20.1).

3) -ten

> SOMETIMES THE GENITIVE PLURAL ENDING IS -ten, WHICH IS ADDED TO A CONSONANT STEM

BASIC FORM		INFLECTIONAL STEM (gen. sing.) §		GENITIVE PLURAL	OR (FOR MOST TYPES SELDOM):
kieli	language	kiele/n	18.3	kiel/**ten**	∼ kiel/i/**en** (cf. 1)
pieni	small	piene/n	18.3	pien/**ten**	∼ pien/i/**en**
nuori	young	nuore/n	18.3	nuor/**ten**	∼ nuor/i/**en**
nainen	woman	naise/n	20.1	nais/**ten**	∼ (nais/i/**en**)
ruotsa-lainen	Swedish	ruotsa-laise/n	20.1	ruotsa-lais/**ten**	∼ (ruotsa-lais/i/**en**)
ostos	purchase	ostokse/n	20.2	ostos/**ten**	∼ ostoks/i/**en**
hammas	tooth	hampaa/n	20.3	hammas/**ten**	∼ hampa/i/**den**
kallis	expensive	kallii/n	20.3	kallis/**ten**	∼ kalli/i/**den**
puhelin	telephone	puhelime/n	20.5	puhelin/**ten**	∼ puhelim/i/**en**
askel	pace	askele/n	20.7	askel/**ten**	∼ askel/i/**en**
mies	man	miehe/n	20.8	mies/**ten**	∼ mieh/i/**en**

§35. *USE OF THE GENITIVE*

The genitive often marks the possessor, belonging to someone or something, or origin.

possessor etc.

Presidenti/**n** nimi on Koivisto.	The *President's* name is Koivisto.
Auli/**n** auto on keltainen.	*Auli's* car is yellow.
Ihmise/**n** elämä on lyhyt.	*Man's* life is short.
Kaarle Kustaa on ruotsalais/**ten** kuningas.	Carl Gustaf is the King *of the Swedes*.
Oletko juonut Aura/**n** olutta?	Have you drunk *Aura* beer?
Mies/**ten** vaatteet ovat pohja-kerroksessa.	*Men's* clothes are on the ground floor.
Öljyma/i/**den** politiikka kovenee.	The policies *of the oil countries* are getting tougher.
Kirjo/j/**en** sisältö on muuttunut.	The content of (the) books has changed.

Genitive expressions like the following are typical to Finnish; in many European languages the corresponding forms are preposition or adjective structures or compound nouns.

NOTE!

Turu/**n** kaupunki	the city *of Turku*
Helsingi/**n** yliopisto	*Helsinki* University
englanni/**n** kieli	the *English* language
Neuvostoliito/**n** ulkoministeri	the Foreign minister *of the Soviet Union*
Summa/**n** taistelut	the battles *of Summa*
Niemise/**n** perhe	the *Nieminen* family
Virtase/**n** Reino	Reino *Virtanen* (colloquial)
Lapi/**n** mies	a man *from Lapland*
maido/**n** hinta	the price *of milk*
Suome/**n** kansa	the *Finnish* people

Pohjoisma/i/den neuvosto	the Council *of the Nordic Countries*
Ranska/n vallankumous	the *French* Revolution
kadu/n mies	the man *in the street*
ruotsi/n kiele/n opettaja	a *Swedish language* teacher
Espanja/n-matka	a trip *to Spain*

as a subject case The genitive is the case of the subject with some verbs of necessity or obligation (*täytyy* 'must', *on pakko* 'have to', etc.), and some verbs with a modal meaning (e.g. *kannattaa* 'be worth (doing sth.)', *sopii* 'may', *onnistuu* 'succeed').

1) expressions of necessity etc.

Minu/n täytyy lähteä.	*I* must leave.
He/i/dän täytyy lähteä.	*They* must leave.
Saksalais/ten täytyy lähteä.	*The Germans* must leave.
Suome/n kannattaa yrittää.	It is worth *Finland* trying.
Vireni/n onnistui voittaa.	*Viren* succeeded in winning.
Mies/ten on pakko poistua.	*The men* have to go away.
Sinu/n ei pidä uskoa kaikkea.	*You* must not believe everything.

(In traditional Finnish grammar these genitives are not always analysed as subjects, but are called dative adverbials. The two basic subject cases are nominative and partitive (§§25.3, 33.1).)

The genitive is also the case of the subject (traditionally: the dative adverbial) in expressions like *on hyvä* 'be good', *on paha* 'be bad' and *on hauska* 'be nice'.

2) *on hyvä* etc.

Minu/n on hyvä olla.	*I* feel good.
Mauno/n oli hauska päästä kotiin.	It was nice *for Mauno* to get home.
Suomalais/ten oli paha palata.	*The Finns* felt bad about returning.
Mikä Tuula/n on?	What's up *with Tuula*?

The subjects of many participle and infinitive constructions also appear in the genitive.

3) participle and infinitive constructions

Talve/n tullessa...	When *winter* comes...
	(lit.: ''winter coming'')
Kesä/n tultua...	*Spring* having come...
kaikk/i/en tuntema kirjailija	a writer known *by everyone*
Näin Ulla/n tulevan.	I saw *Ulla* coming.
Huomasin Kalle/n tulleen.	I noticed *Kalle* had come.

And finally, many postpositions require the genitive for the headwords they modify.

4) postposition + genitive

pöydä/n *alla*	under the table
kesä/n *aikana*	during the summer
auto/n *jäljessä*	after the car
huonee/n *keskellä*	in the middle of the room
äidi/n *luo*	to mother
Virolaise/n *mielestä*	in Virolainen's opinion
talo/n *sisällä*	inside the house
raha/n *tähden*	for the sake of money
isä/n *vieressä*	next to father
tämä/n *yhteydessä*	in connection with this
tori/n *ympärillä*	around the market place

§36. *POSSESSIVE SUFFIXES*

Finnish does not have independent possessive pronouns as such, marking possession for the different grammatical persons; this function is fulfilled by the genitive forms of the personal pronouns.

minä	I	**minu/n**	my
sinä	you	**sinu/n**	your
hän	he, she	**häne/n**	his, her.
me	we	**mei/dän**	our
te	you	**tei/dän**	your
he	they	**hei/dän**	their

The word signifying what is possessed also takes an ending, a possessive suffix, which varies with the person (concord; 3rd person singular and plural have the same ending).

		SINGULAR	PLURAL
possessive	1ST PERSON	**-ni**	**-mme**
suffixes	2ND PERSON	**-si**	**-nne**
	3RD PERSON	**-nsa ~ -nsä**	

GENITIVE PERSONAL PRONOUNS IN THE 1ST AND 2ND PERSONS CAN BE OMITTED WHEN THEY OCCUR TOGETHER WITH A POSSESSIVE SUFFIX

(minun) velje/**ni**	my brother
(minun) äiti/**ni**	my mother
(sinun) sisare/**si**	your sister
hänen poika/**nsa**	his/her son
hänen isä/**nsä**	his/her father
(meidän) talo/**mme**	our house
(meidän) perhee/**mme**	our family
(teidän) paikka/**nne**	your place
(teidän) kirja/**nne**	your book
heidän talo/**nsa**	their house
heidän ystävä/**nsä**	their friend

The omission of the 1st and 2nd person pronouns is particularly common when the person is identical with that of the subject of the sentence and the possessive expression has another function (e.g. object).

Otan kirja/**ni**.	I('ll) take *my book.*
Myyttekö auto/**nne**?	Are you selling *your car*?
Löydätkö avaime/**si**?	Can you find *your key*?
Teemme parhaa/**mme**.	We are doing *our best.*
Emme muuta asunno/sta/**mme**.	We are not moving out of *our flat.*

3rd person pronouns can normally only be omitted when they have the same reference as the subject of the sentence; they then correspond to possessive pronouns in many other languages.

Hän ajaa auto/**nsa** kotiin.	He drives *his car* home.
Kalle ajaa auto/**nsa** kotiin.	Kalle drives *his car* home.
He juovat olue/**nsa**.	They drink *their beer.*
Miehet juovat olue/**nsa**.	The men drink *their beer.*
Presidentti lähtee linna/a/**nsa**.	The President goes to *his palace.*

Compare the following sentences where the 3rd person pronoun does not refer back to the subject.

Kalle ajaa *hänen* auto/**nsa** kotiin.	Kalle drives *his/her car home* (i.e. *someone else's car).*
Amerikkalaiset tapaavat *heidän* edustaja/**nsa**.	The Americans meet *their representatives* (not their own but e.g. the other side's).

Within the word, possessive suffixes always occur after case endings but before enclitic particles.

possessive	auto/lla/**ni**	in *my* car
suffix	auto/sta/**si**	out of *your* car
after	maa/ta/**mme**	*our* country (part.)
case	poika/**nne**/kin	*your* son too
ending	äidi/ltä/**ni**/hän	from *my* mother + emph.
	isä/lle/**si**/kö	to *your* father?

When a possessive suffix occurs after a case-form ending in a consonant the following alternation takes place:

deletion
of final
consonant

> THE FINAL CONSONANT OF A CASE ENDING IS DROPPED WHEN FOLLOWED BY A POSSESSIVE SUFFIX

This deletion particularly applies to the genitive singular -**n**, the genitive plural -**iden**, -**itten**, -**en**, -**ten**, the nominative plural -**t** and the illative -**Vn**, -**hVn**, -**seen**, -**siin**.

ROOT + CASE		ROOT + CASE + POSSESSIVE SUFFIX	
laiva/**n**	of the ship	laiva/ /ni	my ship's
tytö/**n**	of the girl	tyttö/ /mme	our girl's
talo/**t**	the houses	talo/ /nne	your houses
lauku/**t**	the bags	laukku/ /si	your bags
auto/**on**	into the car	auto/**o**/ni	into my car
maa/**han**	into the country	maa/**ha**/nsa	into his country

Note especially that on account of this dropping of the final consonant several case-forms look the same when followed by a possessive suffix: nominative singular and plural, accusative singular and plural, and genitive singular.

coinciding forms		
	Veneeni on uusi.	*My boat* is new.
	Veneeni ovat uudet.	*My boats* are new.
	Veneeni nimi on Tarantella.	*My boat's* name is Tarantella.
	Oletko nähnyt *veneeni*?	Have you seen *my boat(s)*?

Notice that it is the concord in the verb that differentiates the first two sentences above (*on* 'is' and *ovat* 'are').

It is apparent from what has been said so far that consonant gradation does not occur directly before a possessive suffix; cf. the inflection of the noun *laukku* 'bag'.

(minun) laukku/ni   (meidän) laukku/mme
(sinun) laukku/si   (teidän) laukku/nne
hänen laukku/nsa   heidän laukku/nsa

Because of the deletion of the final consonant, (*minun*) *laukku/ni* for instance may mean 'my bag', 'my bags', or 'of my bag'.

In the nominative singular the possessive suffix is always added to the inflectional stem.

	BASIC FORM	INFLECTIONAL STEM + POSSESSIVE SUFFIX		Cf. §
inflectional	ovi	ove/mme	our door	18.2
stem +	ääni	ääne/si	your voice	18.3
possessive	käsi	käte/ni	my hand	18.4
suffix	kone	konee/nne	your machine	19
	hevonen	hevose/nsa	his/her/their horse	20.1
	kysymys	kysymykse/si	your question	20.2
	kirves	kirvee/nsä	his/her/their axe	20.3

-Vn in the 3rd person... If the 3rd person possessive suffix occurs after a case ending in a short vowel other than the final vowel of the stem, its form is usually -**Vn** (vowel + -**n**), where the vowel is identical with the immediately preceding vowel. The ending -**nsa** ∼ -**nsä** is occasionally also possible with such forms, and it is always the ending used after cases other than those ending in a short vowel of the type mentioned.

heidän talo/ssa/**an**   in their house
hänen auto/lla/**an**   in his/her car
heidän isä/lle/**en**   to their father
hänen äidi/ltä/**än**   from his/her mother
äiti/ä/**än**   his/her mother (part.)
pää/tä/**än**   his/her head (part.)
maa/ta/**an**   his/her country (part.)

Compare the following forms where the 3rd person possessive suffix is not preceded by a case ending of the type defined above.

heidän talo/ssa/**an**   into their house
hänen auto/**nsa**   his/her car
heidän isä/ä/**nsä**   their father (part.)
hänen äiti/**nsä**   his/her mother

§37. WHAT IS THE ACCUSATIVE?

The accusative is not a uniform morphological case-form as such, but a collective name given to a certain set of cases when they mark the *object* of the sentence. These cases are: nominative singular, which of course has no ending (*Ø*); genitive singular, with the ending -**n**; the -**t** accusative ending peculiar to personal pronouns; and the nominative plural in -**t**. The accusative, i.e. this set of case-forms, appears as the case of the object in opposition to the *partitive*.

When determining the particular case of the object one must first check whether any of the conditions for the partitive hold (§33.2); if so, the object must be in the partitive. The partitive is thus a "stronger" object case than the accusative. Only after this, if none of the partitive object conditions are fulfilled, can one proceed to determine which of the accusative endings is the correct one.

> THE OBJECT IS IN THE PARTITIVE IF ANY OF THE PARTITIVE
> CONDITIONS (§33.2) HOLD; IF NOT, THE OBJECT TAKES ONE
> OF THE ACCUSATIVE ENDINGS (*Ø*, -**n**, -**t**)

The partitive object occurs in three instances: a) in negative sentences, b) when the action expressed by the verb is irresultative, and c) when the object expresses an indefinite quantity.

a) En tunne tuo/**ta** mies/**tä**.   I don't know *that man*.
   Risto ei lue sanomalehte/**ä**.   Risto does not read *the newspaper*.

b) Reino lukee hyvä/**ä** kirja/**a**.   Reino is reading *a good book*.
   He katsovat ottelu/**a**.   They are watching *the match*.

c) Opiskelemme suomen kiel/**tä**.   We study / are studying *the Finnish language*.

   Ostatteko olut/**ta**?   Will you buy (*some*) *beer*?

The case of the object is therefore accusative only if a) the sentence is affirmative, and also b) the action of the verb is resultative, or c) the object is a whole or a definite quantity. With respect to (c), the accusative may be compared to the nominative when the nominative marks the subject (§25.3).

meaning

> THE ACCUSATIVE EXPRESSES
> a) RESULTATIVE ACTION
> b) A WHOLE or A DEFINITE QUANTITY
> IN AFFIRMATIVE SENTENCES

ACCUSATIVE OBJECT	PARTITIVE OBJECT
a) Tuula kirjoittaa kirjee/**n**.	Tuula kirjoittaa kirje/**ttä**.
Tuula *writes* a/the letter.	Tuula *is writing* a/the letter.

Hän kantoi kassi/**n** kotiin.
He *carried* the bag home.

Hän kantoi kassi/**a**.
He *was carrying* a/the bag.

Suurensin valokuva/**n**.
I *enlarged* the photo
(e.g. to a given size).

Suurensin valokuva/**a**.
I *was enlarging* a/the photo.
Or: I *enlarged* a/the photo (*a bit*, but
I could have made it bigger still).

b) Ostin leivä/**n**.
I bought *the bread / a loaf of bread*.

Ostin leipä/**ä**.
I bought *some bread*.

Syötkö kala/**n**?
Will you eat *a/the fish*[1]?

Syötkö kala/**a**?
Do you eat *fish*?

Tunnen ruotsalaise/**t**.
I know *the Swedes*.

Tunnen ruotsalais/i/**a**.
I know *some Swedes*.

All the accusative endings *∅*, -**n** and -**t** share these basic meanings. The following section deals with the factors determining when each of these endings should be used.

§38. *THE ACCUSATIVE ENDINGS*

When is each accusative ending used? We can formulate three rules:

---

1) THE -**t** ACCUSATIVE ALWAYS MARKS THE OBJECT
   a) IN THE PLURAL
   b) IN PERSONAL PRONOUNS

---

plural -**t**

a) Luen kirja/**t**.
Kansa valitsee kansanedustaja/**t**.

I'll read *the books*.
The people elect *the Members of Parliament*.

Vien kirjee/**t** postiin.
Isä vie lapse/**t** kouluun.
Vie lapse/**t** kouluun.
Lapse/**t** vietiin kouluun.
Tunnetko nämä maa/**t**?
Seija avasi ikkuna/**t**.
Hallitus korvaa vahingo/**t**.

I will take *the letters* to the post.
Father takes *the children* to school.
Take *the children* to school.
The children were taken to school.
Do you know *these countries*?
Seija opened *the windows*.
The government will repay *the damage*.

Huomenna ostan uude/**t** kengä/**t**.
Minun täytyy ostaa kirja/**t**.

Tomorrow I will buy a pair of *new shoes*.
I must buy *the books*.

The use of the plural -**t** here follows exactly the same rules as the plural -**t** for the subject (§25.3).

When they function as the object, personal pronouns take the ending -**t**: minu/**t**, sinu/**t**, häne/**t**; meidä/**t**, teidä/**t**, heidä/**t**.

---

[1] Translator's note: structures like this, with a present tense resultative verb + an accusative object, often correspond to the English future form with *will* rather than the simple present, otherwise the resultative sense is lost. (Finnish has no equivalent future form.)

personal pronouns	b)	Risto vei minu/t elokuviin.	Risto took *me* to the cinema.
		Vie minu/t elokuviin!	Take *me* to the cinema!
		Oletko nähnyt häne/t?	Have you seen *him/her*?
		Neiti Mäkinen saattaa teidä/t ovelle.	Miss Mäkinen will escort *you* to the door.
		Saatanko sinu/t kotiin?	Shall I take *you* home?
		Kyllä Tuula tuntee heidä/t.	Tuula knows *them* all right.
		Tuo häne/t tänne!	Bring *him/her* here!
		Minut/t vietiin elokuviin.	*I* was taken to the cinema.

If the object is *singular* (and is not one of the personal pronouns *minä* : *minu/t, sinä* : *sinu/t, hän* : *häne/t*) there are two possibilities. Sometimes the ending is **-n**, and sometimes there is no ending (∅). A singular object takes no ending if the predicate verb is 1st or 2nd person imperative, passive, or a verb expressing obligation with a subject in the genitive (§35). Otherwise a singular object takes the ending **-n**.

---

2) A SINGULAR ACCUSATIVE OBJECT
   a) USUALLY TAKES -n
   b) TAKES NO ENDING WITH VERBS IN 1ST AND 2ND PERSON IMPERATIVE, PASSIVE VERBS, AND SOME VERBS OF OBLIGATION

2a) -n	(Minä) ostan kirja/n.	I will buy *a/the book*.
	Tunnetko Olli Nuutise/n?	Do you know *Olli Nuutinen*?
	Isä vie lapse/n kouluun.	Father takes *the child* to school.
	Irma avaa ikkuna/n.	Irma opens *the window*.
	Join kupi/n kahvia ja söin leivokse/n.	I drank *a cup* of coffee and ate *a tart*.
	Hallitukse/n muodostaa Martti Miettunen.	*The government* is / will be formed by Martti Miettunen.
	Ilkka ostaa sormukse/n vaimolleen.	Ilkka will buy *a ring* for his wife.
	Pekka Pekkanen saa paika/n.	Pekka Pekkanen gets / will get *the job*.
	Poliisit pysäyttävät liikentee/n.	The police stop *the traffic*.
	Kommunistit esittävät uude/n ehdotukse/n.	The communists put forward *a new proposal*.
	Rakennamme tehtaa/n Tampereelle.	We (will) build *a/the factory* at Tampere.

2b) no ending	Osta *kirja*!	Buy (sing.) *a book*!
	Ostakaa *kirja*!	Buy (pl.) *a book*!
	Ostakaamme *kirja*!	Let us buy *a book*!
	Kirjoita *kirje* loppuun!	Finish writing *the letter*! (lit.: "write the letter to the end")
	Viekää *koira* pois!	Take (pl.) *the dog* away!
	Ostettiin *kirja*.	*A book* was bought. ("one bought a book")
	Ostetaan *kirja*.	Let's buy *a book*. ("one buys a book")
	Koira vietiin pois.	*The dog* was taken away.
	Onko *kirje* kirjoitettu loppuun?	Is *the letter* finished?
	Kalle Nieminen nähtiin viimeksi Kuopiossa.	*Kalle Nieminen* was last seen in Kuopio.
	Minun täytyy ostaa *kirja*.	I must buy *a/the book*.
	Sinun on pakko viedä *kirje* postiin.	You have to take *the letter* to the post.

Nyt *koira* on vietävä ulos.
Teidän pitäisi tavata *Raija*.
Meidän täytyy hyväksyä *tämä*.

Now *the dog* must be taken out.
You should meet *Raija*.
We must accept *this*.

The third important accusative rule concerns numerals:

---

3) NUMERALS (except yksi 'one') HAVE NO ACCUSATIVE ENDING

Kadulla näin *kolme* ihmistä.
Saanko *kaksi* tuoppia olutta?
Väinö söi *kuusi* appelsiinia.
Kansa valitsee *kaksisataa* kansan-
edustajaa.
But: Saanko yhde/**n** kupi/**n** kahvia?
Reijo lainaa yhde/**n** kirja/**n**.

I saw *three* people in the street.
Can I have *two* tankards of beer?
Väinö ate *six* oranges.
The people elect *two hundred*
Members of Parliament.
Can I have *one cup* of coffee?
Reijo borrows *one book*.

Note once again the point made above (§36) concerning possessive suffixes: because of the omission of the final consonant some forms coincide.

the accusative and possessive suffixes

WITHOUT POSSESSIVE SUFFIX

Ostin auto/**n**.
I bought *a/the car*.

Ostin auto/t.
I bought *the cars*.

Ostin auto/**n** moottorin.
I bought the engine *of the car*.

WITH POSSESSIVE SUFFIX

Ostin auto/**ni**.
I bought *my car*.

Ostin auto/**ni**.
I bought *my cars*.

Ostin auto/**ni** moottorin.
I bought the engine *of my car*.

In conclusion it should be stressed that the partitive rules always take precedence over the accusative rules. E.g. in negative sentences the object is always in the partitive regardless of what the accusative ending would be in the corresponding affirmative sentences.

the partitive takes precedence

AFFIRMATIVE
(accusative)

Luen kirja/t.
I read *the books*.
Tunnen nämä maa/t.
I know *these countries*.
Risto vie minu/t elokuviin.
Risto will take *me* to the cinema.
Näen häne/t.
I see *him/her*.
Ostan kirja/**n**.
I (will) buy *a/the book*.
Pekka Virtanen saa paika/**n**.
Pekka Virtanen will get *the job*.
Sinun on pakko viedä *kirje* postiin.

You have to take *the letter* to the post.

NEGATIVE
(partitive)

En lue kirjo/j/**a**.
I don't read *books*.
En tunne nä/i/**tä** ma/i/**ta**.
I don't know *these countries*.
Risto ei vie minu/a elokuviin.
Risto will not take *me* to the cinema.
En näe hän/**tä**.
I don't see *him/her*.
En osta kirja/a.
I will not buy *a/the book*.
Pekka Virtanen ei saa paikka/**a**.
Pekka Virtanen will not get *the job*.
Sinun ei ole pakko viedä kirje/**ttä**
postiin.
You do not have to take *the letter* to
the post.

Pertti ostaa *neljä* vihkoa.
Pertti buys / will buy *four* notebooks.

Pertti ei osta neljä/ä vihkoa.
Pertti does / will not buy *four* notebooks.

Juotko *kaksi* kuppia kahvia?
Will you drink *two* cups of coffee?

Etkö juo kah/**ta** kuppia kahvia?
Won't you drink *two* cups of coffee?

§39. *QUANTITY ADVERBS TAKING AN OBJECT CASE*

There are some expressions of quantity which are similar to objects in that they take partitive or accusative endings in accordance with the normal rules for objects. These expressions include those answering the questions 'how long?', 'how far?', 'how many times?', and 'which time (in order)?'.

Olen ollut Suomessa viiko/**n**.
I have been *a week* in Finland.

En ole ollut Suomessa viikko/**a**.
I have not been *a week* in Finland.

Ole Suomessa *viikko*!
Stay *a week* in Finland!

Suomessa ollaan *viikko*.
We (lit.: "one") will stay *a week* in Finland.

Viren juoksee kilometri/**n**.
Viren will run *a kilometre*.

Viren ei juokse kilometri/**ä**.
Viren will not run *a kilometre*.

Juokse *kilometri*!
Run *a kilometre*!

Olen nähnyt hänet *kaksi* kertaa.
I have seen him/her *twice* ("*two* times").

En ole nähnyt häntä kah/**ta** kertaa.
I have not seen him/her *twice*.

10 The Six Local Cases

General
Inessive
Elative
Illative
Adessive
Ablative
Allative
Directional verbs
Place names

§40. *GENERAL*

Six of the fifteen Finnish cases form a sub-system of their own since their basic function is the expression of *place* and *direction*. This set of local cases consists of the inessive -**ssa** ~ -**ssä**, the elative -**sta** ~ -**stä**, the illative -**Vn**, -**hVn**, -**seen**, -**siin**, the adessive -**lla** ~ -**llä**, the ablative -**lta** ~ -**ltä** and the allative -**lle**.

The system of local cases is structured according to two dimensions. One is location: ''inside'' (or in immediate contact with) vs. ''outside''. And the other is direction: ''static'', ''movement towards'' and ''movement away from''. The six cases can be set out as follows; the diagram includes only one variant for each case-ending.

		LOCATION	
		INSIDE	OUTSIDE
DIREC-TION	STATIC	-ssa	-lla
	AWAY FROM	-sta	-lta
	TOWARDS	-Vn	-lle

The use of the local cases is illustrated in the house-diagram below; **x** indicates ''static'' location.

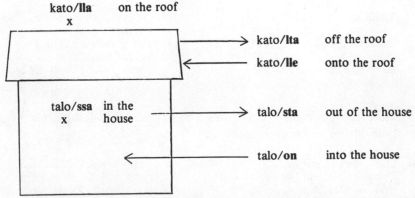

kato/**lla**   on the roof
x

kato/**lta**   off the roof
kato/**lle**   onto the roof

talo/**ssa**   in the
x   house

talo/**sta**   out of the house

talo/**on**   into the house

other meanings It must be remembered that the local cases also have many other meanings apart from place and direction. Some may express e.g. time, reason, instrument or manner.

§41. *INESSIVE*

The inessive ending is -ssa ~ -ssä; in the singular this is added directly to the inflectional stem (§§18—20), and in the plural it is added after the plural -i- following the inflectional stem (§26). Because the inessive ending begins with two consonants the rules of consonant gradation apply in the normal way (§15). In *vene*-words (§19) and words with a basic form ending in a consonant (§20),the inflectional stem appears in the strong grade.

> THE BASIC MEANING OF THE INESSIVE IS 'LOCATION INSIDE SOMETHING', SOMETIMES 'DIRECT CONTACT'

BASIC FORM	INESSIVE SINGULAR		INESSIVE PLURAL	
talo	talo/ssa	in the house	talo/i/ssa	in the houses
puu	puu/ssa	in the tree	pu/i/ssa	etc.
maa	maa/ssa	in the country	ma/i/ssa	
tunti	tunni/ssa	in the hour	tunne/i/ssa	
kivi	kive/ssä	in the stone	kiv/i/ssä	
käsi	käde/ssä	in the hand	käs/i/ssä	
liike	liikkee/ssä	in the shop	liikke/i/ssä	
nainen	naise/ssa	in the woman	nais/i/ssa	
ajatus	ajatukse/ssa	in the thought	ajatuks/i/ssa	
syvyys	syvyyde/ssä	in the depth	syvyyks/i/ssä	
avain	avaime/ssa	in the key	avaim/i/ssa	

It is fairly rare for the inessive to mean 'direct contact', but there are a few common expressions of this kind.

'direct contact'

Minulla on sukat jala/ssa.	I have socks on my feet (lit.: "in the foot").
Pekalla on hansikkaat käde/ssä.	Pekka has gloves on his hands ("in the hand").
Venee/ssä on kaksi mastoa.	The boat has two masts ("in the boat...").
Tuopi/ssa on korvat.	The tankard has handles ("in the tankard...").
Onko sinulla hattu pää/ssä?	Do you have a hat on your head ("in the head")?
Laiva on laituri/ssa.	The ship is at ("in") the quay.

The inessive is common in expressions of time, when it indicates the period of time during which an action takes place.

expressions of time

Luin kirjan tunni/ssa.	I read the book *in an hour*.
Pimenee kymmene/ssä minuuti/ssa.	It gets dark *in ten minutes*.
Hän luki lääkäriksi viide/ssä vuode/ssa.	He qualified as a doctor *in five years*.
Päivä/ssä pääsee Helsingistä Kuopioon.	One can get from Helsinki to Kuopio *in a day*.
Tulen Norjaan ensi kuu/ssa.	I'm coming to Norway *next month*.

Sometimes the inessive is used to mark a substance covering something.

Talo on tule/ssa.	The house is on ("in") fire.
Nenä oli vere/ssä.	The nose was bloody ("in blood").
Aurajoki on jää/ssä.	The river Aura is frozen ("in ice").
Lasi on huurtee/ssa.	The glass is covered with frost ("is in frost").

Concord rules apply in the normal way: pronouns and adjectival modifiers inflect in the same case and number as the headword (§31).

concord

iso/ssa talo/ssa	in the big house
tä/ssä talo/ssa	in this house
piene/ssä auto/ssa	in the small car
iso/i/ssa talo/i/ssa	in the big houses
tavallise/ssa liikkee/ssä	in an ordinary shop
tavallis/i/ssa liikke/i/ssä	in ordinary shops
toise/ssa maa/ssa	in another country
tois/i/ssa ma/i/ssa	in other countries

§42. *ELATIVE*

The elative ending is -sta ~ -stä, which is added to the inflectional stem and causes consonant gradation in the same way as the inessive. The basic meaning of the elative is 'out from inside'.

basic
meaning

> THE BASIC MEANING OF THE ELATIVE IS 'OUT FROM IN-SIDE', SOMETIMES 'ORIGIN' OR 'DIRECTION AWAY FROM SURFACE CONTACT'

BASIC FORM	ELATIVE SINGULAR		ELATIVE PLURAL
talo	talo/sta	out of the house	talo/i/sta
maa	maa/sta	out of the country	ma/i/sta
kivi	kive/stä	out of the stone	kiv/i/stä
vesi	vede/stä	out of the water	ves/i/stä
ihminen	ihmise/stä	out of the person	ihmis/i/stä
tiede	tietee/stä	out of science	tiete/i/stä

The sentences below illustrate this basic meaning.

'out from
inside'

Sylvi nousee sängy/stä kello 8.	Sylvi gets *out of bed* at 8 o'clock.
Noudan paketin posti/sta.	I'll fetch the parcel *from the post office.*
Mi/stä Teuvo tulee?	*Where* does Teuvo come *from*?
Hän tulee Kemi/stä.	He comes *from Kemi.*
Nousemme juna/sta satamassa.	We get *out of the train* at the harbour.
Älä juo olutta pullo/sta!	Don't drink beer *from the bottle*!
Pekka tulee koulu/sta.	Pekka comes *from school.*

Merimiehet karkasivat laiva/**sta**. The sailors deserted (''from'') *the ship*.
Vesi loppuu kaivo/**sta**. *The well* runs out of water (''the water finishes from the well'').

Tulen hammaslääkäri/**stä**. I am coming *from the dentist*.
Mi/**stä** löysit kynäsi? (''From'') *Where* did you find your pen?

Otan hatun pää/**stä**/ni. I take my hat *off my head*.
Jyväskylä/**stä** Helsinkiin. *From Jyväskylä* to Helsinki.
Johtaja on palannut Brasilia/**sta**. The director has returned *from Brazil*.

The elative is also often used for adverbials occurring after certain verbs. These verbs include those of speaking, writing, thinking, understanding and knowing.

more abstract elative	Pentti kertoo matka/**sta**/an.	Pentti tells *about his trip*.
	Hän puhuu kokemuks/i/**sta**/an.	He speaks *of his experiences*.
	Mitä ajattelet Vennamo/**sta**?	What do you think *of Vennamo*?
	Mitä luulet tä/**stä**?	What do you think *of this*?
	En pidä musta/**sta** kahvi/**sta**.	I don't like *black coffee*.
	Minä pidän Liisa/**sta**.	I like *Liisa*.
	Mi/**stä** sen tiedät?	*How* (''from what'') do you know?

The elative can also indicate the substance something is made of, origin, and cause.

'substance, origin, cause'	Pöytä on tehty puu/**sta**.	The table is made *of wood*.
	Teen puvun villa/**sta**.	I will make the dress *out of wool*.
	Häne/**stä** tulee lääkäri.	*He* will be (''out of him will come'') a doctor.
	Isä/**stä** poikaan.	*From father* to son.
	Kolme/**sta** neljään kilometriä.	*From three* to four kilometres.
	Witold on Puola/**sta**.	Witold is *from Poland*.
	Lapsi itkee pelo/**sta**.	The child is crying *with* (''from'') *fear*.
	Hän hymyili onne/**sta**.	He smiled *with happiness*.
	Mi/**stä** syy/**stä** Ahti lähti?	*For* (''from'') *what reason* did Ahti leave?

Note also the following additional functions of the elative.

special expressions	Kaksi te/i/**stä**.	Two *of you*.
	Viisi nais/i/**sta**.	Five *of the women*.
	Kiitos ruua/**sta**.	Thank you *for the food*.
	Haluan kiittää kahvi/**sta**.	I want to thank (you) *for the coffee*.
	Maksan 100 mk taki/**sta**.	I will pay 100 marks *for the coat*.
	Minu/**sta** hän on sairas.	*In my opinion* (''of me'') he is ill.
	Aamu/**sta** iltaan.	From morning to evening.
	Hän on ollut täällä viime vuode/**sta**.	He has been here since last year.

Concord rules operate in the usual way (§31).

piene/**stä** talo/**sta** out of the small house
varhaise/**sta** aamu/**sta** from early morning
tä/**stä** auto/**sta** out of this car
mu/*i*/**sta** ma/*i*/**sta** from other countries

§43. *ILLATIVE*

The illative has three different endings: **-Vn** and **-hVn** (where "V" is always a vowel identical with the immediately preceding vowel), and **-seen**. The plural ending is also occasionally **-siin**. Consonant gradation does not occur before the illative ending (§15). The basic meaning is 'into'.

basic
meaning

> THE BASIC MEANING OF THE ILLATIVE IS '(DIRECTION) INTO', SOMETIMES 'END POINT OF A CHANGE OR MOVEMENT'

1) -Vn

> THE ENDING **-Vn** OCCURS AFTER INFLECTIONAL STEMS ENDING IN A SHORT VOWEL (also in the plural; if the plural stem ends in two vowels the illative ending is **-hVn**)

BASIC FORM	ILLATIVE SINGULAR		ILLATIVE PLURAL
talo	talo/**on**	into the house	talo/i/hin
koulu	koulu/**un**	to school	koulu/i/hin
kaupunki	kaupunki/**in**	to the town	kaupunke/i/hin
lehti	lehte/**en**	into the newspaper	leht/i/**in**
kivi	kive/**en**	into the stone	kiv/i/**in**
käsi	käte/**en**	into the hand	käs/i/**in**
meri	mere/**en**	into the sea	mer/i/**in**
kunta	kunta/**an**	into the commune	kunt/i/**in**
ihminen	ihmise/**en**	into the person	ihmis/i/**in**
ajatus	ajatukse/**en**	into the thought	ajatuks/i/**in**
avain	avaime/**en**	into the key	avaim/i/**in**
korkea	korkea/**an**	into the high	korke/i/hin (-siin)
sairaala	sairaala/**an**	into (the) hospital	sairaalo/i/hin

2) -hVn

> THE ENDING **-hVn** OCCURS AFTER MONOSYLLABIC INFLECTIONAL STEMS (both singular and plural) AND ALSO AFTER PLURAL STEMS ENDING IN TWO VOWELS

BASIC FORM	ILLATIVE SINGULAR		ILLATIVE PLURAL
maa	maa/**han**	into the country	ma/i/**hin**
tie	tie/**hen**	to the road	te/i/**hin**
työ	työ/**hön**	to work	tö/i/**hin**
suu	suu/**hun**	into the mouth	su/i/**hin**
tämä	tä/**hän**	into this	nä/i/**hin**
tuo	tuo/**hon**	into that	no/i/**hin**
joka	jo/**hon**	into which	jo/i/**hin**
mikä	mi/**hin**	into which	mi/**hin**
pullo	pullo/on	into the bottle	pullo/i/**hin**
kala	kala/an	into the fish	kalo/i/**hin**
vaikea	vaikea/an	into the difficult	vaike/i/**hin** (-siin)
purkki	purkki/in	into the tin	purkke/i/**hin**

> **THE ENDING -seen OCCURS AFTER POLYSYLLABIC INFLEC-TIONAL STEMS ENDING IN A LONG VOWEL; THE ILLATIVE PLURAL IS THEN EITHER -siin OR -hin**

BASIC FORM	ILLATIVE SINGULAR		ILLATIVE PLURAL
vapaa	vapaa/**seen**	into the free	vapa/i/**siin** (**-hin**)
harmaa	harmaa/**seen**	into the grey	harma/i/**siin** (**-hin**)
perhe	perhee/**seen**	into the family	perhe/i/**siin** (**-hin**)
tiede	tietee/**seen**	into science	tiete/i/**siin** (**-hin**)
rikas	rikkaa/**seen**	into the rich	rikka/i/**siin** (**-hin**)
taivas	taivaa/**seen**	to heaven / into the sky	taiva/i/**siin** (**-hin**)

The examples below illustrate the use of the illative in its basic meaning.

'into'

Isä ajaa auton autotalli/**in**.	Father drives the car *into the garage*.
Panetko sokeria kahvi/**in**?	Do you put sugar *into (your) coffee*?
Hän pani avaimen lukko/**on**.	He put the key *into the lock*.
Kyllä minä vastaan puhelime/**en**.	Yes, I (will) answer *the phone*.
Lähetän kirjeen Tukholma/**an**.	I (will) send a letter *to Stockholm*.
Seija laski paketin maa/**han**.	Seija put the parcel *on the ground*.
Kesällä aion matkustaa Tanska/**an**.	In the summer I intend to travel *to Denmark*.
Kuningatar lähtee Lontoo/**seen**.	The queen is going *to London*.
Lintu rakensi pesänsä puu/**hun**.	The bird built its nest *in the tree*.
Mi/**hin** ma/i/**hin** Koivisto lähtee tänä vuonna?	*Which countries* is Koivisto going *to* this year?
Aurinko laskee länte/**en**.	The sun sets *in the west*.
Aamulla kaikki menevät työ/**hön**.	In the morning everyone goes *to work*.
Pekka menee koulu/**un**.	Pekka goes *to school*.
Aion mennä sänky/**yn**.	I intend to go / am going *to bed*.
Muutamme uute/**en** paikka/**an**.	We are moving *to a new place*.
Nixon ei joutunut vankila/**an**.	Nixon did not have to go *to prison*.

The illative is also used for the end point of a movement or change, or the surface which a movement is directed towards and comes into direct contact with.

'end point, direct contact'

Käte/**en** tuli haava.	*The hand* was wounded ("into the hand came a wound").
Lamppu ripustetaan katto/**on**.	The light is hung *from* ("into") *the ceiling*.
Emäntä panee ruuan pöytä/**än**.	The hostess puts the food *onto the table*.
Lapsi panee lakin pää/**hän**.	The child puts the cap *on (his) head*.
Pane kengät jalka/**an**!	Put shoes *on your feet* ("into the foot")!
Opettaja löi nyrkin pöytä/**än**.	The teacher banged his fist *on the table*.

The illative also occurs in time expressions, indicating the later of two time limits or the time by which an action has not taken place.

time expressions	Viikosta viikko/**on**.	From week *to week*.
	Aamusta ilta/**an**.	From morning *to evening*.
	Tammikuusta maaliskuu/**hun**.	From January *to March*.
	En ole käynyt Ruotsissa vuote/**en**.	I haven't been to Sweden *for a year*.
	Pekka ei ole ollut kotona kolme/**en** viikko/**on**.	Pekka has not been home *for three weeks*.
	En ole nähnyt häntä pari/**in** tunti/**in**.	I haven't seen him *for a couple of hours*.

Concord rules operate in the normal way.

concord	piene/**en** kaupunki/**in**	into a small town
	pien/*i*/**in** kaupunke/*i*/**hin**	into small towns
	korkea/**an** puu/**hun**	into a high tree
	kaikk/*i*/**in** kone/*i*/**siin**	into all the machines

The final consonant of the illative ending is dropped before possessive suffixes (§36).

final consonant dropped	talo/**on**	into the house
	talo/**o**/ni	into my house
	talo/**o**/mme	into our house
	talo/i/**hin**	into the houses
	talo/i/**hi**/nne	into your houses

§44. *ADESSIVE*

The three cases presented above, the inessive, elative and illative, are the internal local cases: *talo/ssa* 'in the house', *talo/sta* 'out of the house', *talo/on* 'into the house'. The corresponding external local cases are the adessive, ablative and allative, cf. *kadu/lla* 'in the street', *kadu/lta* 'from the street', *kadu/lle* 'to the street', and *Peka/lla* ' "at" Pekka', *Peka/lta* 'from Pekka', *Peka/lle* 'to Pekka'.

basic meanings	THE ADESSIVE OFTEN MEANS LOCATION 'ON TOP OF' OR 'NEAR', 'OWNER', OR 'INSTRUMENT' BY MEANS OF WHICH AN ACTION IS PERFORMED

BASIC FORM	ADESSIVE SINGULAR		ADESSIVE PLURAL
pöytä	pöydä/**llä**	on the table	pöyd/i/**llä**
katu	kadu/**lla**	in the street	kadu/i/**lla**
auto	auto/**lla**	by car	auto/i/**lla**
ihminen	ihmise/**llä**	"at" the person	ihmis/i/**llä**
kone	konee/**lla**	with a machine	kone/i/**lla**
vastaus	vastaukse/**lla**	with the answer	vastauks/i/**lla**

105

The basic meanings of the adessive are illustrated in the sentences below.

'on'
Matto on lattia/**lla**.
Kupit ovat pöydä/**llä**.
Onko juna jo asema/**lla**?
Vaatteeni ovat tuoli/**lla**.
Auto on jo lauta/**lla**.

The mat is *on the floor*.
The cups are *on the table*.
Is the train already *at the station*?
My clothes are *on the chair*.
The car is already *on the ferry*.

'near, at'
Kokous on Ylioppilastalo/**lla**.
Vainikkala on Neuvostoliiton raja/**lla**.
Penkki on peräseinä/**llä**.
Puukko on vyö/**llä**.

The meeting is *at the Student House*.
Vainikkala is *at the* Soviet *border*.
The bench is *on the back wall*.
The knife is *in the belt*.

'owner'
Poja/**lla**/ni on kolme lasta.
Minu/**lla** ei ole rahaa.
Perti/**llä** on uusi vene.
Isä/**llä** on harmaat hiukset.

My son has three children.
I have no money.
Pertti has a new boat.
(My) *father* has grey hair.

'instrument'
Matkustamme Kuopioon juna/**lla**.
Hän kirjoittaa kynä/**llä**.
Syön keittoa lusika/**lla**.

We travel to Kuopio *by train*.
He writes *with a pen*.
I eat soup *with a spoon*.

The adessive is also used in time expressions, especially those where the head-word is not preceded by attributes (time expressions containing attributes are often in the essive -**na** ~ -**nä**, §49). If the headword is *hetki* 'moment', *tunti* 'hour', *viikko* 'week', *kausi* 'period', or *vuosisata* 'century', however, the case is invariably the adessive.

time expressions
Talve/**lla** voi hiihtää.
Päivä/**llä** teen työtä.
Yö/**llä** pitäisi nukkua.
Tä/**llä** hetke/**llä** en voi tulla.
Viime tunni/**lla** puhuimme objektista.
Ensi viiko/**lla** lähden Lappiin.

In winter one can ski.
In the day I work.
At night one should sleep.
At the moment I can't come.
In the last hour / lesson we spoke about the object.
Next week I am going to Lapland.

The adessive can also express manner.

manner
Tä/**llä** tava/**lla** ei voi tehdä.
Puhukaa kova/**lla** ääne/**llä**.
Tulen miele/**llä**/ni.

One can't do (it) *this way*.
Speak *in a loud voice*.
I'll come *with pleasure*.

Attributes agree in the normal way.

concord
kolme/**lla** auto/**lla**
pitkä/**llä** kadu/**lla**
tä/**llä** pöydä/**llä**
vanha/**lla** miehe/**llä**

in (''with'') three cars
in the long street
on this table
''at'' the old man

§45. ABLATIVE

The ablative ending is -lta ~ -ltä, which is added to the inflectional stem in both singular and plural and causes consonant gradation.

basic
meanings

THE ABLATIVE EXPRESSES MOVEMENT 'OFF OR FROM A SURFACE' OR 'FROM NEAR' OR 'FROM SOMEONE'

BASIC FORM	ABLATIVE SINGULAR		ABLATIVE PLURAL
maa	maa/lta	from the country	ma/i/lta
pöytä	pöydä/ltä	off the table	pöyd/i/ltä
meri	mere/ltä	from the sea	mer/i/ltä
ihminen	ihmise/ltä	from the person	ihmis/i/ltä
mies	miehe/ltä	from the man	mieh/i/ltä

There follow a few examples of the use of the ablative.

'off, from a surface', 'from near'

Juna lähtee asema/lta.	The train leaves *from the station*.
Otatko maton lattia/lta?	Will you take the mat (up) *off the floor*?
Reino nousi penki/ltä.	Reino got up *from the bench*.
Linja-auto ajoi tie/ltä.	The bus drove *off the road*.
Tuula tulee kaupungi/lta.	Tuula comes *from the town*.
Huomenna johtaja palaa kesäloma/lta/an.	Tomorrow the director is returning *from his summer holiday*.
Raitiovaunu kääntyy Aura-kadu/lta Eerikinkadulle.	The tram turns *from Aura Street* into Eric's Street.
Tänään tuli kirje poja/lta/ni.	Today there came a letter *from my son*.
Lainaan rahaa äidi/ltä.	I'll borrow money *from mother*.
Kysy häne/ltä, missä posti on.	Ask (''from'') *him* where the post office is.
Ostan auton Niemise/ltä.	I will buy the car *from Nieminen*.
Pyydän sinu/lta anteeksi.	I beg your pardon (''pardon *from you*'').
Anoin rehtori/lta lupaa.	I applied for permission *from the headmaster*.
Laulaja/lta meni ääni.	*The singer* lost (''from the singer went'') his voice.
Poja/lta katkesi jalka.	*The boy* broke his leg (''from the boy broke the leg'').
Kaikki jää minu/lta kesken.	*I* never finish anything (''everything remains unfinished from me'').

The ablative also expresses time, measure, and sometimes a property of something.

time expressions

Viini on vuode/lta 1879.	The wine is *from the year* 1879.
Lopetamme tä/ltä päivä/ltä.	We will finish *for today*.
Opetus alkaa kello yhdeksä/ltä.	Teaching begins *at nine o'clock*.
Lounas on kello kahde/lta/toista.	Lunch is *at twelve o'clock*.

'measure'	Perunat maksavat markan kilo/**lta**.	The potatos cost a mark *a kilo*.
	Maito maksaa kaksi markkaa litra/**lta**.	Milk costs two marks *a litre*.
	Kankaan hinta on 25 mk metri/**ltä**.	The price of the material is 25 marks *a metre*.

'property'	Hän on luontee/**lta**/an vilkas.	He is lively *by nature*.
	Olen paino/**lta**/ni normaali.	I am *of* normal *weight* (''normal of my weight'').

Particular attention should be paid to the sense-perception verbs *näyttää* 'seem, look', *tuntua* 'seem, feel', *maistua* 'taste' and *kuulostaa* 'sound', which take an ablative adverbial (complement).

NB!	Tämä näyttää kumma/**lta**.	This looks *odd*.
	Puku näyttää hyvä/**ltä**.	The dress looks *good*.
	Ehdotus tuntuu huono/**lta**.	The suggestion seems *bad*.
	Laulu tuntui mukava/**lta**.	The song seemed *nice*.
	Ruoka maistuu huono/**lta**.	The food tastes *bad*.
	Kuulostaa mainio/**lta**.	(That) sounds *excellent*.

Concord rules operate as usual.

concord	mi/**ltä** laituri/**lta**?	from what platform?
	likaise/**lta** lattia/**lta**	from the dirty floor
	tuo/**lta** vanha/**lta** naise/**lta**	from that old lady

§46. *ALLATIVE*

The allative ending is -**lle**, which is added to the inflectional stem in the singular and plural and causes consonant gradation.

basic meanings	THE ALLATIVE EXPRESSES MOVEMENT 'TOWARDS A SURFACE' OR 'TO SOMEONE'

BASIC FORM	ALLATIVE SINGULAR		ALLATIVE PLURAL
katto	kato/**lle**	onto the roof	kato/i/**lle**
tuoli	tuoli/**lle**	onto the chair	tuole/i/**lle**
nainen	naise/**lle**	to the woman	nais/i/**lle**
tyttö	työt/**lle**	to the girl	tytö/i/**lle**

The use of the allative is illustrated in the following sentences.

'onto'	Kirja putosi lattia/**lle**.	The book fell *onto the floor*.
	Pane tyynyt sohva/**lle**!	Put the cushions *on the sofa*!
	Istuudun tuoli/**lle**.	I sit down *on the chair*.
	Lähdemmekö ostoks/i/**lle**?	Shall we go *shopping* (''to the purchases'')?
	Kuka vie koiran kävely/**lle**?	Who will take the dog *for a walk*?
	Menen parvekkee/**lle**.	I am going *onto the balcony*.

108

Älä sylje lattia/**lle**!	Don't spit *on the floor*!
Tapio lähtee matka/**lle** huomenna.	Tapio is going *away* ("to a trip") tomorrow.
Illalla menemme Ylioppilastalo/**lle**.	In the evening we are going *to the Student House*.
Lähdemmekö asema/**lle**?	Shall we go *to the station*?
Hän on muuttanut Kauppiaan-kadu/**lle**.	He has moved *to Merchant's Street*.
Oikea/**lle** vai vasemma/**lle**?	*To the right* or *to the left*?
Puhun sinu/**lle**.	I talk *to you*.

'to someone'

Kerro asia minu/**lle**.	Tell *me* about it ("tell the matter to me").
Annan lahjan vaimo/**lle**/ni.	I give a present *to my wife*.
Näytän te/i/**lle** tien.	I'll show *you* the way.
Tarjoamme viera/i/**lle** illallisen.	We offer *the guests* a dinner.
Opetan suomea skandinaave/i/**lle**.	I teach Finnish *to Scandinavians*.

The perception verbs taking a structure with the ablative (§45) can also take the allative, but in the standard language the ablative is more common.

Tämä näyttää kumma/**lle** ~ kumma/**lta**.	This looks odd.
Ruoka maistui huono/**lle** ~ huono/**lta**.	The food tasted bad.

Finally, a few examples of concord.

concord

tä/**lle** miehe/**lle**	to this man
pitkä/**lle** kävely/**lle**	for a long walk
likaise/**lle** lattia/**lle**	onto the dirty floor
kaik/*i*/**lle** nä/*i*/**lle** laps/*i*/**lle**	to all these children

§47. *DIRECTIONAL VERBS*

The set of local cases has a natural threefold division (§40): both internal and external local cases can express static location, movement towards or movement away from. In Finnish, adverbials associated with some verbs expressing change or direction appear in one of the directional cases (elative, illative, ablative, allative), whereas in many Indo-European languages the equivalent expression would contain a "static" preposition. These verbs include *etsiä* 'look for', *jättää* 'leave', *jäädä* 'stay', *löytää* 'find', *ostaa* 'buy', *pysähtyä* 'stop (intrans.)', *pysäyttää* 'stop (trans.)', *rakentaa* 'build' and *unohtaa* 'forget'.

Hän etsii avainta tasku/**sta**.	He looks *in his pocket* for the key.
Hän löytää koliko/n kadu/**lta**.	He finds the coin *in the street*.
Hän löytää avaimen tasku/**sta**.	He finds the key *in his pocket*.
Elanno/**sta** löysin uudet kengät.	I found new shoes *at Elanto*.
Aion jäädä Ruotsi/**in**.	I inted to stay *in Sweden*.
Paavo jäi luoka/**lle**.	Paavo failed to pass into the next form ("stayed *in the class*").
Jätän auton autotalli/**in**.	I will leave the car *in the garage*.

Onko hän unohtanut avaimen lukko/**on**?	Has he left (''forgotten'') the key *in the lock*?
Unohdin kirjat huonee/**see**/ni.	I left (''forgot'') the books *in my room*.
Ostan olutta Alko/**sta**.	I'll buy some beer *in Alko*.
Ostammeko kartan kirjakaupa/**sta**?	Shall we buy a map *at the bookshop*?
Rakennamme uuden hotellin Turku/**un**.	We shall build a new hotel *in Turku*.
Juna pysähtyi asema/**lle**.	The train stopped *at the station*.
Poliisi pysäytti auton kadunkulma/**an**.	The policeman stopped the car *at the corner* of the street.

§48. PLACE NAMES

Place names decline either in the internal local cases (inessive, elative, illative) or in the external ones (adessive, ablative, allative). The internal cases are more common. The names of *countries* almost always decline in the internal local cases.

countries

Suome/**ssa**	in Finland
Suome/**sta**	from Finland
Suome/**en**	to Finland
Tanska/**ssa**	in Denmark
Unkari/**in**	to Hungary
Sveitsi/**stä**	from Switzerland
Englanti/**in**	to England
Neuvostoliito/**ssa**	in the Soviet Union
Neuvostoliitto/**on**	to the Soviet Union
Yhdysvallo/i/**sta**	from the United States
Yhdysvalto/i/**hin**	to the United States
NB: Venäjä/**llä**	in Russia

The names of most towns and other municipalities also decline in the internal local cases, but there are some exceptions.

Helsingi/**ssä**	in Helsinki
Turu/**ssa**	in Turku
Oulu/**sta**	from Oulu
Pori/**in**	to Pori
Jyväskylä/**ssä**	in Jyväskylä
Kuopio/**sta**	from Kuopio
Tukholma/**an**	to Stockholm
Moskova/**ssa**	in Moscow
Lontoo/**seen**	to London
Pariisi/**ssa**	in Paris
Tamperee/**lla**	in Tampere
Tamperee/**lta**	from Tampere
Tamperee/**lle**	to Tampere
Rauma/**lla**	in Rauma
Riihimäe/**ltä**	from Riihimäki
Rovanieme/**llä**	in Rovaniemi
Seinäjoe/**lla**	in Seinäjoki

NB: Tampere etc.

11 Other cases

Essive
Translative
Abessive, comitative and instructive

§49. *ESSIVE*

NB: no consonant gradation

meaning

The essive ending is **-na** ~ **-nä**, which is added to the inflectional stem in the singular and plural. The structure of the essive ending is such that it does not cause consonant gradation (§15.2). The essive usually expresses a (temporary) state or function, sometimes circumstances, conditions or causes. The essive is also used in time expressions.

BASIC FORM	ESSIVE SINGULAR		ESSIVE PLURAL
auto	auto/**na**	as a car	auto/i/**na**
ihminen	ihmise/**nä**	as a person	ihmis/i/**nä**
nuori	nuore/**na**	(as a) young	nuor/i/**na**
vanha	vanha/**na**	(as an) old	vanho/i/**na**

'state' etc.

Heikki on Jämsässä lääkäri/**nä**. — Heikki is (working as) *a doctor* in Jämsä.

Olemme siellä vuokralais/i/**na**. — We are *lodgers* there.

Lähetän ilmoituksen pikakirjee/**nä**. — I will send the notice *as an express letter*.

Kuka siellä on apu/**na**? — Who is *helping* ("as a help") there?

Pidämme ehdotusta järkevä/**nä**. — We regard the proposal *as sensible*.

Olen Suomessa turisti/**na**. — I am *a tourist* in Finland.

Pentti oli kolme viikkoa sairaa/**na**. — Pentti was *ill* for three weeks.

Viini kelpaa kylmä/**nä**/kin. — Wine is good *even when cold*.

Minulla on tapa/**na** polttaa vain illalla. — I have *a habit* of smoking only in the evening.

Pekka lähti iloise/**na** luennolle. — Pekka went *cheerfully* ("as cheerful") to the lecture.

Syön puuron kuuma/**na**. — I will eat the porridge *hot*.

Pysyykö ilma kirkkaa/**na**? — Will the air stay *clear*?

Arto tuli väsynee/**nä** kotiin. — Arto came home *tired*.

The essive is used in time expressions when the reference is to festivals and days of the week, and usually when the headword denoting time is preceded by an attribute (cf. §44).

festivals and days of the week

Joulu/**na** olin kotona. — *At Christmas* I was at home.

Itsenäisyyspäivä/**nä** presidentillä on vastaanotto. — *On Independence Day* the president has a reception.

Juhannukse/**na** aion purjehtia. — *At midsummer* I'm going sailing.

Tuletko meille lauantai/**na**? — Will you come round ("to us") *on Saturday*?

111

Perjantai/**na** kaikki menevät saunaan.	*On Friday* everyone goes to sauna.
Minulla on luento maanantai/**na**.	I have a lecture *on Monday*.
Sunnuntai/**na** täytyy levätä.	*On Sunday* one must rest.

time-words with an attribute	*Viime* talve/**na** olin sairaana.	*Last winter* I was ill.
	Ensi kesä/**nä** lähden Italia/an.	*Next summer* I'm going to Italy.
	Erää/**nä** päivä/**nä** tapasin hänet.	*One day* I met him/her.
	Kahte/**na** yö/**nä** on ollut hallaa.	*On two nights* there has been frost.
	Mi/**nä** päivä/**nä** hän tulee?	*What day* is he coming?
	Kuum/i/**na** kes/i/**nä** on paljon kärpäsiä.	*In hot summers* there are lots of flies.
	Tä/**nä** vuon/**na** inflaatio on taas noussut.	*This year* inflation has risen again.
	Tammikuun seitsemänte/**nä** päivä/**nä**.	*On the seventh (day)* of January.

Note that the words *ensi* 'next' and *viime* 'last' do not obey the concord rules for attributes, c.f. *ensi talve/na* 'next winter', *viime talve/na* 'last winter'.

§50. *TRANSLATIVE*

basic meanings	The translative ending is -**ksi**, which is added to the inflectional stem in the singular and plural and causes consonant gradation (the ending begins with two consonants). The translative generally expresses a state, property, function or position into which something or someone enters, or the end point of a movement or change.

BASIC FORM	TRANSLATIVE SINGULAR		TRANSLATIVE PLURAL
auto	auto/**ksi**	to (become) a car	auto/i/**ksi**
pieni	piene/**ksi**	to (become) little	pien/i/**ksi**
lahja	lahja/**ksi**	to (become) a present, as a present	lahjo/i/**ksi**
rengas	renkaa/**ksi**	to (become) a ring	renka/i/**ksi**

state etc. entered into	Lauri tuli iloise/**ksi**.	Lauri became *pleased*.
	Isä on tullut vanha/**ksi**.	Father has become *old*.
	Tuletko kipeä/**ksi**?	Are you becoming *ill*?
	Tyttö aikoo insinööri/**ksi**.	The girl intends to become *an engineer*.
	Pekka antoi kirjan lahja/**ksi**.	Pekka gave the book *as a present*.
	Juotko lasin tyhjä/**ksi**?	Will you empty your glass ("drink your glass *empty*")?
	Poikasi on kasvanut pitkä/**ksi**.	Your son has grown *tall*.
	Jalat käyvät kanke/i/**ksi**.	(One's) legs go *stiff*.
	Kirjoitan kirjan valmii/**ksi**.	I shall finish writing the book ("write the book *finished*").
	Olot muuttuvat normaale/i/**ksi**.	The conditions become *normal*.
	Pääsetkö opettaja/**ksi** Helsinkiin?	Will you be able *to become a teacher* in Helsinki?
	Tämä riittää perustelu/**ksi**.	This suffices *as an explanation*.
	Auli luuli minua norjalaise/**ksi**.	Auli thought me *a Norwegian*.
	Turkua sanotaan vanha/**ksi** kaupungi/**ksi**.	Turku is said to be *an old city*.
	Vennamoa ei saa kutsua idiooti/**ksi**.	Vennamo must not be called *an idiot*.

Opettaja puhuu suome/**ksi**.	The teacher speaks *in Finnish*.
Kaikki esitelmät ovat ruotsi/**ksi**.	All the lectures are *in Swedish*.
Mitä 'auto' on englanni/**ksi**?	What is "auto" *in English?*
Tule vähän lähemmä/**ksi**!	Come a bit *closer!*
Siirtykää hiukan kauemma/**ksi**!	Move a little *further away!*
Nouse ylemmä/**ksi**!	Get up *higher!*

The translative also expresses time, in particular time by which something happens or during which something happens, or the point of time until which something is postponed.

time	Tulen kotiin joulu/**ksi**.	I'll come home *for Christmas*.
expressions	Onko meillä ohjelmaa iltapäivä/**ksi**?	Do we have a programme *for the afternoon?*
	Minun täytyy ehtiä kotiin kello kolme/**ksi**.	I must get home *by three*.
	Pekka lähtee Espanjaan viiko/**ksi**.	Pekka is going to Spain *for a week*.
	Poistun kahde/**ksi** tunni/**ksi**.	I shall be away *for two hours*.
	Ostatko ruokaa sunnuntai/**ksi**?	Will you buy some food *for Sunday?*
	Lykkäämme kokouksen huomise/**ksi**.	We shall postpone the meeting *until tomorrow.*
	Maksu siirtyy myöhemmä/**ksi**.	The payment is transferred *to a later date* ("to later").

Note the contrast between the essive and the translative in pairs such as the following.

essive/	Tulen kotiin joulu/**ksi**.	I'll come home *for Christmas*.
translative	Joulu/**na** olen kotona.	*At Christmas* I am / shall be at home.
	Ostatko ruokaa sunnuntai/**ksi**?	Will you buy some food *for Sunday?*
	Sunnuntai/**na** emme mene kirkkoon.	*On Sunday* we do not go to church.
	Kesä/**ksi** lähden Suomeen.	I am going to Finland *for the summer*.
	Kesä/**llä** olen Suomessa.	*In the summer* I shall be in Finland.

When the translative ending is followed by a possessive suffix the final -**i** changes to -**e**-.

NB: -**kse**-	Tuletko vaimo/**kse**/ni?	Will you become *my wife?*
before a	Laulan oma/ksi ilo/**kse**/ni.	I sing *for my own pleasure*.
possessive	Juomme maljan sinun kunnia/**kse**/si.	We drink a toast *in* ("to") *your honour.*
suffix		
	He ottavat lapsen oma/**kse**/en.	They adopt ("take") the child *as their own*.

§51. *ABESSIVE, COMITATIVE AND INSTRUCTIVE*

These three cases are all rare; the instructive and the comitative appear mainly in fixed expressions like idioms.

abessive   The abessive ending is -**tta** ~ -**ttä**, which is added to the inflectional stem in the singular and plural and causes consonant gradation. Its meaning is 'without'.

113

'without'	Hän lähti ulkomaille raha/**tta** ja passi/**tta**.	He went abroad *without money* and *without a passport*.
	Hänet tuomittiin syy/**ttä**.	He was condemned *without cause*.
	Joka kuri/**tta** kasvaa, se kunnia/**tta** kuolee.	He who grows up *without discipline* will die *without honour*.

The preposition *ilman* 'without' is usually used instead of the abessive; it takes the partitive, e.g. *ilman raha/a* 'without money', *ilman passi/a* 'without a passport'.

instructive   The instructive ending is **-n**. It occurs almost exclusively in a few fixed plural expressions.

fixed expressions	om/i/**n** silm/i/**n**	with (one's) own eyes
	kaik/i/**n** puol/i/**n**	in all respects
	palja/i/**n** pä/i/**n**	with bare head
	näillä ma/i/**n**	in these parts (areas)
	kaks/i/**n** käs/i/**n**	with both hands

comitative   The comitative ending is **-ine-**, and this as always followed by a possessive suffix. Because the -i- of the ending is in fact a fossilized plural -i- (cf. §26), there is no difference between the comitative singular and plural. The meaning of the case is 'with, accompanied by'.

'with'	Läsnä oli Veikko Väätäinen vaimo/**ine**/en.	Present was Veikko Väätäinen *with his wife*.
	Läsnä olivat Veikko Väätäinen ja Esko Kallio vaimo/**ine**/en.	Present were Veikko Väätäinen and Esko Kallio, *accompanied by their wives*.
	Rauma on mukava kaupunki vanho/**ine** talo/**ine**/en ja kape/**ine** katu/**ine**/en.	Rauma is a pleasant town *with its old houses* and *narrow streets*.

12 Numerals

Cardinal numbers
Ordinal numbers

§52. CARDINAL NUMBERS

§52.1. Inflection of cardinal numbers

All cardinal numbers decline like nouns, adjectives and pronouns: they inflect
for number and case. Several sound alternations occur in the inflected forms.

	BASIC FORM	INFLECTIONAL STEM (no consonant gradation)	INFLECTIONAL STEM (with consonant gradation)	PARTITIVE SINGULAR
1—10	1 yksi	yhte/en	yhde/n	yh/tä
	2 kaksi	kahte/en	kahde/n	kah/ta
	3 kolme	kolme/en		
	4 neljä	neljä/än		
	5 viisi	viite/en	viide/n	viit/tä
	6 kuusi	kuute/en	kuude/n	kuut/ta
	7 seitsemän	seitsemä/än		
	8 kahdeksan	kahdeksa/an		
	9 yhdeksän	yhdeksä/än		
	10 kymmenen	kymmene/en		kymmen/tä

The cardinal numbers 11—19 are formed from the numbers 1—9 by the addition of the invariable form *toista* (cf. *toinen* '(an) other, second').

11—19	11 yksitoista
	12 kaksitoista
	13 kolmetoista
	14 neljätoista
	15 viisitoista
	16 kuusitoista
	17 seitsemäntoista
	18 kahdeksantoista
	19 yhdeksäntoista

Endings are added to the inflectional stem of the first part of the number.

invariable -toista	yhde/ssä/toista	in 11
	kolme/n/toista	of 13
	viide/stä/toista	out of 15
	seitsemä/ä/toista	17 (partitive)
	yhdeksä/lle/toista	to 19

The tens from 20 upward are formed from the cardinal numbers 2—9 followed by *kymmentä* (cf. *kymmenen* 'ten').

20—100	20 kaksikymmentä
	30 kolmekymmentä
	40 neljäkymmentä
	50 viisikymmentä
	60 kuusikymmentä
	70 seitsemänkymmentä
	80 kahdeksankymmentä
	90 yhdeksänkymmentä
	100 sata
	27 kaksikymmentäseitsemän
	39 kolmekymmentäyhdeksän
	52 viisikymmentäkaksi
	76 seitsemänkymmentäkuusi
	99 yhdeksänkymmentäyhdeksän

Note that *kymmentä* (*kymmenen*) declines together with the other parts of the numeral.

-kymmentä	kahde/**n**/kymmene/**n**	of 20
declines	kolme/**lle**/kymmene/**lle**	to 30
	viide/**stä**/kymmene/**stä**	out of 50
	kuute/**na**/kymmene/**nä**	as 60
	yhdeksä/**llä**/kymmene/**llä**	with 90
	kahde/**lta**/kymmene/**ltä**/kolme/**lta**	from 23
	seitsemä/**stä**/kymmene/**stä**/kahdeksa/**sta**	out of 78

The cardinal numbers continue in the same way. The hundreds and thousands are formed from the numbers 2—9 followed by *sataa* '100', *tuhatta* '1,000', *miljoonaa* '1,000,000', which all inflect for number and case like the other parts of the numeral.

200—	200 kaksisataa
	300 kolmesataa
	700 seitsemänsataa
	1 000 tuhat (tuhante/en, tuhanne/n, tuhat/ta)
	3 000 kolmetuhatta
	9 000 yhdeksäntuhatta
	238 kaksisataakolmekymmentäkahdeksan
	711 seitsemänsataayksitoista
	902 yhdeksänsataakaksi
	2 134 kaksituhatta satakolmekymmentäneljä
	9 876 yhdeksäntuhatta kahdeksansataaseitsemänkymmentäkuusi
	87 100 kahdeksankymmentäseitsemäntuhatta sata
	456 302 neljäsataaviisikymmentäkuusituhatta kolmesataakaksi
	1 000 000 miljoona
	4 000 000 neljä miljoonaa

Case-endings are added to all the parts of a cardinal number, but in long numerals the ending is often added to the last element only.

kahde/**n**/sada/**n**	of 200
kolme/**lle**/sada/**lle**	to 300
viide/**stä**/tuhanne/**sta**	out of 5000
kolme/**lla**/tuhanne/**lla** sada/**lla**/kahde/**lla**	with 3102
kolmetuhatta satakahde/**lla**	with 3102

116

§52.2. *Use of cardinal numbers*

When a cardinal number is the subject, object or complement, i.e. when it occurs in the nominative or partitive, the rest of the phrase it modifies takes the partitive singular, e.g. *kolme talo/a* 'three houses'.

> **WHEN A CARDINAL NUMBER IS THE SUBJECT, OBJECT OR COMPLEMENT THE WORDS IT MODIFIES TAKE THE PARTITIVE SINGULAR**

A second important rule for the use of cardinals is the following:

> **WHEN THE NUMERAL EXPRESSION IS THE SUBJECT, THE PREDICATE VERB IS IN THE SINGULAR**

subject	Kadulla seisoo *kolme mies/tä.*	There are *three men* standing in the street.
	Minulla on *kaksi velje/ä.*	I have *two brothers.*
	Neljä ministeri/ä erosi hallituksesta.	*Four ministers* resigned from the cabinet.
	Kuusitoista ihmis/tä sai surmansa lento-onnettomuudessa.	*Sixteen people* died in the plane crash.
object	Ostan *kolme pullo/a* punaviiniä.	I will buy *three bottles* of red wine.
	Eilen kirjoitin *seitsemän sivu/a.*	Yesterday I wrote *seven pages.*
	En omista *kah/ta auto/a.*	I don't own *two cars.*
	Opiskelen *kolme/a kiel/tä.*	I am studying *three languages.*
	Viit/tä/kymmen/tä osanottaja/a emme voi hyväksyä.	*Fifty participants* we cannot accept.
	Hän ei anna *kolme/a/tuhatta markka/a* koneesta.	He/she will not give *three thousand marks* for the machine.
complement	Hinta on *yhdeksän markka/a* kilolta.	The price is *nine marks* per kilo.

When a cardinal number is an attribute or an adverbial, i.e. appears in cases other than nominative or partitive, its case is determined by that of the headword (the noun), and all the parts of a compound numeral are similarly inflected. With the exception of invariable plurals these expressions are always singular.

> **CARDINAL NUMBERS AGREE WITH THE HEADWORD IN THE GENITIVE, ALL SIX LOCAL CASES, THE ESSIVE AND THE TRANSLATIVE**

	Matkallani käyn kolme/**ssa** maa/**ssa**.	On my trip I shall visit three countries (*"in three countries"*).
	Neljä/**n** litra/**n** hinta on seitsemän markkaa.	The price *of four litres* is seven marks.
NB: concord!	En ole käynyt Suomessa viite/**en**/toista vuote/**en**.	I have not been to Finland *for fifteen years.*

117

Hän on kahde/n piene/n lapse/n äiti.	She is the mother *of two small children.*
Verotoimistot palauttavat rahaa seitsemä/**lle**/sada/**lle**/tuhanne/**lle** suomalaise/**lle**.	The tax offices (will) refund money *to 700,000 Finns.*
Tuhanne/n ja yhde/n yö/n tarinat.	A thousand and one nights (''the stories of...'').
Yhte/**nä** päivä/**nä** viikossa olen Helsingissä.	I am in Helsinki *one day* a week.
Olen kolme/**n**/kymmene/**n**/kahde/**n** vuode/**n** ikäinen.	I am *32 years old.*
Kuude/**ssa**/toista tapaukse/**ssa** sairas kuoli.	*In 16 cases* the patient died.
Kirje tuli kahde/**lta** ystävä/**ltä**/ni.	The letter came *from two of my friends.*
Kahde/**lla**/tuhanne/**lla** marka/**lla** pääsee jopa Afrikkaan.	*For 2,000 marks* one can even get to Africa.

NB: invariable plurals!

Minulla on kahde/t sakse/t.	I have *two pairs of scissors.*
Tänä lauantaina on vain yhde/t hää/t.	This Saturday there is only *one wedding.*
Tämä kangas pitää leikata kaks/i/**lla** saks/i/**lla**.	This cloth has to be cut *with two pairs of scissors.*

When the numeral expression is the subject, the verb, as was said above, is generally in the singular, e.g. *Kolme tyttöä juokse/e* 'Three girls run'. But when the numeral expression is preceded e.g. by the words *nämä* 'these' or *nuo* 'those' (which make the phrase definite), the verb is then in the plural.

plural verb

Nämä kolme miestä seiso/**vat** kadulla.	These three men *are standing* in the street.
Nuo kaksi o/**vat** naimisissa.	Those two *are* married.
Nämä neljä ehdotusta o/**vat** yhtä hyviä.	These four proposals *are* equally good.

In other contexts too the verb may be in the plural when the subject is a definite numeral expression.

Kuusi paikallissijaa tuli/**vat** esille luvussa 10.
The six local cases *were discussed* in chapter 10.

Kolmetoista maata pääsi/**vät** eilen sopimukseen.
The thirteen countries *reached* an agreement yesterday.

§53. ORDINAL NUMBERS

sound alternations

The nominative of ordinal numbers is formed by adding the ending -s to the inflectional stem of the corresponding cardinal number (exceptions are *ensimmäinen* 'first' and *toinen* 'second'). In the ordinal inflectional stem -s is replaced by -**nte**-, which alternates with -**nne**- in accordance with the sound alternation rules. The partitive singular has the ending -**ta** ~ -**tä**, and -s then changes to -**t**-.

	BASIC FORM	INFLECTIONAL STEM (no consonant gradation)	INFLECTIONAL STEM (with consonant gradation)	PARTITIVE SINGULAR
	1. ensimmäi-nen	ensimmäise/en		ensimmäis/tä
	2. toinen	toise/en		tois/ta
NB:	3. kolma/s	kolma/**nte**/en	kolma/**nne**/n	kolma/**t**/ta
kolme :	4. neljäs	neljänteen	neljännen	neljättä
kolma/s!	5. viides	viidenteen	viidennen	viidettä
	6. kuudes	kuudenteen	kuudennen	kuudetta
	7. seitsemäs	seitsemänteen	seitsemännen	seitsemättä
	8. kahdeksas	kahdeksanteen	kahdeksannen	kahdeksatta
	9. yhdeksäs	yhdeksänteen	yhdeksännen	yhdeksättä
	10. kymmenes	kymmenenteen	kymmenennen	kymmenettä
invariable	11. yhdestoista	yhdenteentoista	yhdennentoista	yhdettätoista
-toista	12. kahdestoista	kahdenteentoista	kahdennentoista	kahdettatoista
	13. kolmastoista	kolmanteentoista	kolmannentoista	kolmattatoista
	16. kuudestoista	kuudenteentoista	kuudennentoista	kuudettatoista
	20. kahdes-kymmenes	kahdenteen-kymmenenteen	kahdennen-kymmenennen	kahdetta-kymmenettä
	50. viides-kymmenes	viidenteen-kymmenenteen	viidennen-kymmenennen	viidettä-kymmenettä
	100. sadas	sadanteen	sadannen	sadatta
	300. kolmas-sadas	kolmanteen-sadanteen	kolmannen-sadannen	kolmatta-sadatta
	1 000. tuhannes	tuhannenteen	tuhannennen	tuhannetta
	9 000. yhdeksäs-tuhannes	yhdeksänteen-tuhannenteen	yhdeksännen-tuhannennen	yhdeksättä-tuhannetta

In long compound ordinal numbers often only the last element is given an ending.

long ordinals

3,134th kolmetuhatta satakolmekymmentäneljä/**s**
(cf. kolma/s/tuhanne/s sada/s/kolma/s/kymmene/**s**/neljä/**s**)
kolmetuhatta satakolmekymmentäneljä/**nne**/n
(cf. kolma/**nne**/n/tuhanne/**nne**/n sada/**nne**/n/kolma/**nne**/n/-
kymmene/**nne**/n/neljä/**nne**/n)

Ordinal numbers function like adjectives and agree with the headword in case and number.

concord

Miettusen kolma/**nne**/ssa hallituksessa on viisi uutta ministeriä.
In Miettunen's *third* Cabinet there are five new ministers.

Vasta *toinen* yritys onnistui.
Only the *second* attempt succeeded.

Tammikuun neljä/**nte**/nä päivänä.
(*On*) the *4th* (day) of January.

Helmikuun seitsemä/**nte**/nä/toista päivänä.
(*On*) the *17th* of February.

Olen syntynyt joulukuun kahde/**nte**-na/kymmene/**nte**/nä/kuude/**nte**/na päivänä.
I was born *on* the *26th* of December.

Poikani on *ensimmäise/llä* luokalla.
My son is *in* the *first* class.

Hissi menee viide/**nte**/en kerrokseen.
The lift goes *to* the *fifth* floor.

Joka seitsemä/**nne**/llä suomalaisella on liian pitkä työmatka.
Every *seventh* Finn has too long a journey to work.

13 Pronouns

Personal pronouns
Demonstrative pronouns
Interrogative pronouns
Indefinite pronouns
Relative pronouns

functions of pronouns

Finnish pronouns inflect for number and case. Some pronouns function like nouns, as independent words (a), while others are like adjectives and agree with their headword in the normal way (b).

a) **Tämä** on kirja.   *This* is a book.
   Tuo ei ole totta.   *That* is not true.
   Hän on näyttelijä.   *He* is an actor.

b) Asun **tä/ssä** talo/**ssa**.   I live *in this* house.
   Mi/ssä talo/**ssa** asut?   *In which* house do you live?
   Mi/nä päivä/**nä** lähdette? *What day* are you leaving?

exceptions

There often occur exceptional forms in the declension of pronouns: these are indicated below in *italics*. Note in particular the pronouns **joka** 'who, which', **mikä** 'which, what' and **tämä** 'this', where the last syllable **-ka, -kä, -mä** occurs only in the nominative singular and plural and the genitive singular. In all other forms this syllable is dropped: cf. *tämä* 'this' : *tämä/n* 'of this' : *tä/ssä* 'in this' : *tä/llä* 'on this' etc.

In the following sections the pronouns are presented in five groups. For each pronoun the most important case-forms are given in the singular and plural (if they occur), together with examples of how they are used.

§54. PERSONAL PRONOUNS

	SINGULAR			PLURAL		
nom.	minä I	sinä you	hän he, she	me we	te you	he they
gen.	minu/n	sinu/n	häne/n	me/i/dän	te/i/dän	he/i/dän
acc.	*minu/t*	*sinu/t*	*häne/t*	*me/i/dät*	*te/i/dät*	*he/i/dät*
part.	minu/a	sinu/a	*hän/tä*	me/i/tä	te/i/tä	he/i/tä
iness.	minu/ssa	sinu/ssa	häne/ssä	me/i/ssä	te/i/ssä	he/i/ssä
elat.	minu/sta	sinu/sta	häne/stä	me/i/stä	te/i/stä	he/i/stä
illat.	minu/un	sinu/un	häne/en	me/i/hin	te/i/hin	he/i/hin
adess.	minu/lla	sinu/lla	häne/llä	me/i/llä	te/i/llä	he/i/llä
ablat.	minu/lta	sinu/lta	häne/ltä	me/i/ltä	te/i/ltä	he/i/ltä
allat.	minu/lle	sinu/lle	häne/lle	me/i/lle	te/i/lle	he/i/lle

Note accusative!

Sinu/ssa ei ole mitään vikaa.	There is nothing wrong *with you*.
Minä rakastan te/i/tä.	I love *you* (plural, or polite singular).
Anna kirje häne/lle!	Give the letter *to him/her*!
Minu/lla on kova nälkä.	*I* am very hungry.
He/i/hin ei voi luottaa.	One cannot trust *them*.
Minu/sta ehdotus on hyvä.	*In my opinion* the proposal is good.
Näin häne/t ravintolassa.	I saw *him/her* in the restaurant.
Tämä on he/i/dän kirjansa.	This is *their* book.
Saatte vastauksen me/i/ltä huomenna.	You will receive an answer *from us* tomorrow.
Saatamme te/i/dät kotiin.	We will see *you* home.
Ettekö enää tunne minu/a?	Don't you know *me* any longer?

For concord between personal pronouns and verbs see §24, and for the possessive forms and the possessive suffixes see §36.

itse   The Finnish reflexive pronoun is **itse** 'self', which inflects for case and is followed by the appropriate possessive suffix. It has no separate plural forms.

Haen sen itse.	I will fetch it *myself*.
Ajan itse partani.	I shave ("my beard") *myself*.
Annan kirjeen hänelle itse/lle/en.	I will give the letter *to him himself*.
Saitko kirjeen häneltä itse/ltä/än?	Did you get a letter *from him himself*?
Pidätkö itse/ä/si viisaana?	Do you regard *yourself* as wise?
Pohdin asiaa itse/kse/ni.	I will consider the matter for by *myself*.
Itse/e/nsä ei voi luottaa.	One cannot trust *oneself*.
Ole oma itse/si!	Be *yourself*! ("your own self")

toinen —
toinen   The combination **toinen — toinen** 'one — the other / another' is used to express the reciprocal sense 'each other, one another'. The first word of the pair is indeclinable but the second occurs in the singular followed by the necessary case-ending and possessive suffix. Another way of expressing reciprocity is to use only the one word **toinen**, in the plural and inflected for the appropriate case-ending and possessive suffix.

Lähetämme kirjeitä **toinen toise/lle/mme** (~ tois/i/lle/mme).	We send letters *to each other*.
Rakastatteko **toinen tois/ta/nne** (~ tois/i/a/nne)?	Do you love *each other*?
Ajamme **toinen toise/mme** (~ tois/te/mme) autoilla.	We drive in *each other's* cars.

§55. *DEMONSTRATIVE PRONOUNS*

The main demonstrative pronouns are **tämä** 'this' and **tuo** 'that'. The pronoun **se** 'it' refers primarily to something previously mentioned. The plural forms of all these pronouns are irregular (the initial consonant changes, etc.). In the declension of **tämä** the syllable -**mä** occurs only in the nominative singular and plural and the genitive singular.

	SINGULAR			PLURAL		
nom.	tämä this	tuo that	se it	*nämä* these	*nuo* those	*ne* they
gen.	*tämä/n*	tuo/n	se/n	nä/i/den	no/i/den	ni/i/den
part.	tä/tä	tuo/ta	si/tä	nä/i/tä	no/i/ta	ni/i/tä
iness.	tä/ssä	tuo/ssa	*sii/nä*	nä/i/ssä	no/i/ssa	ni/i/ssä
elat.	tä/stä	tuo/sta	*sii/tä*	nä/i/stä	no/i/sta	ni/i/stä
illat.	tä/hän	tuo/hon	*sii/hen*	nä/i/hin	no/i/hin	ni/i/hin
adess.	tä/llä	tuo/lla	si/llä	nä/i/llä	no/i/lla	ni/i/llä
ablat.	tä/ltä	tuo/lta	si/ltä	nä/i/ltä	no/i/lta	ni/i/ltä
allat.	tä/lle	tuo/lle	si/lle	nä/i/lle	no/i/lle	ni/i/lle
ess.	tä/nä	tuo/na	si/nä	nä/i/nä	no/i/na	ni/i/nä
transl.	tä/ksi	tuo/ksi	si/ksi	nä/i/ksi	no/i/ksi	ni/i/ksi

NB: se

Tämä kirja on minun.	*This* book is mine.
Tämä on kirja.	*This* is a book.
Tuo nainen on Tyyne Nyrkiö.	*That* woman is Tyyne Nyrkiö.
Onko **tuo** sinun autosi?	Is *that* your car?
Se on minun autoni.	*It* is my car.
Se auto on Tyynen.	*That* car is Tyyne's.
Tä/ssä on leipää ja juustoa.	*Here* is (some) bread and (some) cheese.
Tä/ssä ravintolassa on hyvä ruoka.	*This* restaurant has good food.
Hän meni **tuo/hon** taloon.	He/she went *into that* house.
Miksi puhut **tuo/lla** tavalla?	Why do you speak *in that* way?
Si/llä tavalla ei saa puhua!	One must not speak like that ("*in that* way").
Si/nä päivänä aurinko paistoi.	*On that* day the sun shone.
Sii/nä huoneessa ei voi olla.	One can't stay *in* (i.e. 'use') *that* room.
Tauno meni **sii/hen** huoneeseen missä Ristokin oli.	Tauno went *into the* room where Risto was too.
Sii/tä asia/sta en tiedä mitään.	*About that* matter I know nothing.
Tunnetko **no/i/ta** miehiä?	Do you know *those* men?
En tunne **he/i/tä**.	I don't know *them*.
He/i/llä on uusi talo.	*They* have a new house.
En kerro **he/i/lle** tästä.	I won't tell *them* about this.
Nämä kukat maksavat viisi markkaa.	*These* flowers cost five marks.
Mitä **nuo** maksavat?	What do *those* cost?
Ne/kin maksavat viisi markkaa.	*They also* cost five marks.
Nä/i/den kukkien hinta on kolme markkaa.	The price *of these* flowers is three marks.
Entä **no/i/den**?	And *of those*?
Ni/i/nä aiko/i/na asuin kotona.	*At that* time ("those times") I was living at home.

tällainen
etc.

Tällainen 'of this kind', **tuollainen** 'of that kind', **sellainen** 'such' and **semmoinen** 'such' all decline like **ihminen**-nominals (§20.1).

Tällaise/lla autolla ei voi ajaa.	One cannot drive in a car *like this*.
Paljonko **tuollainen** auto maksaa?	How much does *that kind* of car cost?
Oletko syönyt **tällais/ta** ruokaa ennen?	Have you eaten *this kind* of food before?
En ole syönyt **sellais/ta** ruokaa.	I have not eaten *such* food.
Sellais/i/a ihmisiä ei ole paljon.	There are not many *such* people.
Tällaise/ssa tilanteessa täytyy olla varovainen.	*In this kind of* situation one must be careful.
En lue **tuollais/i/a** kirjoja.	I don't read books *of that kind*.

§56. INTERROGATIVE PRONOUNS

kuka, mikä

Interrogative pronouns were briefly introduced in §30.2 above. Many of the question words are actually inflected forms of the interrogative pronouns **kuka** 'who' and **mikä** 'which, what'. The singular forms of **kuka** are based on the stem **kene-** (NB: partitive singular **ke/tä**), and the plural forms on the stem

irregular forms

ke-. Note in particular the accusative singular **kene/t** and the nominative plural **ke/t/kä**. In the declension of **mikä** the syllable -kä is dropped in all cases except the nominative singular and plural and the genitive singular (**mikä, mi/n/kä, mi/t/kä**). Almost all the plural forms of **mikä** are the same as the singular.

	SINGULAR		PLURAL	
nom.	*kuka* who	*mikä* which, what	*ke/t/kä*	*mi/t/kä*
gen.	kene/n	*mi/n/kä*	ke/i/den	(also acc.)
acc.	*kene/t*	mi/n/kä	ke/t/kä	(other forms as
part.	*ke/tä*	mi/tä	ke/i/tä	singular)
iness.	kene/ssä	mi/ssä	ke/i/ssä	
elat.	kene/stä	mi/stä	ke/i/stä	
illat.	kene/en	mi/hin	ke/i/hin	
adess.	kene/llä	mi/llä	ke/i/llä	
ablat.	kene/ltä	mi/ltä	ke/i/ltä	
allat.	kene/lle	mi/lle	ke/i/lle	
ess.	kene/nä	mi/nä	ke/i/nä	
transl.	kene/ksi	mi/ksi	ke/i/ksi	

Kuka tuo mies on?	*Who* is that man?
Kene/n kynä tämä on?	*Whose* pen is this?
Mi/ssä talossa asut?	*In which* house do you live?
Mi/tä kieltä opiskelemme?	*What* language are we studying?
Mi/hin ravintolaan mennään?	*Which* restaurant shall we go *to*?
Kene/ssä vika on?	*Whose* fault is it ("*in whom* is the fault")?
Mi/n/kä omenan valitset?	*Which* apple do you choose?
Ke/t/kä nuo ihmiset ovat?	*Who* are those people?
Kene/ltä voimme kysyä?	*Whom* ("*from whom*") could we ask?
Mi/hin kaupunkeihin matkustat?	*Which* towns are you travelling *to*?
Mi/tä ihmisiä tapasit siellä?	*What* people did you meet there?
Ke/i/lle lähetämme kirjat?	*Whom* shall we send the books *to*?
Mi/ltä sää näyttää?	*What* does the weather look like?
Mi/tä tämä on?	*What* is this?
Kene/t näit?	*Whom* did you see?
Mi/nä päivänä he tulevat?	*What* day are they coming?

kumpi

Kumpi 'which of two' declines like the comparative forms of adjectives (see §85).

	SINGULAR	PLURAL
nom.	kumpi which (of two)	kumma/t
gen.	kumma/n	kump/i/en
part.	kumpa/a	kump/i/a
iness.	kumma/ssa	kumm/i/ssa
elat.	kumma/sta	kumm/i/sta
illat.	kumpa/an	kump/i/in
adess.	kumma/lla	kumm/i/lla
ablat.	kumma/lta	kumm/i/lta
allat.	kumma/lle	kumm/i/lle
ess.	kumpa/na	kump/i/na
transl.	kumma/ksi	kumm/i/ksi

Note the alternation -i : -a-!

Kumma/lla puolella olet?	*Which* side are you *on*?
Kumma/ssa huoneessa Reino on?	*In which* room (of the two) is Reino?
Kumma/t kengät ostat?	*Which* shoes (of the two pairs) will you buy?
Kumpa/an kaupunkiin muutat?	*Which* town (of the two) are you moving *to*?
Kumma/lle annat lahjan?	*To whom* (of the two) will you give the present?

millainen, minkälainen The interrogative pronouns **millainen** and **minkälainen** 'what kind of' decline like **ihminen**-nominals (§20.1).

Millainen sää on ulkona?	*What is* the weather *like* outside?
Minkälais/ta lihaa teillä on?	*What kind of* meat do you have?
Millaise/n palkan saat?	*What kind of* salary do you get?
Minkälaise/ssa lentokoneessa pääministeri saapuu?	*In what kind of* aeroplane is the Prime Minister arriving?
Millais/i/a vieraita teille tulee?	*What kind of* guests are you having (''are coming to you'')?

§57. *INDEFINITE PRONOUNS*

The most common indefinite pronouns are **joku** 'someone', **jokin** 'something', **(ei) kukaan** 'no one', **(ei) mikään** 'nothing', **jompikumpi** 'either', **kumpikin** 'each (of two)' and **kukin** 'each one, everyone'.

joku **Joku** is a two-part pronoun: both **jo-** and **-ku** inflect for a given ending.

	SINGULAR	PLURAL
nom.	joku someone	jo/t/ku/t
gen.	jo/n/ku/n	jo/*i*/den/ku/*i*/**den**
part.	jo/ta/ku/ta	jo/i/ta/ku/i/ta
iness.	jo/ssa/ku/ssa	jo/i/ssa/ku/i/ssa
elat.	jo/sta/ku/sta	jo/i/sta/ku/i/sta
illat.	jo/hon/ku/hun	jo/i/hin/ku/i/hin
adess.	jo/lla/ku/lla	jo/i/lla/ku/i/lla
ablat.	jo/lta/ku/lta	jo/i/lta/ku/i/lta
allat.	jo/lle/ku/lle	jo/i/lle/ku/i/lle
ess.	jo/na/ku/na	jo/i/na/ku/i/na
transl.	jo/ksi/ku/ksi	jo/i/ksi/ku/i/ksi

(*Note double inflection!*)

Joku koputtaa oveen.	*Someone* is knocking at the door.
Olet saanut kirjeen **jo/lta/ku/lta**.	You have got a letter *from someone*.
Tunnetko **jo/ta/ku/ta** hyvää lääkäriä?	Do you know *a* (''any'') good doctor?
Jo/i/den/ku/i/den mielestä meidän pitäisi lähteä jo nyt.	In the opinion *of some* we ought to leave right now.
Jo/lla/ku/lla on avaimet.	*Someone* has the keys.
Jo/i/hin/ku/i/hin ei voi luottaa.	*Some people* cannot be trusted.
Pitäisin enemmän **jo/sta/ku/sta** toisesta.	I would prefer *someone* else.

jokin In the pronoun **jokin** 'something', **-kin** is an enclitic particle, so that number and case-endings are placed in the middle of the word. In case-forms ending in **-a** (e.g. **-lla**, **-ta**, **-sta**) the **-k-** of this particle may be dropped, especially in the spoken language but also often in the written language.

	SINGULAR			PLURAL	
NB:	nom.	jokin	something	jo/t/kin	
endings	gen.	jo/**n**/kin		jo/*i*/den/kin	
before	part.	jo/ta/kin	(~ jotain)	jo/i/ta/kin	(~ joitain)
-kin!	iness.	jo/ssa/kin	(~ jossain)	jo/i/ssa/kin	(~ joissain)
	elat.	jo/sta/kin	(~ jostain)	jo/i/sta/kin	(~ joistain)
	illat.	jo/hon/kin		jo/i/hin/kin	
	adess.	jo/lla/kin	(~ jollain)	jo/i/lla/kin	(~ joillain)
	ablat.	jo/lta/kin	(~ joltain)	jo/i/lta/kin	(~ joiltain)
	allat.	jo/lle/kin		jo/i/lle/kin	
	ess.	jo/na/kin	(~ jonain)	jo/i/na/kin	(~ joinain)
	transl.	jo/ksi/kin		jo/i/ksi/kin	

Olohuonessa liikkuu **jokin**.	*Something* is moving in the livingroom.
Jo/na/kin sunnuntaina lähden hiihtämään.	*One* Sunday I'll go skiing.
Jo/lla/kin tavalla aion myydä sen.	*Some*how I'm going to sell it.
Sinulla on aina **jo/i/ta/kin** esteitä.	There is always something that prevents you ("you always have *some* obstacles").
Söisin mielelläni **jo/ta/kin**.	I would like to eat *something*.
Jo/t/kin asiat ovat hyvin tärkeitä.	*Some* things are very important.
Olen lukenut sen **jo/sta/kin**.	I have read it ("from") *somewhere*.
Jo/i/hin/kin ihmisiin ei voi uskoa.	*Some* people cannot be believed.
Jo/i/lle/kin asioille ei voi mitään.	There are *some* things one can't do anything about.
Olli on **jo/ssa/kin** ulkona.	Olli is *somewhere* outside.

As the examples show, **jokin** may sometimes be used to refer to people as well, especially in the spoken language.

(ei)
kukaan

The negative equivalent of **joku** is **(ei) kukaan** 'no one, anyone. **-kaan ~ -kään** is an enclitic particle, and so the other endings appear before it. **Kukaan** usually occurs together with the negation verb. The stem for most of the singular forms is **kene-**, and for the plural forms **ke-**; cf. the declension of **kuka** above (§56). There are also some shorter alternative forms in the singular.

SINGULAR			PLURAL
nom.	*(ei) kukaan*	no one	*(eivät) ke/t/kään*
gen.	(ei) kene/n/kään		(ei) ke/i/den/kään
part.	*(ei) ke/tä/än*		*(ei) ke/i/tään*
iness.	(ei) kene/ssä/kään	(~ kessään)	(ei) ke/i/ssä/kään
elat.	(ei) kene/stä/kään	(~ kestään)	(ei) ke/i/stä/kään
illat.	(ei) kene/en/kään	(~ kehenkään)	(ei) ke/i/hin/kään
adess.	(ei) kene/llä/kään	(~ kellään)	(ei) ke/i/llä/kään
ablat.	(ei) kene/ltä/kään	(~ keltään)	(ei) ke/i/ltä/kään
allat.	(ei) kene/lle/kään	(~ kellekään)	(ei) ke/i/lle/kään

Kukaan ei usko minua.	*No one* believes me.
En usko **ke/tä/än**.	I don't believe *anyone*.
Kene/ssä/kään ei ole vikaa.	It's *no one's* fault.
Onko täällä **ke/tä/än**?	Is there *anybody* here?
Ke/i/tään ei ole näkynyt.	*No one* was to be seen.
Älä tee **kene/lle/kään** pahaa!	Do no harm *to anyone*.
Tämä ei ole **kene/stä/kään** hyvää.	*No one* thinks this is good ("this is not good *in anyone's opinion*").
Ke/t/kään eivät kannata ehdotusta.	*Nobody* support the proposal.
En saa apua **kene/ltä/kään**.	I get no help *from anyone*.
Ke/i/llä/kään ei ole varaa tähän.	*No one* can afford this.

(ei) mikään

The declension of **(ei) mikään** 'nothing', the negative equivalent of **jokin**, is similar; cf. **mikä** (§56). For both **mikä** and **(ei) mikään** almost all the plural forms are the same as the corresponding singular ones.

SINGULAR

nom	*(ei) mikään*	nothing
gen.	(ei) mi/n/kään	
part.	(ei) mi/tä/än	
iness.	(ei) mi/ssä/än	
elat.	(ei) mi/stä/än	
illat.	(ei) mi/hin/kään	
adess.	(ei) mi/llä/än	
ablat.	(ei) mi/ltä/än	
allat.	(ei) mi/lle/kään	
ess.	(ei) mi/nä/än	
transl.	(ei) mi/ksi/kään	

PLURAL

(eivät) mi/t/kään
(other forms as singular)

Mikään ei auta.	*Nothing* helps.
En näe **mi/tä/än**.	I don't see *anything*.
Siellä ei ole **mi/tä/än**.	There is *nothing* there.
Hän ei välitä **mi/stä/än**.	He/she doesn't care *about anything*.
Tyynestä ei ole **mi/hin/kään**.	Tyyne is not good *for anything*.
En voi auttaa teitä **mi/llä/än** tavalla.	I cannot help you *in any* way.
Siitä ei ole **mi/tä/än** hyötyä.	That is *no* use.
Mi/t/kään selitykset eivät auta.	*No* explanations help.
Mi/stä/än maasta ei tule enemmän edustajia kuin Suomesta.	From *no* country are there coming more representatives than from Finland.
Mi/n/kään koneen ominaisuudet eivät ole paremmat kuin tämän.	*No* machine has better qualities than this one (''the qualities *of no* machine are...'').
Mi/ssä/än tapauksessa en suostu tähän.	*On no* account do I agree to this.
Ei ole **mi/tä/än** hyviä keinoja.	There are *no* good methods.
Mi/nä/än vuonna ei ole satanut niin paljon kuin tänä vuonna.	*In no* year has it rained as much as this year.

jompi-kumpi

Jompikumpi 'either, one or the other' is similar to **joku** in that both **jompi** and **kumpi** decline. In **kumpikin** 'each of two, both', the first part declines exactly like the pronoun **kumpi** (§56) and the particle -**kin** is added. **Kumpikaan** 'neither' declines like **kumpikin**.

	SINGULAR	PLURAL
nom.	jompikumpi either	jomma/t/kumma/t
gen.	jomma/n/kumma/n	jomp/i/en/kump/i/en
part.	jompa/a/kumpa/a	jomp/i/a/kump/i/a
iness.	jomma/ssa/kumma/ssa	jomm/i/ssa/kumm/i/ssa
elat.	jomma/sta/kumma/sta	jomm/i/sta/kumm/i/sta
illat.	jompa/an/kumpa/an	jomp/i/in/kump/i/in
adess.	jomma/lla/kumma/lla	jomm/i/lla/kumm/i/lla
ablat.	jomma/lta/kumma/lta	jomm/i/lta/kumm/i/lta
allat.	jomma/lle/kumma/lle	jomm/i/lle/kumm/i/lle
ess.	jompa/na/kumpa/na	jomp/i/na/kump/i/na
transl.	jomma/ksi/kumma/ksi	jomm/i/ksi/kumm/i/ksi

	SINGULAR		PLURAL
kumpikin (-kaan)	nom.	kumpikin each of two	kumma/t/kin
	gen.	kumma/n/kin	kump/i/en/kin
	part.	kumpa/a/kin	kump/i/a/kin
	iness.	kumma/ssa/kin	kumm/i/ssa/kin
	elat.	kumma/sta/kin	kumm/i/sta/kin
	illat.	kumpa/an/kin	kump/i/in/kin
	adess.	kumma/lla/kin	kumm/i/lla/kin
	ablat.	kumma/lta/kin	kumm/i/lta/kin
	allat.	kumma/lle/kin	kumm/i/lle/kin
	ess.	kumpa/na/kin	kump/i/na/kin
	transl.	kumma/ksi/kin	kumm/i/ksi/kin

Jompikumpi ehdotus voittaa.	*One or the other* proposal will win.
Kumpikaan ei voita.	*Neither* will win.
En tunne **kumpa/a/kaan** heistä.	I don't know *either* of them.
Jomma/ssa/kumma/ssa tapauksessa.	*In either* case.
Pidän **kumma/sta/kin**.	I like *both* of them.
Tulen **jompa/na/kumpa/na** pääsiäis-päivänä.	I'll come *on one* of the Easter holidays (i.e. the Sunday or the Monday).
En tule **kumpa/na/kaan** päivänä.	I'm not coming *on either* day.
Kumma/sta/kin talosta tulee yksi mies.	*From each of the (two)* houses comes one man.
Kumpa/an/kin perheeseen syntyi tyttö.	*Into both* families a girl was born.
Voit ottaa **jomma/t/kumma/t** kengät.	You can take *either* pair of shoes.
Kumma/t/kin häät ovat ennen joulua.	*Both* weddings are before Christmas.
En pidä **kumma/sta/kaan** kirjasta.	I don't like *either* of the books.
Sain kirjan **jomma/lta/kumma/lta**, en muista keneltä.	I got a letter *from one* of them, I don't remember which.
Hän ei osaa **kumpa/a/kaan** kieltä.	He/she does not speak *either* language.
Kumma/n/kin kengät ovat eteisessä.	The shoes *of both* are in the hall.

kukin Similarly, in the declension of **kukin** 'each, everyone' the case-endings are placed before the particle **-kin**.

SINGULAR	
nom.	kukin each
gen.	ku/n/kin
part.	ku/ta/kin
iness.	ku/ssa/kin
elat.	ku/sta/kin
illat.	ku/hun/kin
adess.	ku/lla/kin
ablat.	ku/lta/kin
allat.	ku/lle/kin
ess.	ku/na/kin
transl.	ku/ksi/kin

Kukin saa yhden voileivän.	*Everyone* gets one sandwich.
Annamme **ku/lle/kin** yhden voileivän.	We will give *everyone* one sandwich.
Ku/lla/kin on huolensa.	*Everyone* has his worries.
Ku/ssa/kin talossa asuu neljä perhettä.	*In each* house there live four families.
Ku/n/kin täytyy tehdä kaikkensa.	*Everyone* must do his best ("his all").
Maksamme seitsemän markkaa **ku/lta/kin** sivulta.	We pay seven marks *for each* page.
Perehdymme **ku/hun/kin** tapaukseen erikseen.	We investigate *each* case separately.

Note further the following words which decline like the corresponding nouns and adjectives.

other important words	BASIC FORM		GENITIVE	PARTITIVE
	eräs	a certain	erää/n	eräs/tä
	jokainen	every, each one	jokaise/n	jokais/ta
	kaikki	all, everything	kaike/n	kaikke/a
	molemma/t	both	molemp/i/en	molemp/i/a
	moni	many (a)	mone/n	mon/ta
	muutama	some, a few	muutama/n	muutama/a
	muu	other, else	muu/n	muu/ta
	toinen	another, other	toise/n	tois/ta
	usea	many (a), several	usea/n	usea/a

Molemma/t, muutama and **usea** occur in both singular and plural.

Melkein **jokaise/lla** perheellä on televisio.	Almost *every* family has a television.
Kaikki tulevat meille illalla.	*Everyone* comes to us in the evening.
Kaik/i/lla on hauskaa.	*Everyone* has a nice time.
Molemma/t lapset ovat koulussa.	*Both* the children are at school.
Annan banaanin **molemm/i/lle.**	I (will) give a banana *to both*.
Erää/nä päivänä viime viikolla.	*One / a certain* day last week.
Teos on **erää/llä** tavalla hyvä.	*In one* way the work is good.
Eräs toinen tyttö tuli sisään.	*Another* (''*a certain* other'') girl came in.
Tiedän **kaike/n**.	I know *everything*.
Moni yritys epäonnistuu.	*Many an* attempt fails.
Tuli **mon/ta** vierasta.	There came *many* guests.
Olen ollut **mon/i/ssa** maissa (~ **mone/ssa** maassa).	I have been *in many* countries.
Mon/i/en mielestä tämä on huono ehdotus.	In *many people's* opinion this is a bad proposal.
Mone/lla yrittäjällä on vaikeuksia.	*Many an* entrepreneur has difficulties.
Tunnen **mon/i/a** ihmisiä.	I know *many* people.
Muu/t ovat eri mieltä.	*The others / the rest* are of a different opinion.
Olen käynyt **mu/i/ssa/kin** Pohjois-maissa.	I have also visited *the other* Nordic countries.
Ostin takin **muutama/lla** markalla.	I bought a coat *for a few* marks.
Muutama/t ihmiset väittävät, että...	*Some / a few* people claim that...
Työ on valmis **muutama/ssa** minuutissa.	The work will be ready *in a few* minutes.
Muutam/i/a vuosia sitten.	*A few* years ago.
Selitän asian **muutama/lla** sanalla.	I will explain the matter *in a few* words.
Tämä on **toinen** asia.	This is *another* matter.
Usea/t ihmiset sanovat, että...	*Many / several* people say that...
Use/i/ssa tapauksissa.	*In many / several* cases.
Use/i/den mielestä hallitus on kelvoton.	In *many people's* opinion the government is no good.
En ole nähnyt Osmoa **use/i/hin** vuosiin.	I haven't seen Osmo *for several* years.

§58. RELATIVE PRONOUNS

joka

The most common relative pronoun is **joka** 'who, which', the final syllable of which occurs only in the nominative singular and plural and the genitive singular.

SINGULAR		PLURAL
nom.	joka who, which, that	*jo/t/ka*
gen.	*jo/n/ka*	jo/i/den
part.	jo/ta	jo/i/ta
iness.	jo/ssa	jo/i/ssa
elat.	jo/sta	jo/i/sta
illat.	jo/hon	jo/i/hin
adess.	jo/lla	jo/i/lla
ablat.	jo/lta	jo/i/lta
allat.	jo/lle	jo/i/lle
ess.	jo/na	jo/i/na
transl.	jo/ksi	jo/i/ksi

mikä

Mikä (mentioned above as an interrogative pronoun, §56) is also used as a relative pronoun. With the exception of the nominative and accusative the plural forms are the same as the corresponding singular ones; otherwise it declines like **joka**.

SINGULAR		PLURAL
nom.	mikä which, that	*mi/t/kä* (other forms as singular)
gen.	*mi/n/kä*	
part.	mi/tä	
iness.	mi/ssä	
elat.	mi/stä	
illat.	mi/hin	
adess.	mi/llä	
ablat.	mi/ltä	
allat.	mi/lle	
ess.	mi/nä	
transl.	mi/ksi	

Joka is a more common relative pronoun than **mikä**, and it is mainly, but not always, used to refer to entities that are alive. **Mikä** is mostly used only for inanimate entities; it is also used when the reference is to a clause or to an expression containing a superlative.

Hän on mies, **joka** ei pelkää.	He is a man *who* does not fear.
Tämä on kirja, **jo/ta** en halua lukea.	This is a book *that* I don't want to read.
Talo **jo/ssa** asun on Vilhonkadulla.	The house *where* I live is in Vilho's Street.
Sain lahjan, **jo/sta** on hyötyä.	I got a present *which* is useful ("*of which* is use").
Ne olivat aikoja, **jo/t/ka** eivät palaa.	They were times *that* will never return.
Tapahtumat **jo/i/sta** kuulin olivat kauheita.	The events *which* I heard *about* were terrible.
Se on paras paikka **mi/n/kä** tiedän.	It is the best place *that* I know.
Tässä ovat kirjeet **mi/t/kä** lähetit minulle.	Here are the letters *that* you sent to me.
Tuo on kertomus, **jo/hon** en usko.	That is a story *that* I don't believe.
Tuli sade, **mikä** esti matkamme.	It rained, *which* prevented our trip.

14 Tenses

§59. *PRESENT*

Finnish has four tenses: two simple (present and past) and two compound (perfect and pluperfect). Cf. present *sano/n* 'I say', past *sano/i/n* 'I said', perfect *ole/n sano/nut* 'I have said' and pluperfect *ol/i/n sano/nut* 'I had said'.

The *present* is used for non-past time: usually a time simultaneous with the moment of utterance, and sometimes also future time, i.e. later than the moment of utterance. It is also used for general "timeless" truths of the kind *Leijona on eläin* 'The lion is an animal; *Leijonat ovat eläimiä* 'Lions are animals'.

There is no separate ending for the present. But note that in the 3rd person singular the short final vowel of the stem lengthens, i.e. doubles (§24). Otherwise only the normal personal endings are added to the inflectional stem (§23).

NB:
vowel
length-
ening

Kalle on ulkona.	Kalle is outside.
(Minä) ole/n kotona.	I am at home.
(Me) lue/mme sanomalehteä.	We are reading the newspaper.
Pertti luke/e sanomalehteä.	Pertti is reading the newspaper.
Mitä sano/tte?	What do you say?
Auto seiso/o tallissa.	The car is standing in the garage.
Ritva halua/a olutta.	Ritva wants some beer.
Tuula ja Leena lähte/vät Espanjaan.	Tuula ja Leena are going to Spain.
Mattikin lähte/e sinne.	Matti is going there too.

§60. *PAST*

The past tense is used for past time, to express an action which took place before the moment of utterance. The past tense ending is -i, which is added to the inflectional stem (§23) and is followed by the personal ending.

-i

> THE PAST TENSE ENDING IS -i, WHICH IS ADDED TO THE INFLECTIONAL STEM (§23)

The verbs *sano/a* 'say', *puhu/a* 'speak' and *anta/a* 'give' thus conjugate as follows in the past tense. For consonant gradation see §15.

<table>
<tr><td>NB:
consonant
gradation</td><td>1ST P. SING.</td><td>(minä)</td><td>sano/i/n
puhu/i/n
anno/i/n</td><td>I said
I spoke
I gave</td></tr>
<tr><td></td><td>2ND P. SING.</td><td>(sinä)</td><td>sano/i/t
puhu/i/t
anno/i/t</td><td>you said
you spoke
you gave</td></tr>
<tr><td></td><td>3RD P. SING.</td><td>hän
äiti
Kalle</td><td>sano/i
puhu/i
anto/i</td><td>he/she said
mother spoke
Kalle gave</td></tr>
<tr><td></td><td>1ST P. PL.</td><td>(me)</td><td>sano/i/mme
puhu/i/mme
anno/i/mme</td><td>we said
we spoke
we gave</td></tr>
<tr><td></td><td>2ND P. PL.</td><td>(te)</td><td>sano/i/tte
puhu/i/tte
anno/i/tte</td><td>you said
you spoke
you gave</td></tr>
<tr><td></td><td>3RD P. PL.</td><td>he
naiset
miehet</td><td>sano/i/vat
puhu/i/vat
anto/i/vat</td><td>they said
the women spoke
the men gave</td></tr>
</table>

NB:
vowel
changes!

Before the past tense -i the usual vowel change rules apply (§16); cf. above **anno/i/n** etc. The table below gives first the basic form of the verb (1st infinitive), then the 3rd person singular of the present as an example of the inflectional stem, and the section number (§) explaining the vowel change in question, and finally the 3rd person singular of the past tense (without consonant gradation) and the 1st person singular of the past tense (with consonant gradation).

	INFINITIVE			3RD P. SING. PRESENT	CF.§	3RD P. SING. PAST	1ST P. SING. PAST
anta/a- verbs	kerto/a	tell		kerto/o	16.1	kerto/i	kerro/i/n
	asu/a	live		asu/u	"	asu/i	asu/i/n
-e, -i, -ä dropped	pysy/ä	stay		pysy/y	"	pysy/i	pysy/i/n
	luke/a	read		luke/e	16.5	luk/i	lu/i/n
	etsi/ä	look for		etsi/i	16.6b	ets/i	ets/i/n
	oppi/a	learn		oppi/i	"	opp/i	op/i/n
	vetä/ä	pull		vetä/ä	16.7	vet/i	ved/i/n
	yrittä/ä	try		yrittä/ä	"	yritt/i	yrit/i/n
-a → o	anta/a	give		anta/a	16.8c	anto/i	anno/i/n
	sata/a	rain		sata/a	"	sato/i	—
	jaka/a	divide		jaka/a	"	jako/i	jao/i/n
-a dropped	muista/a	remember		muista/a	16.8c	muist/i	muist/i/n
	otta/a	take		otta/a	"	ott/i	ot/i/n
	rakasta/a	love		rakasta/a	"	rakast/i	rakast/i/n
	osta/a	buy		osta/a	"	ost/i	ost/i/n
saa/da- verbs	saa/da	get		saa	16.2	sa/i	sa/i/n
	myy/dä	sell		myy	"	my/i	my/i/n
	voi/da	be able		voi	16.4	vo/i	vo/i/n
deletion	juo/da	drink		juo	16.3	jo/i	jo/i/n
	pysäköi/dä	park		pysäköi	16.4	pysäkö/i	pysäkö/i/n
	luennoi/da	lecture		luennoi	"	luenno/i	luenno/i/n

nous/ta-,	nous/ta	rise	nouse/e	16.5	nous/i	nous/i/n
tul/la-	tul/la	come	tule/e	"	tul/i	tul/i/n
verbs	men/nä	go	mene/e	"	men/i	men/i/n
-e dropped	ajatel/la	think	ajattele/e	"	ajattel/i	ajattel/i/n
	kierrel/lä	circle	kiertele/e	"	kiertel/i	kiertel/i/n
	julkais/ta	publish	julkaise/e	"	julkais/i	julkais/i/n
	tarvit/a	need	tarvitse/e	"	tarvits/i	tarvits/i/n
	häirit/ä	disturb	häiritse/e	"	häirits/i	häirits/i/n
	paet/a	flee	pakene/e	"	paken/i	paken/i/n

In some verbs of the **anta/a**-type, where because of the deletion of -**a** or -**ä** the short consonant -**t**- occurs immediately before the past tense ending, this -**t**- changes to -**s**-. This most often happens when the -**t**- occurs after two vowels or after **l, n** or **r**.

> -t- SOMETIMES CHANGES TO -s- IF, AFTER THE DELETION OF
> -a OR -ä, IT OCCURS IMMEDIATELY BEFORE THE PAST TENSE
> -i

	INFINITIVE		3RD P. SING. PRESENT	3RD P. SING. PAST	1ST P. SING. PAST
	tietä/ä	know	tietä/ä	ties/i	ties/i/n
	löytä/ä	find	löytä/ä	löys/i	löys/i/n
	huuta/a	shout	huuta/a	huus/i	huus/i/n
-t ~ -s-	piirtä/ä	draw	piirtä/ä	piirs/i	piirs/i/n
	työntä/ä	push	työntä/ä	työns/i	työns/i/n
	lentä/ä	fly	lentä/ä	lens/i	lens/i/n
	kiertä/ä	turn	kiertä/ä	kiers/i	kiers/i/n
	pyytä/ä	ask	pyytä/ä	pyys/i	pyys/i/n
	kiiltä/ä	shine	kiiltä/ä	kiils/i	kiils/i/n

Verbs to which this rule does not apply include *pitä/ä* 'keep', *vetä/ä* 'pull', *sietä/ä* 'bear', *hoita/a* 'take care of', cf. *hän pit/i* 'he/she kept', *pid/i/n* 'I held', *Reijo vet/i* 'Reijo pulled', *ved/i/n* 'I pulled', etc.

The important group of **huomat/a**-verbs form their past tense according to the following special change.

special rule

> THE PAST TENSE OF **huomat/a**-VERBS IS FORMED BY CHANG-
> ING THE LAST -a OR -ä OF THE INFLECTIONAL STEM TO -s-,
> AND THEN ADDING THE PAST TENSE -i

	INFINITIVE		3RD P. SING. PRESENT	3RD P. SING. PAST	1ST P. SING. PAST
	huomat/a	notice	huomaa	huomas/i	huomas/i/n
	osat/a	know how	osaa	osas/i	osas/i/n
	hypät/ä	jump	hyppää	hyppäs/i	hyppäs/i/n
huomat/a-	pelät/ä	fear	pelkää	pelkäs/i	pelkäs/i/n
verbs	maat/a	lie	makaa	makas/i	makas/i/n
	tavat/a	meet	tapaa	tapas/i	tapas/i/n
	määrät/ä	order	määrää	määräs/i	määräs/i/n
	halut/a	want	halua/a	halus/i	halus/i/n
	tarjot/a	offer	tarjoa/a	tarjos/i	tarjos/i/n

The examples below illustrate the use of the past tense.

Koira makas/i lattialla.	The dog *lay* on the floor.
Oskari anto/i minulle suukon.	Oskari *gave* me a kiss.
Poliisi kysy/i nimeäni.	The policeman *asked* me my name.
Kuka siellä ol/i?	Who *was* there?
Jo/i/t/ko punaviiniä eilen?	*Did you drink* red wine yesterday?
Mitä he tek/i/vät illalla?	What *did they do* in the evening?
Mitä te/i/tte illalla?	What *did you do* in the evening?
Niin me ajattel/i/mme/kin.	That's just what *we thought*.
Ajo/i/n Turusta Helsinkiin kahdessa tunnissa.	*I drove* from Turku to Helsinki in two hours.
Mitä ost/i/t Kaleville lahjaksi?	What *did you buy* as a present for Kalevi?
He läht/i/vät jo aamulla.	*They left* ("already") in the morning.
Ties/i/tte/kö tämän?	*Did you know* this?
Keijo avas/i vieraille oven.	Keijo *opened* the door for the guests.

NB:
käy/dä

Note that the verb **käy/dä** 'go' has an exceptional past tense: **käv/i**, cf. *käv/i/n* 'I went', *he käv/i/vät* 'they went'.

§61. *PERFECT*

The perfect is used for past actions whose influence is in some way still valid at the moment of utterance: the perfect ist the tense of "present relevance". It is formed with the present tense of the auxiliary verb *ol/la* 'be' inflected for person, followed by the past participle in the singular or plural form according to the number of the subject. The participle ending is **-nut ~ -nyt**. E.g. *(minä) ole/n sanonut* 'I have said', *(sinä) ole/t luke/nut* 'you have read', *hän on syö/nyt* 'he/she has eaten'.

formation
of the
past
participle

> THE PAST PARTICIPLE IS FORMED BY ADDING THE ENDING
> - **nut ~ -nyt** TO THE INFINITIVE STEM (§23)

sound
alterna-
tions

> IF THE INFINITIVE STEM ENDS IN A CONSONANT
> a) WHICH IS **l**, **r** OR **s**, THE **n** OF THE PARTICIPLE CHANGES
>   TO A SECOND **l**, **r** OR **s**;
> b) WHICH IS **t**, THIS **t** CHANGES TO **n**

	INFINITIVE		PAST PARTICIPLE	CF. 3RD P. SING. PRESENT
anta/a- verbs	osta/a	buy	osta/**nut**	osta/a
	itke/ä	cry	itke/**nyt**	itke/e
	seiso/a	stand	seiso/**nut**	seiso/o
	tanssi/a	dance	tanssi/**nut**	tanssi/i
	löytä/ä	find	löytä/**nyt**	löytä/ä
	anta/a	give	anta/**nut**	anta/a
	näyttä/ä	show	näyttä/**nyt**	näyttä/ä
	synty/ä	be born	synty/**nyt**	synty/y

	INFINITIVE		PAST PARTICIPLE	CF. 3RD P. SING. PRESENT
saa/da- verbs	saa/da	get	saa/**nut**	saa
	myy/dä	sell	myy/**nyt**	myy
	juo/da	drink	juo/**nut**	juo
	soi/da	ring	soi/**nut**	soi
	vartioi/da	guard	vartioi/**nut**	vartioi
nous/ta-, **tul/la-** verbs	nous/ta	rise	nous/**sut**	nouse/e
	pes/tä	wash	pes/**syt**	pese/e
	tul/la	come	tul/**lut**	tule/e
n- → s, l, r	ol/la	be	ol/**lut**	on
	ajatel/la	think	ajatel/**lut**	ajattele/e
	pur/ra	bite	pur/**rut**	pure/e
	väitel/lä	dispute	väitel/**lyt**	väittele/e
huomat/a- verbs	huomat/a	notice	huoman/**nut**	huomaa
	osat/a	know how	osan/**nut**	osaa
	halut/a	want	halun/**nut**	halua/a
-t → n	veikat/a	bet	veikan/**nut**	veikkaa
	pelät/ä	fear	pelän/**nyt**	pelkää
	hypät/ä	jump	hypän/**nyt**	hyppää
	kelvat/a	be good enough	kelvan/**nut**	kelpaa
	tarvit/a	need	tarvin/**nut**	tarvitse/e
	paet/a	flee	paen/**nut**	pakene/e
	lämmet/ä	become warm	lämmen/**nyt**	lämpene/e
	havait/a	observe	havain/**nut**	havaitse/e

-nee- The inflectional stem of the past participle is formed by changing -ut ~ -yt to -ee-, e.g. sano/**nut** : sano/**nee**-, and any endings are added to this stem. The different persons of the perfect tense are thus as follows.

1ST P. SING.	(minä)	ole/n sano/**nut**	I have said
		ole/n ol/**lut**	I have been
		ole/n huoman/**nut**	I have noticed
2ND P. SING.	(sinä)	ole/t sano/**nut**	you have said
		ole/t ol/**lut**	you have been
		ole/t huoman/**nut**	you have noticed
3RD P. SING.	hän	on sano/**nut**	he/she has said
	hän	on ol/**lut**	he/she has been
	hän	on huoman/**nut**	he/she has noticed
1ST P. PL.	(me)	ole/mme sano/**neet**	we have said
		ole/mme ol/**leet**	we have been
		ole/mme huoman/**neet**	we have noticed
2ND P. PL.	(te)	ole/tte sano/**neet**	you have said
		ole/tte ol/**leet**	you have been
		ole/tte huoman/**neet**	you have noticed
3RD P. PL.	he	ovat sano/**neet**	they have said
	he	ovat ol/**leet**	they have been
	he	ovat huoman/**neet**	they have noticed

Below are some examples of the use of the perfect.

Keihänen **on** matkusta/**nut** Espanjaan.	Keihänen *has travelled* to Spain.
On/ko johtaja men/**nyt** lounaalle?	*Has* the manager *gone* to lunch?
Ole/tte/ko ennen ol/**leet** Suomessa?	*Have* you *been* in Finland before?
Kari ja Pertti **ovat** lähte/**neet** pois.	Kari and Pertti *have gone* away.
Ole/t/ko jo syö/**nyt**?	*Have* you already *eaten*?
Ole/n maan/**nut** sängyssä koko päivän.	I *have lain* in bed all day.
Ole/tte/ko luke/**neet** Salaman uusimman kirjan?	*Have* you *read* Salama's latest book?

condi-
tional
potential

The perfect can also occur in the conditional mood, when the ending -**isi**- is added to the auxilary *olla*, and in the potential mood, which is formed from an exceptional stem of the verb *olla*, **liene**-, followed by a personal ending. After these forms of the auxiliary the past participle follows (see chapter 15).

Ol/**isi**/n ol/**lut** iloinen, jos ol/**isi**/t tul/**lut**.	I *would have been* pleased if you *had* (''*would have*'') *come*.
Ol/**isi**/mme lähte/**neet** Espanjaan, jos meillä ol/**isi** ol/**lut** rahaa.	We *would have gone* to Spain if we *had* (''*would have*'') *had* money.
Kekkonen **liene**/e käy/**nyt** Marokossa.	Kekkonen *has probably been* to Marocco.
He **liene**/vät hankki/**neet** auton.	They (*have*) *probably obtained* a car.

§62. *PLUPERFECT*

ol/**i**- +
-**nut** ~
-**nyt**

The pluperfect is used for actions which have taken place before some point of time in the past. It is formed from the past tense of *ol/la* (*ol/i/n, ol/i/t, ol/i, ol/i/mme, ol/i/tte, ol/i/vat*), followed by the past participle (§61).

Ol/i/n juuri tul/**lut** kotiin, kun soitit.	I *had* just *come* home when you rang.
Ol/i/mme tul/**leet** kotiin...	We *had come* home...
Hän **ol**/i opiskel/**lut** suomea ennen kuin hän tuli Suomeen.	He *had studied* Finnish before he came to Finland.
Kalle **ol**/i odotta/**nut** kymmenen minuuttia kun tulin.	Kalle *had waited / been waiting* ten minutes when I came.
He **ol**/i/vat odotta/**neet**...	They *had waited*...

§63. *NEGATIVE FORMS*

All negative forms are based on the negation verb *en, et, ei, emme, ette, eivät*. The present tense negative has been discussed earlier (§29); here the negation verb is followed by a minimal stem form of the main verb subject to consonant gradation.

present
(§29)

AFFIRMATIVE		NEGATIVE	
kerro/n	I tell	**en** kerro	I do not tell
kerro/t	etc.	**et** kerro	etc.
hän kerto/o		hän **ei** kerro	
kerro/mme		**emme** kerro	
kerro/tte		**ette** kerro	
he kerto/vat		he **eivät** kerro	

The negative of the past tense is formed differently: the negation verb is followed by the past participle (§61).

AFFIRMATIVE		NEGATIVE	
kerro/i/n	I told	en kerto/**nut**	I did not tell
kerro/i/t	etc.	et kerto/**nut**	etc.
hän kerto/i		hän **ei** kerto/**nut**	
kerro/i/mme		**emme** kerto/**neet**	
kerro/i/tte		**ette** kerto/**neet**	
he kerto/i/vat		he **eivät** kerto/**neet**	

Here are some further examples of the formation of the past tense negative.

AFFIRMATIVE		NEGATIVE
tanss/i/n	I danced	en tanssi/**nut**
tanss/i/tte	you (pl.) danced	ette tanssi/**neet**
itk/i/t	you (s.) cried	et itke/**nyt**
hän näytt/i	he/she showed	hän **ei** näyttä/**nyt**
he anto/i/vat	they gave	he **eivät** anta/**neet**
lu/i/n	I read	en luke/**nut**
ol/i/mme	we were	**emme** ol/**leet**
ol/i/t	you (s.) were	et ol/**lut**
nous/i/n	I got up	en nous/**sut**
he nous/i/vat	they got up	he **eivät** nous/**seet**
ajattel/i/mme	we thought	**emme** ajatel/**leet**
Tuula sa/i	Tuula got	Tuula **ei** saa/**nut**
osas/i/mme	we knew how	**emme** osan/**neet**
osas/i/t	you (s.) knew how	et osan/**nut**
hän pelkäs/i	he/she feared	hän **ei** pelän/**nyt**
pelkäs/i/tte	you (pl.) feared	**ette** pelän/**neet**
tarvits/i/n	I needed	en tarvin/**nut**
he häirits/i/vät	they disturbed	he **eivät** häirin/**neet**

The negative of the perfect tense is formed from the negation verb followed by *ole* (without a personal ending) and the past participle of the main verb (singular or plural).

perfect

AFFIRMATIVE		NEGATIVE
ole/n osta/nut	I have bought	en ole osta/**nut**
ole/t osta/nut	you (s.) have bought	et ole osta/**nut**
hän on osta/nut	he/she has bought	hän **ei** ole osta/**nut**
ole/mme osta/neet	we have bought	**emme** ole osta/**neet**
ole/tte osta/neet	you (pl.) have bought	**ette** ole osta/**neet**
he ovat osta/neet	they have bought	he **eivät** ole osta/**neet**
ole/n ol/lut	I have been	en ole ol/**lut**
ole/mme ol/leet	we have been	**emme** ole ol/**leet**
ole/t näyttä/nyt	you (s.) have shown	et ole näyttä/**nyt**
he ovat anta/neet	they have given	he **eivät** ole anta/**neet**
ole/mme saa/neet	we have got	**emme** ole saa/**neet**
ole/n ajatel/lut	I have thought	en ole ajatel/**lut**
hän on osan/nut	he/she has known how	hän **ei** ole osan/**nut**
ole/mme pelän/neet	we have feared	**emme** ole pelän/**neet**
ole/n tarvin/nut	I have needed	en ole tarvin/**nut**
ol/isi/n osta/nut	I would have bought	en ol/isi osta/**nut**
ol/isi/tte osta/neet	you (pl.) would have bought	**ette** ol/isi osta/**neet**

he ol/isi/vat osta/neet	they would have bought	he eivät ol/isi osta/neet
hän liene/e osta/nut	he/she has probably bought	hän ei liene osta/nut

The negative of the pluperfect is formed from the negation verb followed by the past participle of *ol/la — ol/lut ~ ol/leet —* and the past participle of the main verb (singular or plural).

	AFFIRMATIVE		NEGATIVE
pluperfect	ol/i/n osta/nut	I had bought	en ol/lut osta/nut
	ol/i/t osta/nut	you (s.) had bought	et ol/lut osta/nut
	hän ol/i osta/nut	he/she had bought	hän ei ol/lut osta/nut
	ol/i/mme osta/neet	we had bought	emme ol/leet osta/neet
	ol/i/tte osta/neet	you (pl.) had bought	ette ol/leet osta/neet
	he ol/i/vat osta/neet	they had bought	he eivät ol/leet osta/neet
	ol/i/n ol/lut	I had been	en ol/lut ol/lut
	ol/i/mme ol/leet	we had been	emme ol/leet ol/leet
	ol/i/t näyttä/nyt	you (s.) had shown	et ol/lut näyttä/nyt
	ol/i/mme osan/neet	we had known how	emme ol/leet osan/neet
	ol/i/t saa/nut	you (s.) had got	et ol/lut saa/nut
	hän ol/i pelän/nyt	he/she had feared	hän ei ol/lut pelän/nyt
	ol/i/mme tul/leet	we had come	emme ol/leet tul/leet
	ol/i/n näh/nyt	I had seen	en ol/lut näh/nyt

And note finally the following sentence examples.

En osta maitoa.	I do / will not buy any milk.
En osta/nut maitoa.	I did not buy any milk.
En ole osta/nut maitoa.	I have not bought any milk.
En ol/lut osta/nut maitoa.	I had not bought any milk.

15 Moods

Indicative
Conditional
Imperative
Potential

§64. *INDICATIVE*

four
moods

The term "mood" refers to certain verb endings expressing the *manner* in which the speaker presents the action of the verb. There are four moods in Finnish: the indicative (which is not marked by a separate ending) is the most common, and expresses the action of the verb "as such". The conditional **-isi-** mostly indicates a hypothetical action; the imperative (several different endings according to person) indicates a command; and the potential **-ne-**, a rare mood, presents an action as probable or conceivable.

The *indicative* is thus the most common mood. It has no ending and presents an action as such, without any indication of the speaker's attitude. Tense and personal endings are added in the normal way.

indicative,
no ending

Nyt *mene/n* kotiin.	Now I'*m going* home.
Lapsi *leikki/i* pihalla.	A/the child *plays* in the yard.
Vieraat *tule/vat* illalla.	The guests *are coming* in the evening.
Eilen *sa/i/n* kaksi kirjettä.	Yesterday I *got* two letters.
Koska *sairastu/i/t*?	When *did* you *fall* ill?
He *o/vat asu/neet* kymmenen vuotta Helsingissä.	They *have lived* in Helsinki for ten years.
Missä *ole/t synty/nyt*?	Where *were* you *born*?
Vuonna 1960 Paasikivi *ol/i* jo *kuol/lut*.	In the year 1960 Paasikivi *had* already *died*.

These verb-forms contain no mood ending, then, only personal and (where necessary) tense endings.

§65. *CONDITIONAL*

The conditional **-isi-** mostly indicates an action that is presented as hypothetical, and occurs most commonly in conditional clauses after *jos* 'if' and in the accompanying main clause.

> **THE CONDITIONAL ENDING IS -isi-, WHICH IS ADDED TO THE INFLECTIONAL STEM (§23)**

NB: vowel changes

The conditional ending does not cause consonant gradation in the stem preceding it (§15.2), but many vowel change rules apply when **-isi-** follows the inflectional stem (§16). The conditional ending is followed by a personal ending, after which there may also be an enclitic particle.

The verbs *sano/a* 'say', *puhu/a* 'speak' and *anta/a* 'give' have the following conditional forms in the three singular persons.

1ST P. SING.	(minä)	sano/**isi**/n	I would say
		puhu/**isi**/n	I would speak
		anta/**isi**/n	I would give
2ND P. SING.	(sinä)	sano/**isi**/t	you would say
		puhu/**isi**/t	you would speak
		anta/**isi**/t	you would give
3RD P. SING.	hän	sano/**isi**	he/she would say
	Kalle	puhu/**isi**	Kalle would speak
	äiti	anta/**isi**	mother would give

Below are examples of the effect of vowel changes before the conditional ending. The table shows first the basic form of the verb, then the 3rd person singular present indicative as an example of the inflectional stem, with the section number (§) explaining the change in the final vowel of the inflectional stem, and finally the 1st person singular of the conditional (the other persons only differ in the personal ending).

	INFINITIVE		3RD P. SING. PRESENT INDICATIVE	CF.§	1ST P. SING. CONDITIONAL
anta/a- verbs	kerto/a	tell	kerto/o	16.1	kerto/**isi**/n
	asu/a	live	asu/u	"	asu/**isi**/n
	pysy/ä	stay	pysy/y	"	pysy/**isi**/n
	luke/a	read	luke/e	16.5	luk/**isi**/n
-e and -i dropped	tunte/a	know, feel	tunte/e	"	tunt/**isi**/n
	oppi/a	learn	oppi/i	16.6	opp/**isi**/n
	salli/a	allow	salli/i	"	sall/**isi**/n
	näyttä/ä	show	näyttä/ä	16.7	näyttä/**isi**/n
	vetä/ä	pull	vetä/ä	"	vetä/**isi**/n
	jaka/a	divide	jaka/a	16.8	jaka/**isi**/n
	otta/a	take	otta/a	"	otta/**isi**/n
	rakasta/a	love	rakasta/a	"	rakasta/**isi**/n
huomat/a- verbs contraction	huomat/a	notice	huom**aa**	16.2	huoma/**isi**/n
	hypät/ä	jump	hyp**pää**	"	hyppä/**isi**/n
	pelät/ä	fear	pel**kää**	"	pelkä/**isi**/n
	tavat/a	meet	ta**paa**	"	tapa/**isi**/n
saa/da- verbs	saa/da	get	**saa**	16.2	sa/**isi**/n
	tuo/da	bring	**tuo**	16.3	to/**isi**/n
	vie/dä	take	**vie**	"	ve/**isi**/n
deletion	syö/dä	eat	**syö**	"	sö/**isi**/n
	voi/da	be able	**voi**	16.4	vo/**isi**/n
	pysäköi/dä	park	**pysäköi**	"	pysäkö/**isi**/n
nous/ta-, tul/la- verbs	nous/ta	rise	nouse/e	16.5	nous/**isi**/n
	tul/la	come	tule/e	"	tul/**isi**/n
	men/nä	go	mene/e	"	men/**isi**/n
	ajatel/la	think	ajattele/e	"	ajattel/**isi**/n
	hymyil/lä	smile	hymyile/e	"	hymyil/**isi**/n
-e dropped	tarvit/a	need	tarvitse/e	"	tarvits/**isi**/n
	vanhet/a	grow old	vanhene/e	"	vanhen/**isi**/n

Below are some examples of the use of the conditional.

Ol/**isi**/n iloinen, jos tul/**isi**/t.   I *would be* pleased if you *came.*
Jo/**isi**/n mielelläni kahvia.   I *would* love some coffee
    (''I *would drink* with pleasure'').
Jos vesi ol/**isi** lämmintä, sa/**isi**/t uida.   If the water *were* warm you *could*
    swim.
Väittä/**isi**/n, että...   I *would claim* that...
Muutta/**isi**/t/ko pois Suomesta?   *Would* you *move* away from Finland?
Tul/**isi**/vat/ko he jos pyytä/**isi**/mme?   *Would* they *come* if we *asked* (them)?
Kyllä Kantanen voitta/**isi** jos halua/**isi**.   Kantanen *would* certainly *win* if he
    wanted to.

The conditional is often used to show politeness.

politeness   Kaata/**isi**/t/ko lisää teetä?   *Would* you *pour* some more tea?
Kysy/**isi**/n, onko teillä...   *May* I *ask* whether you have...
Läht/**isi**/mme/kö jo kotiin?   *Shall* we *go* home now?
Ruoka ol/**isi** nyt valmista.   The meal *is* ready now (in the sense
    'dinner is served').

As was mentioned above (§61), the conditional also occurs in the perfect. These structures consist of the forms *ol/isi/n ~ ol/isi/t* etc. followed by the past participle of the main verb.

condi-   Ol/**isi**/n ol/**lut** iloinen, jos...   I *would have been* pleased if...
tional   Ol/**isi**/n mielelläni lähte/**nyt** Ruotsiin,   I *would have gone* to Sweden with
perfect   jos ol/**isi**/n voi/**nut**.   pleasure if I *had been able* to.
Ol/**isi**/t/ko tul/**lut** meille?   *Would* you *have come* to us?
Ol/**isi**/vat/ko he suostu/**neet** tähän?   *Would* they *have agreed* to this?
Ol/**isi**/n sairastu/**nut**, ellei Martti   I *would have fallen ill* if Martti *had*n't
ol/**isi** autta/**nut** minua.   *helped* me.

The negative forms of the conditional are constructed from the negation verb *en ~ et* etc. and the main verb with the ending -isi- but without a personal ending.

	AFFIRMATIVE		NEGATIVE
condi-	ol/isi/n	I would be	en ol/**isi**
tional	tul/isi/t	you would come	et tul/**isi**
negative	he anta/isi/vat	they would give	he **eivät** anta/**isi**
	kerto/isi/mme	we would tell	**emme** kerto/**isi**
	halua/isi/n	I would like	en halua/**isi**
	sata/isi	it would rain	ei sata/**isi**
	sö/isi/n	I would eat	en sö/**isi**
	luk/isi/mme	we would read	**emme** luk/**isi**
	he vetä/isi/vät	they would pull	he **eivät** vetä/**isi**
	ol/isi/n otta/nut	I would have taken	en ol/**isi** otta/**nut**
	ol/isi/tte syö/neet	you would have eaten	**ette** ol/**isi** syö/**neet**
	he ol/isi/vat lähte/neet	they would have left	he **eivät** ol/**isi** lähte/**neet**.

§66. IMPERATIVE

The imperative is primarily used for commands, requests and exhortations, and in the 3rd person also wishes. There is no imperative form for the 1st person singular.

		SINGULAR	PLURAL
endings	1ST P.	—	**-kaamme** ~ **-käämme**
	2ND P.	(no ending)	**-kaa** ~ **-kää**
	3RD P.	**-koon** ~ **-köön**	**-koot** ~ **-kööt**

The 2nd person singular and plural forms, e.g. *sano* and sano/**kaa**, are the most common. The 3rd person forms occur mostly in the literary language.

2nd p. sing. imperative

> THE 2ND PERSON SINGULAR OF THE IMPERATIVE HAS THE SAME FORM AS THE 1ST PERSON SINGULAR OF THE PRESENT INDICATIVE, WITHOUT THE FINAL -n

This form is also identical with that of the main verb in the present indicative negative (§63), cf. *sano*/n 'I say', *tule*/n 'I come', *pelkää*/n 'I fear' — en *sano* 'I do not say', en *tule* 'I do not come', en *pelkää* 'I do not fear' — *sano* 'say!', *tule* 'come!', *pelkää* 'fear'!'.

the other imperative forms

> THE OTHER IMPERATIVE FORMS ARE BASED ON THE INFINITIVE STEM (§22)

The imperative forms of the verbs *sano/a* 'say', *men/nä* 'go' and *kerto/a* 'tell' are thus as follows.

	SINGULAR		PLURAL	
1ST P.			sano/**kaamme**	let us say
			men/**käämme**	let us go
			kerto/**kaamme**	let us tell
2ND P.	*sano*	say!	sano/**kaa**	say!
	mene	go!	men/**kää**	go!
	kerro	tell!	kerto/**kaa**	tell!
3RD P.	sano/**koon**	may he say	sano/**koot**	may they say
	men/**köön**	may he go	men/**kööt**	may they go
	kerto/**koon**	may he tell	kerto/**koot**	may they tell

The table below shows the infinitive, the 1st person singular present, and the 2nd person singular and plural of the imperative.

	INFINITIVE		1ST P. SING. PRESENT	2ND P. SING. IMPERATIVE	2ND P. PL. IMPERATIVE
anta/a- verbs	anta/a	give	anna/n	*anna*	anta/**kaa**
	osta/a	buy	osta/n	*osta*	osta/**kaa**
	unohta/a	forget	unohda/n	*unohda*	unohta/**kaa**
	luke/a	read	lue/n	*lue*	luke/**kaa**
	vetä/ä	pull	vedä/n	*vedä*	vetä/**kää**
	sulke/a	close	sulje/n	*sulje*	sulke/**kaa**
	herättä/ä	wake	herätä/n	*herätä*	herättä/**kää**
huomat/a- verbs	avat/a	open	avaa/n	*avaa*	avat/**kaa**
	maat/a	lie	makaa/n	*makaa*	maat/**kaa**
	tavat/a	meet	tapaa/n	*tapaa*	tavat/**kaa**
	määrät/ä	order	määrää/n	*määrää*	määrät/**kää**
	hakat/a	hew	hakkaa/n	*hakkaa*	hakat/**kaa**
	tarjot/a	offer	tarjoa/n	*tarjoa*	tarjot/**kaa**
saa/da- verbs	myy/dä	sell	myy/n	*myy*	myy/**kää**
	syö/dä	eat	syö/n	*syö*	syö/**kää**
	ui/da	swim	ui/n	*ui*	ui/**kaa**
	teh/dä	do	tee/n	*tee*	teh/**kää**
	pysäköi/dä	park	pysäköi/n	*pysäköi*	pysäköi/**kää**
nous/ta-, **tul/la-** verbs	nous/ta	rise	nouse/n	*nouse*	nous/**kaa**
	tul/la	come	tule/n	*tule*	tul/**kaa**
	men/nä	go	mene/n	*mene*	men/**kää**
	juos/ta	run	juokse/n	*juokse*	juos/**kaa**
	ajatel/la	think	ajattele/n	*ajattele*	ajatel/**kaa**
	harkit/a	consider	harkitse/n	*harkitse*	harkit/**kaa**
	paet/a	flee	pakene/n	*pakene*	paet/**kaa**

object
of the
imperative

The object of an imperative verb is in the partitive if any of the normal partitive rules apply (§33.2). The accusative object of an imperative takes no ending if the imperative is 1st or 2nd person, but the ending -**n** if the imperative is 3rd person, cf. §38.

The examples below illustrate the use of the imperative.

Mene kotiin!	*Go* home! (sing.)
Men/**kää** kotiin!	*Go* home! (pl.)
Tule tänne!	*Come* here! (sing.)
Tul/**kaa** tänne!	*Come* here! (pl.)
Osta minulle *kuppi* kahvia!	*Buy* me *a cup* of coffee!
Anta/**kaa** meille vettä.	*Give* us some water!
Anna minulle *lusikka*!	*Give* me *a spoon*!
Ol/**kaa** hyvä!	Please. (lit.: ''*Be* good!'') (pl.)
Ole hyvä!	Please. (''*Be* good!'') (sing.)
Ole hyvä ja *avaa ovi*!	Please *open the door*. (''*Be* good and open...'')
Teh/**käämme** kuten hän sanoo.	*Let us do* as he says.
Varat/**kaa** meillekin *pöytä*!	*Reserve a table* for us, too!
Elä/**köön** Suomi!	*Long live* Finland! (''*May* Finland live'')
Onneksi ol/**koon**!	Congratulations! (''*May it be* to (your) happiness'')
Puhu/**kaamme** suomea.	*Let us speak* Finnish.
Juo/**kaamme** Kekkosen *malja*!	*Let us drink a toast* to Kekkonen!
Tul/**koot** he tänne.	*Let* them *come* here.

Men/**kööt** he sinne, me jäämme kotiin.		*Let* them *go* there, we are staying at home.		

Men/**kööt** he sinne, me jäämme
kotiin.
Ajattele asiaa!
Nous/**kaa** ylös!
Kukin teh/**köön** kuten haluaa.
Luke/**kaa** *läksy* kunnolla!

Lue läksy kunnolla!

Let them *go* there, we are staying at
home.
Think about the matter!
Get up!
Let everyone *do* as he likes.
Do ("read") *your homework*
properly! (pl.)
Do your homework properly! (sing.)

In the spoken language the passive is always instead of the 1st person plural imperative form, e.g. *sanotaan* 'one says' but often also 'let's say', *mennään* 'let's go', *tehdään* 'let's do' for *sanokaamme, menkäämme, tehkäämme*.

The negative forms of the imperative are constructed differently; here too the 2nd person singular is unlike the other forms.

imperative
negative

> THE 2ND PERSON SINGULAR IMPERATIVE NEGATIVE IS FORMED FROM THE WORD **älä**, PLACED BEFORE THE IMPERATIVE AFFIRMATIVE FORM

	AFFIRMATIVE		NEGATIVE	
2nd p.	osta	buy!	**älä** osta	don't buy!
sing.	lue	read!	**älä** lue	etc.
	vedä	pull!	**älä** vedä	
	avaa	open!	**älä** avaa	
	makaa	lie!	**älä** makaa	
	syö	eat!	**älä** syö	
	tule	come!	**älä** tule	

> THE OTHER IMPERATIVE NEGATIVE FORMS ARE BASED ON THE STEM **äl-** WITH THE APPROPRIATE IMPERATIVE ENDING, FOLLOWED BY THE INFINITIVE STEM OF THE MAIN VERB WITH THE ENDING -**ko** ~ -**kö**

The negation words are thus **älköön** (3rd person singular), **älkäämme** (1st person plural), **älkää** (2nd person plural) and **älkööt** (3rd person plural).

	INFINITIVE		IMPERATIVE NEGATIVE	
2nd person	sano/a	say	**älkää** sano/**ko**	don't say!
plural	otta/a	take	**älkää** otta/**ko**	etc.
	pelät/ä	fear	**älkää** pelät/**kö**	
	määrät/ä	order	**älkää** määrät/**kö**	
	maat/a	lie	**älkää** maat/**ko**	
	tuo/da	bring	**älkää** tuo/**ko**	
	tul/la	come	**älkää** tul/**ko**	
	men/nä	go	**älkää** men/**kö**	
	ajatel/la	think	**älkää** ajatel/**ko**	

Examples of the imperative negative follow below. The object is in the partitive, in accordance with the normal rules (§33.2).

Älä pelkää koiraa!	*Don't be afraid of* the dog! (sing.)
Älkää syö/kö niin nopeasti!	*Don't eat* so quickly! (pl.)
Älä polta täällä!	*Don't smoke* here! (sing.)
Älkää poltta/ko täällä!	*Don't smoke* here! (pl.)
Älkää lähte/kö kotiin vielä!	*Don't go* home yet! (pl.)
Älä lyö minua!	*Don't hit* me! (sing.)
Älkää lyö/kö minua!	*Don't hit* me! (pl.)
Älkäämme ajatel/ko sitä enää.	*Let us not think* about it any longer.
Älä tanssi Uolevin kanssa!	*Don't dance* with Uolevi! (sing.)
Älköön kukaan usko/ko, että...	*Let* no one *believe* that...
Älkää avat/ko tuota ikkunaa!	*Don't open* that window! (pl.)
Älä sylje lattialle!	*Don't spit* on the floor! (sing.)

§67. *POTENTIAL*

The potential, which has the ending -ne-, is a rare mood and thus of less importance. It indicates that the action of the verb is probable, possible or conceivable.[1]

THE ENDING OF THE POTENTIAL IS -ne-, WHICH IS ADDED TO THE INFINITIVE STEM (§22)

The potential is thus formed in the same way as the past participle, the ending of which is -nut ~ -nyt (§61). The sound alternations are also the same.

sound
alter-
nations

IF THE INFINITIVE STEM ENDS IN A CONSONANT
a) WHICH IS l, r, s, THE n OF THE -ne- ENDING CHANGES TO A
   SECOND l, r, s;
b) WHICH IS t, THIS t CHANGES TO n

After the ending -ne- the personal ending follows.

	INFINITIVE		3RD P. SING. POTENTIAL	CF. 3RD P. SING. PRESENT INDIC.
anta/a- verbs	anta/a	give	anta/ne/e	anta/a
	löytä/ä	find	löytä/ne/e	löytä/ä
	luke/a	read	luke/ne/e	luke/e
saa/da- verbs	saa/da	get	saa/ne/e	saa
	voi/da	be able	voi/ne/e	voi
	vartioi/da	guard	vartioi/ne/e	vartioi

---

[1] Translator's note: The potential is normally glossed 'may' in isolation (e.g. in appendix 2 below); but in context the degree of probability implied is often more accurately rendered by 'probably'.

nous/ta-,	nous/ta	rise	nous/se/e	nouse/e
tul/la-	tul/la	come	tul/le/e	tule/e
verbs	ajatel/la	think	ajatel/le/e	ajattele/e
huomat/a-	huomat/a	notice	huoman/ne/e	huomaa
verbs	kohdat/a	meet	kohdan/ne/e	kohtaa
etc.	leikat/a	cut	leikan/ne/e	leikkaa
	tarvit/a	need	tarvin/ne/e	tarvitse/e
	valit/a	choose	valin/ne/e	valitse/e
	häirit/ä	disturb	häirin/ne/e	häiritse/e

The potential forms of the verb *ol/la* 'be' are exceptional. They are based on the stem **liene-**, which is followed by the personal endings: **liene/n, liene/t, liene/e, liene/mme, liene/tte, liene/vät.**

The following examples illustrate the use of the potential.

Presidentti Husak saapu/**ne**/e huomenna.	President Husak *will probably arrive* tomorrow.
Eduskunta valin/**ne**/e Helteen puhemieheksi.	Parliament *will probably elect* Helle Speaker.
Kekkonen **liene**/e ulkomailla.	Kekkonen *may be / is probably* abroad.
Utsjoki sijain/**ne**/e pohjoisessa.	Utsjoki *is probably* ("situated") in the north.
He **liene**/vät samaa mieltä kanssamme.	They *are probably* of the same opinion as we are.
Hyväksy/**ne**/tte päätöksemme.	You *will probably accept* our decision.

The potential also occurs in the perfect, when the structure is **liene-** plus the past participle of the main verb (§61).

perfect	Kekkonen **liene**/e käy/**nyt** Brasiliassa.	Kekkonen *has probably been* to Brazil.
	Hän **liene**/e ol/**lut** myös Marokossa.	He *has probably* also *been* to Marocco.
	Liene/mme näh/**neet** tämän elokuvan aikaisemmin.	We *may have seen / have probably seen* this film before.

The negative forms of the potential are constructed in the normal way. In the present the negation verb **en, et** etc. is followed by the potential form without a personal ending, e.g. *en osta/ne* 'I shall probably not buy'. The negative of the potential perfect follows the same pattern: negation verb + *liene* (without) personal ending) + past participle, e.g. *en liene osta/nut* 'I have probably not bought'.

perfect negative	Virtanen **ei** syö/**ne** tällaista ruokaa.	Virtanen *probably does not eat* this kind of food.
	Emme uskalta/**ne** tehdä näin.	We *probably do not dare* to do (it like) this.
	Utsjoki **ei** sijain/**ne** Pohjanmaalla.	Utsjoki *is probably not* in Ostrobothnia.
	He **eivät liene** soitta/**neet** vielä.	They *probably have not rung* yet.

16 The Passive

§68. GENERAL

meaning   The Finnish passive is a very common and important verb-form. It indicates that the action of the verb is performed by an unspecified person, i.e. that the agent is **impersonal**. It thus roughly corresponds to Swedish and German *man*, French *on* and English *one*.

endings   The passive has two endings: the passive marker itself, which is **-tta-** ∼ **-ttä-** or **-ta-** ∼ **-tä-**, and a special personal ending **-Vn**, e.g. sano/**ta**/**an** 'one says, it is said'.

Passive sentences should be distinguished from generic sentences expressing a general truth or law or state of affairs. The predicate verb of generic sentences appears in the 3rd person singular and there is no separate subject:

generic sentences	
Usein *kuule/e*, että...	*One* often *hears* that...
Siellä *saa* hyvää kahvia.	*One gets* good coffee there.
Tästä *näke/e* hyvin.	*You / One can see* well from here.
Jos *juokse/e* joka aamu, *tule/e* terveeksi.	If *you run* every morning *you will become* healthy.

The passive occurs in all tenses (present, past, perfect and pluperfect) and also all moods (indicative, conditional, imperative and potential). The basic pattern of the passive forms is illustrated in the table below.

	ROOT	+ PASSIVE	+ TENSE, MOOD	+ PERSON	+ PARTICLE		
	sano	ta		an		one says	(pass. pres.)
structure	sano	tt	i	in		one said	(pass. past)
	sano	tta	isi	in		one would say	(pass. cond.)
	sano	tta	ne	en		one may say	(pass. pot.)
	sano	tta	ko	on		let one say	(pass. imp.)
	sano	ta		an	han	one does say	(pass. pres.)
	sano	tt	i	in	ko	did one say?	(pass. past)

146

In this chapter, however, the formation of the passive will not be described as the addition of these endings: we do not need to say e.g. that the passive present is formed by adding the endings -ta- and -Vn: sano/**ta**/**an** 'one says'. Instead, we shall make use of a number of "short cuts" which are available because the passive happens to resemble several forms we have already discussed, in particular the infinitive. In this way many of the complex sound alternations in the passive can be derived automatically.

§69. *PASSIVE PRESENT*

With the exception of **anta/a**-verbs, the passive present can be formed according to the following simple rule:

> THE PASSIVE PRESENT IS FORMED BY ADDING THE ENDING -**Vn** TO THE (1ST) INFINITIVE (does not apply to **anta/a**-verbs)

This rule thus covers **huomat/a-**, **saa/da-**, **nous/ta-**, **tul/la-** and **lämmet/ä-** verbs. The oblique lines in the examples below indicate the positions of the passive endings proper.

	INFINITIVE	PASSIVE PRESENT	
huomat/a	huomat/a	huomat/a/an	one notices
	osat/a	osat/a/an	one knows how
	hypät/ä	hypät/ä/än	one jumps
	määrät/ä	määrät/ä/än	one orders
	pelät/ä	pelät/ä/än	one fears
saa/da	saa/da	saa/da/an	one gets
	myy/dä	myy/dä/än	one sells
	voi/da	voi/da/an	one can
	teh/dä	teh/dä/än	one does
nous/ta,	nous/ta	nous/ta/an	one rises
tul/la	men/nä	men/nä/än	one goes
	tul/la	tul/la/an	one comes
	ajatel/la	ajatel/la/an	one thinks
	julkais/ta	julkais/ta/an	one publishes
tarvit/a,	tarvit/a	tarvit/a/an	one needs
lämmet/ä	valit/a	valit/a/an	one chooses
	paet/a	paet/a/an	one flees

The passive present of **anta/a**-verbs is formed by adding the passive endings -**ta**/**an** ~ -**tä**/**än** to the 1st person singular stem of the active, e.g. **sano**/**n** : **sano**/**ta**/**an** 'one says'; immediately before the passive endings the usual consonant gradation rules apply (cf. §15.2, rule B:a). If the final vowel of the stem is -**a** or -**ä**, this changes to -**e**.

anta/a-
verbs

THE PASSIVE PRESENT OF anta/a-VERBS IS FORMED
a) BY ADDING -ta/an ~ -tä/än TO THE 1ST PERSON SINGULAR STEM AND
b) CHANGING THE FINAL -a OR -ä OF THE STEM TO -e

INFINITIVE	1ST P. PRESENT	PASSIVE PRESENT	
sano/a	sano/n	sano/ta/an	one says
osta/a	osta/n	oste/ta/an	one buys
etsi/ä	etsi/n	etsi/tä/än	one looks for
kysy/ä	kysy/n	kysy/tä/än	one asks
nukku/a	nuku/n	nuku/ta/an	one sleeps
anta/a	anna/n	anne/ta/an	one gives
sulke/a	sulje/n	sulje/ta/an	one closes
lentä/ä	lennä/n	lenne/tä/än	one flies
unohta/a	unohda/n	unohde/ta/an	one forgets
otta/a	ota/n	ote/ta/an	one takes
luke/a	lue/n	lue/ta/an	one reads
pyytä/ä	pyydä/n	pyyde/tä/än	one requests

The negative forms of the passive present consist of the negation verb **ei** followed by the passive form without the personal ending -Vn.

negative
forms

AFFIRMATIVE	NEGATIVE	
huomat/a/an	ei huomat/a	one does not notice
osat/a/an	ei osat/a	one does not know how
saa/da/an	ei saa/da	one does not get
teh/dä/än	ei teh/dä	one does not do
men/nä/än	ei men/nä	one does not go
nous/ta/an	ei nous/ta	one does not get up
tarvit/a/an	ei tarvit/a	one does not need
sano/ta/an	ei sano/ta	one does not say
anne/ta/an	ei anne/ta	one does not give
pyyde/tä/än	ei pyyde/tä	one does not request
ote/ta/an	ei ote/ta	one does not take

The sentences below illustrate the use of the passive present.

Suomessa juo/da/an sekä maitoa että olutta.	In Finland *people drink* both milk and beer.
Ravintolassa tanssi/ta/an kello yhteentoista.	In the restaurant *there is dancing* ("*one dances*") until 11 o'clock.
Tanskassa puhu/ta/an tanskaa.	In Denmark *they speak* Danish.
Ei/kö täällä puhu/ta ruotsia?	*Isn't* Swedish *spoken* here?
Nyt näh/dä/än, että...	Now *one sees* that...
Mitä täällä teh/dä/än?	What *is being done* here?
Täällä ei tarjot/a olutta.	Beer *is not served* here.
Pelät/ä/än, että Suomi häviää.	*It is feared* that Finland will lose.
Väite/tä/än, että hän on sairas.	*It is claimed* / *They claim* that he / she is ill.

The singular accusative object of a passive verb has no ending (§38).

<table>
<tr><td>NOTE
accusative
object!</td><td>Huomiseksi lue/ta/an *seuraava*
kappale.
Kirja pan/na/an pöydälle.
Ovi sulje/ta/an avaimella.
Auto voi/da/an ajaa pihalle.</td><td>*The next chapter* will be read for
tomorrow.
The book is put on the table.
The door is closed with a key.
The car can be driven into the yard.</td></tr>
</table>

In the spoken language it is very common for the passive forms to be used in place of the 1st person plural indicative and imperative.

<table>
<tr><td>Note
spoken
forms!</td><td>WRITTEN LANGUAGE</td><td></td><td>SPOKEN LANGUAGE (often)</td></tr>
<tr><td></td><td>(me) juo/mme
(me) kerro/mme
(me) halua/mme
(me) ajattele/mme</td><td>we drink
we tell
we want
we think</td><td>(me) juo/daan
(me) kerro/taan
(me) halut/aan
(me ajatel/laan</td></tr>
<tr><td></td><td>juo/kaamme!
kerto/kaamme!
ajatel/kaamme!
lähte/käämme</td><td>let us drink!
let us tell!
let us think!
let us leave!</td><td>juo/daan!
kerro/taan!
ajatel/laan!
lähde/tään!</td></tr>
</table>

§70. *PASSIVE PAST*

The past tense of the passive is formed from one of the endings -**tta**- ∼ -**ttä**- or -**ta**- ∼ -**tä**-, with the final vowel then being dropped before the past tense -**i**- (§16). After the passive ending come the past tense -**i**- and the personal ending -**Vn**. To make the description simpler these combinations of endings will henceforth be given as -**ttiin** and -**tiin**. The passive past can be derived from the passive present by the following rule:

formation

> a) -**ttiin** IS USED IN PLACE OF THE PASSIVE PRESENT -**taan** ∼ -**tään**;
>
> b) -**tiin** IS USED IN PLACE OF OTHER PASSIVE PRESENT ENDINGS

Examples:

<table>
<tr><td></td><td>INFINITIVE</td><td>1ST. P.
PRESENT</td><td>PASSIVE
PRESENT</td><td>PASSIVE
PAST</td><td>MEANING</td></tr>
<tr><td>a)
anta/a</td><td>sano/a
osta/a
vaati/a
anta/a
pyytä/ä
rakasta/a</td><td>sano/n
osta/n
vaadi/n
anna/n
pyydä/n
rakasta/**n**</td><td>sano/taan
oste/taan
vaadi/taan
anne/taan
pyyde/tään
rakaste/taan</td><td>sano/**ttiin**
oste/**ttiin**
vaadi/**ttiin**
anne/**ttiin**
pyyde/**ttiin**
rakaste/**ttiin**</td><td>one said
one bought
one demanded
one gave
one requested
one loved</td></tr>
<tr><td>b)
huomat/a</td><td>huomat/a
osat/a
palat/a
pelät/ä</td><td>huomaa/n
osaa/n
palaa/n
pelkää/n</td><td>huomat/aan
osat/aan
palat/aan
pelät/ään</td><td>huomat/**tiin**
osat/**tiin**
palat/**tiin**
pelät/**tiin**</td><td>one noticed
one knew how
one returned
one feared</td></tr>
</table>

saa/da	saa/da	saa/n	saa/daan	saa/**tiin**	one got
	vie/dä	vie/n	vie/dään	vie/**tiin**	one took
	syö/dä	syö/n	syö/dään	syö/**tiin**	one ate
	tuo/da	tuo/n	tuo/daan	tuo/**tiin**	one brought
nous/ta,	nous/ta	nouse/n	nous/taan	nous/**tiin**	one rose
tul/la	tul/la	tule/n	tul/laan	tul/**tiin**	one came
	men/nä	mene/n	men/nään	men/**tiin**	one went
	ajatel/la	ajattele/n	ajatel/laan	ajatel/**tiin**	one thought
	ol/la	ole/n	ol/laan	ol/**tiin**	one was
tarvit/a,	tarvit/a	tarvitse/n	tarvit/aan	tarvit/**tiin**	one needed
lämmet/ä	paet/a	pakene/n	paet/aan	paet/**tiin**	one fled
	ansait/a	ansaitse/n	ansait/aan	ansait/**tiin**	one earned
	harkit/a	harkitse/n	harkit/aan	harkit/**tiin**	one considered

The negative forms of the passive past have the following structure: **ei** + past participle passive (§71). The examples below illustrate the use of the passive past in the affirmative.

Viime vuonna Suomeen tuo/**tiin** enemmän kuin Suomesta vie/**tiin**.	Last year more *was imported* to Finland than *was exported* from Finland.
Ol/**tiin** sitä mieltä, että...	*One was* of the opinion that...
Pian havait/**tiin**, että Eero oli lähtenyt.	*One / We* soon *noticed* that Eero had left. (Or: *It was* soon *noticed*..)
Meille anne/**ttiin** monta hyvää neuvoa.	We *were given* much good advice.
Tul/**tiin** Helsinkiin aamulla.	*We came* to Helsinki in the morning.
Maahan valit/**tiin** uusi presidentti.	The country *elected* a new president ("a new president *was elected* to the country").
Tukholmasta lenne/**ttiin** Osloon.	From Stockholm *we flew* to Oslo.
Nuku/**ttiin** eri huoneissa.	*One / We slept* in different rooms.

It will be evident from these examples that the passive often has the meaning 'we', especially in the spoken language.

§71. PASSIVE PERFECT AND PLUPERFECT

The passive perfect and pluperfect have the structure **on** (perfect) or **oli** (pluperfect) + past participle passive (for the past participle active see §61). The past participle passive can be formed most conveniently from the past tense by the following rule:

formation

> **THE PAST PARTICIPLE PASSIVE IS FORMED BY CHANGING THE PASSIVE PAST -iin TO -u OR -y**

INFINITIVE	1ST P. SING.	PASSIVE PAST	PASSIVE PAST PARTICIPLE	MEANING
osta/a	osta/n	oste/ttiin	oste/**ttu**	bought
anta/a	anna/n	anne/ttiin	anne/**ttu**	given
nukku/a	nuku/n	nuku/ttiin	nuku/**ttu**	slept
pyytä/ä	pyydä/n	pyyde/ttiin	pyyde/**tty**	requested
huomat/a	huomaa/n	huomat/tiin	huomat/**tu**	noticed
määrät/ä	määrää/n	määrät/tiin	määrät/**ty**	ordered
pelät/ä	pelkää/n	pelät/tiin	pelät/**ty**	feared
saa/da	saa/n	saa/tiin	saa/**tu**	got
syö/dä	syö/n	syö/tiin	syö/**ty**	eaten
myy/dä	myy/n	myy/tiin	myy/**ty**	sold
nous/ta	nouse/n	nous/tiin	nous/**tu**	risen
ol/la	ole/n	ol/tiin	ol/**tu**	been
men/nä	mene/n	men/tiin	men/**ty**	gone
tarvit/a	tarvitse/n	tarvit/tiin	tarvit/**tu**	needed

The use of these forms is illustrated below.

On sano/**ttu**, että Suomi on tuhansien järvien maa.
It has been said that Finland is the land of a thousand lakes.

Ol/i sano/**ttu**, että...
It had been said that...

On väite/**tty**, ettei hän eroa koskaan.
It has been stated that he will never resign.

Tähän **on** tul/**tu**.
One has come to this.

Ol/i anne/**ttu** sellainen neuvo, että...
There had been given such advice that...

Kouluissa **on** lue/**ttu** saksaa jo pitkään.
German *has* long *been studied* in the schools.

Ol/i huomat/**tu**, että laiva uppoaa.
It had been noticed that the ship was sinking.

Ol/i jo syö/**ty**, kun vieraat tulivat.
One / We had already *eaten* when the guests came.

On esite/**tty** kolme ehdotusta.
Three suggestions *have been put forward*.

Tätä **on** pelät/**ty** monta vuotta.
This *has been feared* for many years.

On ol/**tu** myös sitä mieltä, että...
People *have* also *been* of the opinion that...

On/ko nyt men/**ty** liian pitkälle?
Has one / Have we now *gone* too far?

Auto **ol/i** oste/**ttu** jo eilen.
The car *had* already been *bought* yesterday.

Autot **ol/i** oste/**ttu**..
The cars *had been bought*...

151

The form of the passive perfect negative is **ei ole** + the past participle passive of the main verb; the corresponding pluperfect is **ei ol/lut** + the same participle (cf. §63).

	AFFIRMATIVE	NEGATIVE	MEANING
perfect	on saa/tu	**ei ole** saa/**tu**	one has not got
and	ol/i saa/tu	**ei ol/lut** saa/tu	one had not got
pluperfect	on sano/ttu	ei ole sano/ttu	one has not said
negative	ol/i sano/ttu	ei ol/lut sano/ttu	one had not said
	on määrät/ty	ei ole määrät/ty	one has not ordered
	ol/i määrät/ty	ei ol/lut määrät/ty	one had not ordered
	on ol/tu	ei ole ol/tu	one has not been
	ol/i ol/tu	ei ol/lut ol/tu	one had not been

Special attention should be given to the past tense passive negative, which consists of the negation verb **ei** followed by the past participle passive (cf. § 70).

	AFFIRMATIVE	NEGATIVE	MEANING
NB:	sano/ttiin	**ei** sano/**ttu**	one did not say
past	oste/ttiin	ei oste/ttu	one did not buy
negative	kysy/ttiin	ei kysy/tty	one did not ask
	huomat/tiin	ei huomat/tu	one did not notice
	osat/tiin	ei osat/tu	one did not know how
	pelät/tiin	ei pelät/ty	one did not fear
	saa/tiin	ei saa/tu	one did not get
	syö/tiin	ei syö/ty	one did not eat
	tul/tiin	ei tul/tu	one did not come
	ol/tiin	ei ol/tu	one was not
	men/tiin	ei men/ty	one did not go
	tarvit/tiin	ei tarvit/tu	one did not need

The use of the passive negative is further illustrated below.

NB:
partitive
object

Tätä **ei ole** tarvit/**tu** ennenkään.	This *has not been needed* before, either.
Ei/kö **ole** oste/**ttu** ruokaa?	*Has* no food *been bought*?
Keneltäkään **ei** kysy/**tty** neuvoa.	No one *was asked* for advice.
50 vuotta sitten Suomen kouluissa **ei** opiskel/**tu** englantia.	50 years ago English was not studied in Finnish schools.
Virtasta **ei** valit/**tu** puheenjohtajaksi.	Virtanen *was not elected* chairman.
Häntä **ei ol/lut** näh/**ty** kaupungilla.	He /she *had not been seen* in town.
Lakon aikana **ei** saa/**tu** sähköä.	During the strike *we didn't get* any electricity.
Läksyä **ei** osat/**tu** hyvin.	The homework *was not known* well.
Paitaanne **ei** vielä **ole** pes/**ty**.	Your shirt *has not* yet *been washed*.
Seurauksia **ei ol/lut** ote/**ttu** huomioon.	The consequences *had not been taken* into consideration.
Ehdotusta **ei** ymmärre/**tty**.	The proposal *was not understood*.
Sotaa ei koskaan unohde/**ttu**.	The war *was never forgotten*.

152

§72. *PASSIVE MOODS*

There is no mood ending for the indicative: for these forms see §69, e.g. *sano/ta/an* 'one says', *kerro/ta/an* 'one tells', *tul/la/an* 'one comes'. The other moods, i.e. the conditional (-isi-), the imperative (-ko- ∼ -kö-) and the potential (-ne-), are all formed from the passive past tense (cf. §70) as follows:

formation

> CHANGE THE PASSIVE PAST TENSE -iin TO -a OR -ä AND ADD THE REQUIRED MOOD ENDING AND THE PERSONAL ENDING -Vn

From the passive past *sano/tt/i/in* 'one said' we can thus derive the conditional *sano/tta/isi/in* 'one would say', the imperative *sano/tta/ko/on* 'let one say' and the potential *sano/tta/ne/en* 'one may say'.

INFINITIVE	PASSIVE PAST	PASSIVE CONDITIONAL	PASSIVE POTENTIAL	PASSIVE IMPERATIVE	MEANING
katso/a	katso/ttiin	katso/ttaisiin	katso/ttaneen	katso/ttakoon	look
tunte/a	tunne/ttiin	tunne/ttaisiin	tunne/ttaneen	tunne/ttakoon	feel
odotta/a	odote/ttiin	odote/ttaisiin	odote/ttaneen	odote/ttakoon	wait
avat/a	avat/tiin	avat/taisiin	avat/taneen	avat/takoon	open
lisät/ä	lisät/tiin	lisät/täisiin	lisät/täneen	lisät/täköön	add
juo/da	juo/tiin	juo/taisiin	juo/taneen	juo/takoon	drink
saa/da	saa/tiin	saa/taisiin	saa/taneen	saa/takoon	get
ol/la	ol/tiin	ol/taisiin	ol/taneen	ol/takoon	be
men/nä	men/tiin	men/täisiin	men/täneen	men/täköön	go
hävit/ä	hävit/tin	hävit/täisiin	hävit/täneen	hävit/täköön	disappear

The corresponding negative forms are as follows: in the conditional and potential the negation verb **ei** is followed by the appropriate passive form without the personal ending -Vn; in the imperative, **älköön** is followed by the passive form without the personal ending (cf. §66).

negative forms

AFFIRMATIVE	NEGATIVE	
juo/ta/isi/in	ei juo/ta/isi	one would not drink
ol/ta/isi/in	ei ol/ta/isi	one would not be
men/tä/neen	ei men/tä/ne	one may not / probably will not go
sano/tta/koon	älköön sano/tta/ko	let one not say
teh/tä/isi/in	ei teh/tä/isi	one would not do
rakene/tta/isi/in	ei rakenne/tta/isi	one would not build
todet/ta/ne/en	ei todet/ta/ne	one may not / probably will not verify

Examples:

Tätä **ei** sano/**tta**/**isi**, jos ei olisi aihetta.
This *would not be said* if there were no cause.
Voi/**ta**/**isi**/**in**/ko tehdä näin?
Could one do it this way?
Ei voi/**ta**/**isi**.
One could not.
Pääte/**ttä**/**ne**/**en**, että...
It may be decided that...

Mitä sano/**tta**/**isi**/**in**, jos...
Ei kai sano/**tta**/**isi** mitään.
Lakko lopete/**tta**/**isi**/**in**, jos
pääs/**tä**/**isi**/**in** sopimukseen.
Ovea **älköön** avat/**ta**/**ko** liian
nopeasti.
Tätä päätöstä **ei** siis teh/**tä**/**ne**.

What *would people say* if...
I suppose nothing *would be said*.
The strike *would be ended* if an
agreement *could be reached*.
Let the door *not be opened* too
quickly.
This decision *will* thus *probably
not be made*.

17   Infinitives

General
1st infinitive
2nd infinitive
3rd infinitive
4th infinitive

§73. *GENERAL*

Infinitives and participles constitute the set of non-finite verb-forms, which all lack personal endings. The basic structure of the infinitives has been presented above (§14). Each of the infinitives has its own marker, a functional ending without any actual meaning. Some infinitives occur also in the passive (particularly the 2nd infinitive), and some may take several case-endings (particularly the 3rd infinitive). Under certain conditions the 1st and 2nd infinitives may also be followed by possessive suffixes. All the infinitives can take enclitic particles. Infinitives are never marked for number.

    The infinitives function in a sentence as nouns, being nominal forms of verbs; the participles function as adjectives. The examples below illustrate the similarities between infinitives and nouns proper.

similarities
between
infinitives
and nouns

Haluan *omena/n*.	I want *an apple*. (noun)
Haluan ui/**da**.	I want *to swim*. (1st inf.)
Haluan osta/**a** omenan.	I want *to buy* an apple. (1st inf.)
Nälkä katoaa *minuuti/ssa*.	Hunger disappears *in a minute*. (noun in inessive)
Nälkä katoaa syö/**de**/ssä.	Hunger disapperas *as one eats* ("in eating"). (2nd inf. in inessive)
Menen *Helsinki/in*.	I'm going *to Helsinki*. (noun in illative)
Menen ulos juokse/**ma**/an.	I'm going out *to run*. (3rd inf. in illative)
Satamaan pääsee myös *linja-auto/lla*.	One can also get to the harbour *by bus*. (noun in adessive)
Oppii myös luke/**ma**/lla.	One also learns *by reading*. (3rd inf. in adessive)

§74. *1ST INFINITIVE*

§74.1. *Basic form of the 1st infinitive*

The 1st infinitive appears in two cases: the basic form, with only the infinitive ending (e.g. sano/**a** '(to) say', saa/**da** '(to) get'); and the translative case, where the infinitive ending is followed by the ending -**kse**- (cf. §50) and a possessive suffix.

The 1st infinitive endings have been given above (§22). This infinitive is the dictionary form of verbs, e.g. in the *Nykysuomen sanakirja* ('Dictionary of Modern Standard Finnish') and many Finnish language textbooks. There are four different endings: 1) -**a** ∼ -**ä**, 2) -**da** ∼ -**dä**, 3) -**ta** ∼ -**tä**, 4) -**la** ∼ -**lä**, -**ra** ∼ -**rä**, -**na** ∼ -**nä**. The forms and their use are illustrated below.

four
endings

1)	osta/**a**	buy	2)	tuo/**da**	bring
	vetä/**ä**	pull		jää/**dä**	stay
	varat/**a**	reserve		saa/**da**	get
	levät/**ä**	rest		kanavoi/**da**	canalize

3)	juos/**ta**	run	4)	ol/**la**	be
	nous/**ta**	rise		kysel/**lä**	ask
	valais/**ta**	light		pur/**ra**	bite
	väris/**tä**	shiver		men/**nä**	go

Aion lähte/**ä** ulos.	I intend *to go* out.
Yritämme ymmärtä/**ä**.	We try *to understand*.
Mitä haluat syö/**dä**?	What do you want *to eat*?
Saat lainat/**a** tämän kirjan.	You may *borrow* this book.
Teillä on oikeus otta/**a** yksi kuva.	You have the right *to take* one picture.
On aika vaikea oppi/**a** suomea.	It is quite difficult *to learn* Finnish.
Onko sinulla jo ollut mahdollisuus tilat/**a**?	Have you already had an opportunity *to order*?
Teidän täytyy tul/**la** meille!	You must *come* to us / our place.
Täytyy aja/**a** varovasti.	One must *drive* carefully.
Anna hänen men/**nä**!	Let him / her *go*!
Antakaa Kallen men/**nä**!	Let Kalle *go*!
Koneessa täytyy ol/**la** vika.	There must *be* some fault in the machine.
Vian täytyy ol/**la** koneessa.	The fault must *be* in the machine.
Minulla on ajatus lähte/**ä** Unkariin ensi kesänä.	I am thinking of *going* ("I have the thought *to go*") to Hungary next summer.
Pakolaisten sallittiin poistu/**a** maasta.	The refugees were allowed *to leave* the country.

NB:
täytyy,
antaa, etc.

Particular attention should be paid to the special verbs of obligation (*täytyy* 'must', *pitää* 'have to') and permission (*antaa x:n tehdä jotakin* 'let x do something'; *sallia* 'allow'), which often co-occur with the genitive (Antakaa Kalle/**n** mennä; Via/**n** täytyy olla koneessa (see the examples above)) and are followed by the 1st infinitive (Antakaa Kallen men/**nä**; Vian täytyy ol/**la** koneessa).

§74.2. *1st infinitive translative*

**-kse- +
possessive
suffix**

The basic form of the 1st infinitive may be followed by the translative ending -kse- and a possessive suffix corresponding to the person of the subject. This structure usually expresses the idea of aim or purpose.

ROOT	1ST INF.	TRANSL. CASE	POSS. SUFF.	ENCLITIC PARTICLE	
sano	a	kse	ni		in order that I shall say
elä	ä	kse	mme		in order that we shall live
oppi	a	kse	en	han	in order to learn + emph. (3rd p.)
tavat	a	kse	si		in order that you shall meet
juo	da	kse	en		in order to drink (3rd p.)
ol	la	kse	nne		in order that you shall be

Examples:

Lähdin Hollantiin levät/**ä**/**kse**/**ni**.	I went to Holland *in order to rest*.
Ihminen syö elä/**ä**/**kse**/**en**.	Man eats *in order to live*.
Elätkö syö/**dä**/**kse**/**si**?	Do you live *in order to eat*?
Pyörähdin men/**nä**/**kse**/**ni**.	I turned round *in order to go*.
Monet suomalaiset menevät Ruotsiin saa/**da**/**kse**/**en** työtä.	Many Finns go to Sweden *in order to find* ("get") work.
Otatko työn teh/**dä**/**kse**/**si**?	Do you undertake *to do* the job?
Muista/**a**/**kse**/**ni** asia on näin.	*As far as I remember* it's like this.
Tietä/**ä**/**kse**/**mme** hän ei ole täällä.	*As far as we know* he/she is not here.
Osku on hyvin voimakas ol/**la**/**kse**/**en** niin pieni.	Osku is very strong for such a small man ("*to be* so small").

§75. *2ND INFINITIVE*

§75.1. *2nd infinitive inessive*

**-ssa ~
-ssä
expressing
time**

The 2nd infinitive has two cases: the inessive -ssa ~ -ssä expressing time, and the instructive -n expressing manner. The instructive form is rarer.

A possessive suffix is often used with the inessive to mark the subject, e.g. sano/e/ssa/**ni** 'when I say'. The inessive form also occurs in the passive, e.g. sano/**tta**/e/ssa 'when one says'. Generally speaking, the 2nd infinitive inessive can be said to correspond to a temporal subordinate clause beginning with **kun** 'when, as'.

The simplest way to form the stem of the 2nd infinitive is given by the following rule (see §14 for some of the different endings).

> **THE 2ND INFINITIVE IS FORMED BY CHANGING THE -a ~ -ä OF THE FIRST INFINITIVE TO -e**

1ST INFINITIVE		2ND INFINITIVE STEM
sano/**a**	say	sano/**e**-
vetä/**ä**	pull	vetä/**e**-
herät/**ä**	wake	herät/**e**-
tilat/**a**	order	tilat/**e**-
saa/**da**	get	saa/**de**-
myy/**dä**	sell	myy/**de**-
ol/**la**	be	ol/**le**-
men/**nä**	go	men/**ne**-
havait/**a**	observe	havait/**e**-

NB: -e → -i If the 1st infinitive stem ends in -e, this changes to -i in the 2nd infinitive.

1ST INFINITIVE		2ND INFINITIVE STEM
luke/**a**	read	luk**i**/e-
itke/**ä**	cry	itk**i**/e-
tunte/**a**	feel	tunt**i**/e-
koke/**a**	experience	kok**i**/e-

The passive forms of the 2nd infinitive can be derived most easily by adding -e- to the passive stem, which is arrived at according to the first rule given in §72 (change the passive past tense -iin to -a ~ -ä; the passive stem *sano/tta-* is thus derived from the form *sano/ttiin*). The forms of the 2nd infinitive are shown in the following table.

	ROOT	PASS.	INF.	CASE	POSS. SUFF.	PART-ICLE	MEANING
	sano		e	ssa	ni		when I say
	sano		e	ssa	nne		when you say
	sano		e	n			saying
	sano	tta	e	ssa			when one says
	sano	tta	e	ssa		han	when one says + emph.
	sano		e	ssa	mme	kin	when we say too
	ol		le	ssa	ni		when I am
	ol	ta	e	essa			when one is
	juo		de	ssa	an		when he/she drinks
	juo	ta	e	ssa			when one drinks
Pekan	herät		e	ssä			when Pekka wakes
	herät	tä	e	ssä			when one wakes
	luki		e	ssa	nne		when you read
Kallen	tunti		e	ssa			when Kalle feels

The 2nd infinitive inessive thus corresponds to a temporal subordinate clause, particularly one in which the action referred to is simultaneous with the action of the verb in the main clause, e.g. *Sano/e/ssa/ni tämän kaikki nousivat* 'As I was saying / When I said this everyone stood up'.

The subject of the temporal clause appears in the inessive construction as follows:

THE SUBJECT IS EXPRESSED
a) BY A POSSESSIVE SUFFIX ALONE, IF THE SUBJECT IS IDENTICAL WITH THAT OF THE MAIN CLAUSE;
b) BY AN INDEPENDENT WORD IN THE GENITIVE, IF THE SUBJECT IS DIFFERENT FROM THAT OF THE MAIN CLAUSE.
c) BY THE GENITIVE FORM OF PERSONAL PRONOUNS (**minun** etc.), ALWAYS FOLLOWED BY A POSSESSIVE SUFFIX ON THE INFINITIVE INESSIVE (unstressed 1st and 2nd personal pronouns may be omitted)

	kun-CLAUSE	2ND INFINITIVE INESSIVE
a) same subject	Kun *oli*/**n** Ruotsissa, tapasi/**n** useita ystäviä. When *I* was in Sweden *I* met many friends.	Ol/**le**/**ssa**/**ni** Ruotsissa tapasin useita ystäviä.
	Kun *Pekka* heräsi, *hän* oli sairas. When *Pekka* woke up *he* was ill.	Herät/**e**/**ssä**/**ään** Pekka oli sairas.
	Kun aja/**t**, *sinun* pitää olla varovainen. When *you* drive *you* must be careful.	Aja/**e**/**ssa**/**si** sinun pitää olla varovainen.
	Kalevi ajattelee paremmin, kun *hän* juo kahvia. *Kalevi* thinks better when *he* drinks coffee.	Kalevi ajattelee paremmin juo/**de**/**sa**/**an** kahvia.
	Ihmiset nauttivat, kun *he* lähtevät lomalle. *People* enjoy themselves when *they* go on holiday.	Ihmiset nauttivat lähti/**e**/**ssä**/**ään** lomalle.
b) different subject	Kun *Pekka* herää, *Liisa* lähtee töihin. When *Pekka* wakes, *Liisa* goes to work.	Peka/**n** herät/**e**/**ssä** Liisa lähtee töihin.
	Viren tuli maaliin, kun *Päivärinta* oli vielä loppusuoralla. *Viren* arrived at the finish when *Päivärinta* was still on the final straight.	Viren tuli maaliin Päivärinna/**n** ol/**le**/**ssa** vielä loppusuoralla.
c) different subject (personal pronoun)	*Muut* nukkuivat, kun *hän* heräsi. *The others* were sleeping when *he/she* woke.	Muut nukkuivat häne/**n** herät/**e**/**ssä**/**än**.
	Vaimoni heräsi, kun *(minä)* tuli/**n** kotiin. *My wife* woke up when *I* came home.	Vaimoni heräsi *(minun)* tul/**le**/**ssa**/**ni** kotiin.

The following examples show the use of the passive form of the inessive structure.

Helsinkiin tul/**ta**/e/ssa satoi.	When *one (we)* came to Helsinki it was raining.
Musiikkia kuunnel/**ta**/e/ssa pitää olla hiljaa.	When listening to music one must be quiet.
Ikkunan pitää olla auki nuku/**tta**/e/ssa.	The window must be open when *one* sleeps.

Tästä setelistä Suomen Pankki maksaa vaadi/**tta**/e/ssa sata mk.	For this note the Bank of Finland will pay 100 marks on demand (''when *one* demands'').

no simul- taneous actions As has been said, this inessive structure is used to refer to an action simultaneous with that of the main clause. If the action of the **kun**-clause has taken place before the action of the main clause a different structure is used: the partitive form of the past participle (§83):

Peka/**n** herät/**ty**/ä Tuula lähti töihin.	*When Pekka had woken up* Tuula went off to work.
Jäät lähtivät kevää/**n** tul/**tu**/**a**.	The ice melted (''left'') *when spring came.*

§75.2. *2nd infinitive instructive*

This form is derived by adding the instructive ending -**n** to the infinitive stem arrived at according to the basic rule (§75.1), e.g. sano/e/**n** 'saying', naura/e/**n** 'laughing', hymyil/le/**n** 'smiling', huomat/e/**n** 'noticing'. This **manner** structure mainly indicates manner, and most commonly occurs in a number of fixed expressions.

Lapsi tuli itki/e/**n** kotiin.	The child came home *crying.*
He astuivat naura/e/**n** sisään ovesta.	They stepped in through the door *laughing.*
Kyllä sinne kävel/**le**/**n**/kin pääsee.	One can also get there *on foot* (''*walking*'') all right.
Kaikesta päättä/e/**n**.	By all accounts (''*deciding* from everything'').
Illan tul/**le**/**n**.	In the evening /*when* the evening *comes.*
Kalle nauroi kaikkien näh/**de**/**n**.	Kalle laughed in full view of everybody (''everybody *seeing*'').
Näin ol/**le**/**n**.	This *being* the case (''so *being*'').

§76. *3RD INFINITIVE*

§76.1. *Formation*

NB: important structure! The 3rd infinitive, which has the ending -**ma**- ∿ -**mä**-, is a common and important form in both the written and spoken language. It occurs in five cases: the inessive -**ssa** ∿ -**ssä**, the elative -**sta** ∿ -**stä**, the illative -**Vn**, the adessive -**lla** ∿ -**llä**, and the abessive -**tta** ∿ -**ttä**.

The inflectional stem can be derived from the 3rd person singular of the present indicative, by detaching the personal ending.

1ST INFINITIVE		3RD P. SING. PRESENT	3RD INFINITIVE STEM
vetä/ä	pull	vetä/ä	vetä/**mä**-
otta/a	take	otta/a	otta/**ma**-
rakenta/a	build	rakenta/a	rakenta/**ma**-
huomat/a	notice	huomaa	huomaa/**ma**-
kaivat/a	long for	kaipaa	kaipaa/**ma**-
levät/ä	rest	lepää	lepää/**mä**-
maat/a	lie	makaa	makaa/**ma**-
lyö/dä	hit	lyö	lyö/**mä**-
ol/la	be	on	ole/**ma**- (NB!)
tul/la	come	tule/e	tule/**ma**-
men/nä	go	mene/e	mene/**mä**-
valit/a	choose	valitse/e	valitse/**ma**-

The following table shows the forms of the 3rd infinitive.

ROOT	INF.	CASE	PART-ICLE	
lepää	mä	ssä		resting
lepää	mä	än		to rest
lepää	mä	än	kö	to rest?
vetä	mä	llä		by pulling
vetä	mä	llä	kin	also by pulling
mainitse	ma	tta		without mentioning
mainitse	ma	tta	kaan	without mentioning, either
teke	mä	stä		from doing

§76.2. *3rd infinitive inessive*

on-going action

The inessive indicates an on-going action or process; it usually occurs together with the verb *ol/la* 'be', and occasionally also with other verbs expressing a state.

Ville on kirjastossa luke/**ma**/**ssa**.
Ville is in the library *reading*.

Veljeni on opiskele/**ma**/**ssa** Tampereella.
My brother is *studying* at Tampere.

Lapset ovat ulkona leikki/**mä**/**ssä**.
The children are outside *playing*.

Olitko jo nukku/**ma**/**ssa** kun soitin?
Were you already *sleeping / asleep* when I rang?

Kalle ja Pekka ovat olutta osta/**ma**/**ssa**.
Kalle and Pekka are *buying* some beer.

Huomenna käyn äitiäni katso/**ma**/**ssa**.
Tomorrow I'll go *and see* my mother.

Istumme juuri syö/**mä**/**ssä**.
Just now we are sitting *eating*.

Pyykki on kuivu/**ma**/**ssa**.
The washing is *drying*.

161

§76.3. *3rd infinitive elative*

meaning

The elative form co-occurs with verbs indicating concrete or abstract movement, e.g. *tul/la* 'come' and *palat/a* 'return', to express coming 'from doing something'. Note in addition the verbs below which are always followed by the 3rd infinitive.

estä/ä	prevent	*pelasta/a*	save
esty/ä	be prevented	*pelastu/a*	be saved
kieltä/ä	forbid	*varo/a*	beware of
kieltäyty/ä	refuse	*varoitta/a*	warn
lakat/a	cease	*vältta/ä*	avoid

Tuula *tuli* rannalta ui/**ma**/**sta**.

Tuula came from the beach, where she had been swimming (*"from swimming"*).

Teuvo *palasi* Helsingistä opiskele/**ma**/**sta**.
Silja *lakkasi* itke/**mä**/**stä**.
Kieltäydyn poltta/**ma**/**sta** savukkeita.
Älä *estä* minua näke/**mä**/**stä**!
Hän *pelasti* minut hukku/**ma**/**sta**.

Teuvo returned *from studying* at (*"from"*) Helsinki.
Silja stopped *crying*.
I refuse *to smoke* cigarettes.
Don't prevent me *from seeing*!
He/she saved me *from drowning*.

§76.4. *3rd infinitive illative*

meaning

The illative form is used after verbs of movement and indicates an action which is about to begin. Note in particular the structure *tul/la* 'come' + 3rd infinitive illative, which refers to future time, e.g. *Tule/n palaa/ma/an* 'I will return'. The most common verbs followed by the 3rd infinitive illative are the following:

NB:
important
verbs

joutu/a	come, be made to	*pysty/ä*	be capable
jättä/ä	leave	*pyytä/ä*	request
jää/dä	stay	*pääs/tä*	get
kehotta/a	urge	*ruvet/a*	begin
kyet/ä	be able	*ryhty/ä*	set about
käske/ä	command	*sattu/a*	happen
pakotta/a	force		

Menen ulos syö/**mä**/**än**.
Tanssi/**ma**/**an**/ko te menette?
Matkustan maalle lepää/**mä**/**än**.
Illalla tulen teille sauno/**ma**/**an**.

Lähden hake/**ma**/**an** lapset koulusta.

Menetkö kotiin nukku/**ma**/**an**?
Tulen lähte/**mä**/**än** pois.
Jätin Kallen kotiin luke/**ma**/**an**.
Jään vielä työskentele/**mä**/**än**.
Kehotan teitä lopetta/**ma**/**an** tupakoimisen.
Poliisi käski meitä poistu/**ma**/**an**.
Pystytkö aja/**ma**/**an** Helsinkiin?
Tuija pyysi minua tanssi/**ma**/**an**.
Illalla rupesi sata/**ma**/**an**.
Reijo sattui ole/**ma**/**an** paikalla.

I'm going out *to eat*.
Are you really going *dancing*?
I'm going into the country *to rest*.
In the evening I'll come to your house *to have a sauna*.
I'll go *and fetch* the children from school.
Are you going home *to sleep*?
I will *go* away.
I left Kalle at home *to read*.
I'll stay a bit longer *to do some work*.
I urge you *to give up* smoking.

The policeman ordered us *to leave*.
Can you *drive* to Helsinki?
Tuija asked me *to dance*.
In the evening it began *to rain*.
Reijo happened *to be* there.

adjectives The 3rd infinitive illative also occurs after certain adjectives, of which the most frequent are: *halukas* 'willing', *innostunut* 'keen', *kiinnostunut* 'interested', *valmis* 'ready'.

Kuka on halukas vastaa/**ma**/**an**?	Who is willing *to answer*?
En ole innokas tule/**ma**/**an**.	I'm not keen *to come*.
Olen kyllä kiinnostunut osta/**ma**/**an** pesukoneen.	Yes, I am interested *in buying* a washing-machine.
Karikin on valmis lähte/**mä**/**än** syö/**mä**/**än**.	Kari too is ready *to go and eat*.

§76.5. *3rd infinitive adessive and abessive*

means The adessive indicates means, and sometimes manner.

Voitin miljoonan veikkaa/**ma**/**lla**.	I won a million *by betting*.
Sinne pääsee mukavasti kävele/**mä**/**llä**.	One can get there easily *on foot* (*"by walking"*).
Hän elää kirjoitta/**ma**/**lla** kirjoja.	He/she lives *by writing* books.
Kieliä oppii parhaiten puhu/**ma**/**lla**.	One learns languages best *by talking*.

without The meaning of the abessive is 'without'; the object takes the partitive (cf. §33.2). If there is a subject it takes the genitive, and if it is a personal pronoun the verb also takes a possessive suffix.

Sehän on sano/**ma**/**tta**/kin selvää.	That goes *without saying* (*"is clear without one saying"*).
Syö/**mä**/**ttä** ja juo/**ma**/**tta** ei elä.	*Without eating* and *drinking* one cannot live.
Kalle teki sen (*meidän*) tietä/**mä**/**ttä**/**mme**.	Kalle did it *without our knowing*.
Myyjä tuli sisään *Leenan* huomaa/**ma**/**tta** mitään.	The seller came in *without Leena noticing* anything.
Koira karkasi *hänen* huomaa/**ma**/**tta**/**an**.	The dog ran away *without his/her noticing*.

The forms in -**ma**- ∼ -**mä**- are also used adjectivally in what is called the agent construction (§84). A few examples:

Kalle/n osta/**ma** auto	the car Kalle *bought / bought* by Kalle
Oletko istunut Kalle/n osta/**ma**/ssa autossa?	Have you sat in the car Kalle *bought*?
En ole nähnyt Kalle/n osta/**ma**/a autoa.	I have not seen the car Kalle *bought*.

§77. 4TH INFINITIVE

-minen The 4th infinitive has the ending -**minen**, which is added to the inflectional stem of the verb (cf. §23; §76.1). Examples:

1ST INFINITIVE		3RD P. SING.	4TH INFINITIVE
tietä/ä	know	tietä/ä	tietä/**minen**
suoritta/a	perform	suoritta/a	suoritta/**minen**
halut/a	want	halua/a	halua/**minen**
todet/a	verify	totea/a	totea/**minen**
lakat/a	cease	lakkaa	lakkaa/**minen**
jää/dä	stay	jää	jää/**minen**
ol/la	be	on	ole/**minen**
juos/ta	run	juokse/e	juokse/**minen**
havait/a	observe	havaitse/e	havaitse/**minen**

The 4th infinitive has only two rare forms: the nominative, indicating obligation, and the corresponding partitive.

rare expressions

Minun on mene/**minen** sinne. (nom.; note genitive minu/**n**)	I must go there.
Tämä tehtävä on suoritta/**minen**. (nom.)	This task must be carried out.
Sinne ei ole mene/**mis**/tä. (part.)	One must not go there.

More common ways of expressing this meaning are e.g.:

more common expressions

Minun *täytyy mennä* ~ *pitää mennä* ~ *on mentävä* sinne.
Tämä tehtävä *on suoritettava* ~ *pitää suorittaa*.
Sinne ei *pidä* mennä.

A much more frequent -**minen** form is that used to mark nouns derived from verbs (deverbal nouns: see further §93.1). A few examples:

Tupakoi/**minen** on täällä kielletty.	*Smoking* is forbidden here.
Auton aja/**minen** on hankalaa.	*Driving* a car is difficult.
Sauno/**minen** on mukavaa.	*Having a sauna* is nice.

18 Participles

§78. GENERAL

two
participles

Like infinitives, participles are non-finite verb-forms: they are not inflected for person. Finnish has two participles, the present and the past. Both have active and passive forms; cf. §14, where all the non-finite forms were introduced. The four participle forms of the verb *sano/a* 'say' are:

	ACTIVE	PASSIVE
PRESENT	sano/**va**	sano/tta/**va**
	'saying'	'which is to be said'
PAST	sano/**nut**	sano/**ttu**
	'said'	'said'

The participles function partly as **verbs**, e.g. (*olen*) *sano/nut* '(I have) said' (§61) and (*on*) *sano/ttu* '(one has) said' (§71), and partly as **adjectives**. In this latter function participles inflect in the normal adjectival way for number and case:

adjectival
expres-
sions

pitkä mies	a tall man
syö/**vä** mies	an eating man
syö/**nyt** mies	a man who has eaten
lyö/**tä/vä** mies	a man who is to be hit
lyö/**ty** mies	a man who was hit / a beaten man

pitkä/t miehe/t	the tall men
syö/**vä**/t miehe/t	the eating men
syö/**nee**/t miehe/t	the men who have eaten
lyö/tä/**vä**/t miehe/t	the men who are to be hit
lyö/**dy**/t miehe/t	the men who were hit

As premodifiers, participles are thus subject to the normal rules of concord for attributes (§31).

Participles also have other uses. For instance, all the participles (inflected in the genitive) can be used in what is called the participial construction, which corresponds to an *että* 'that' -clause (§82):

165

participial construction	Näen, että Pekka tulee. I see that Pekka is coming.	∼ Näen Peka/n tule/**va**/n. I see Pekka *coming*.
	Näen, että Pekka on tullut. I see that Pekka has come.	∼ Näen Peka/n tul/**lee**/n. I see that Pekka *has come*.

The past participle passive, inflected in the partitive, may be used to replace a temporal subordinate clause indicating an action previous to that of the main clause (§83; cf. also §75.1):

temporal construction	Nukahdin, kun Pekka oli tullut. I fell asleep when Pekka had come.	Nukahdin Peka/n tul/**tu**/a. I fell asleep "Pekka *having come*" / when Pekka *had come*.

The 3rd infinitive stem (-**ma**- ∼ -**mä**-, see §76.1) is used in the agent construction to replace a relative clause:

agent construction	Peka/n osta/**ma** auto the car *bought* by Pekka	auto, jonka Pekka oli ostanut the car which Pekka had bought

§79. PRESENT PARTICIPLE ACTIVE

incomplete action
This form has the ending -**va**- ∼ -**vä**-, which is added to the inflectional stem of the verb (§23). It indicates a continuing action or process.

1ST INFINITIVE	3RD P. SING.	PRESENT PARTICIPLE	MEANING
kerto/a	kerto/o	kerto/**va**	telling
kylpe/ä	kylpe/e	kylpe/**vä**	bathing
luvat/a	lupaa	lupaa/**va**	promising
kadot/a	katoa/a	katoa/**va**	disappearing
määrät/ä	määrää	määrää/**vä**	ordering
soi/da	soi	soi/**va**	ringing
men/nä	mene/e	mene/**vä**	going
ol/la	on	ole/**va**	being
häirit/ä	häiritse/e	häiritse/**vä**	disturbing
ratkais/ta	ratkaise/e	ratkaise/**va**	deciding

The present participle often corresponds to a relative clause with a present-tense verb:

Pihalla seiso/**va** auto on sininen.   Auto, *joka seisoo* pihalla, on sininen.
The car *standing* / *which is standing* in the yeard is blue.

Oletko nähnyt pihalla seiso/**va**/n auton?   Oletko nähnyt auton, *joka seisoo* pihalla?
Have you seen the car *standing* / *which is standing* in the yard?

työtä teke/**vä** luokka   luokka, *joka tekee* työtä
the *working* class

Pihalla on huuta/**v**/**i**/**a** lapsia.   Pihalla on lapsia, *jotka huutavat*.
In the yard there are children *shating* / *who are shating*.

Ratkaise/va/t päätökset tehdään
iltapäivällä.
The *final* decisions / decisions *which are final* are made in the afternoon.

Päätökset, *jotka ovat ratkaisevia,*
tehdään iltapäivällä.

hyvää musiikkia soitta/va yhtye
a bund *playing / which plays* good music

yhtye, *joka soittaa* hyvää musiikkia

premodifiers

The examples also show that where a particle functioning as an attribute takes an object or adverbial, these appear *before* the participle (*musiikkia* soittava yhtye (object); *pihalla* seisova auto (adverbial)).

§80. *PRESENT PARTICIPLE PASSIVE*

This form is most conveniently derived from the past tense passive (cf. §80) by the following rule (which is the same as that for the derivation of the passive moods, §72).

formation

> CHANGE THE PASSIVE PAST TENSE -**iin** TO -**a** OR -**ä** AND ADD
> -**va**- ~ -**vä**-

Example: *sano/ttiin* 'one said' → *sano/tta/va*. These participles have various special meanings. Usually they correspond to the following types of relative clause:

NB:
meanings!

sano/**tta**/**va** asia   1) a thing that *must / has to be / is to be said*
2) a thing that *can be said*
3) a thing that *will be said*
4) a thing that *is said*

1ST INFINITIVE	PAST TENSE PASSIVE	PRESENT PARTICIPLE PASSIVE	MEANING	
kerto/a	kerro/ttiin	kerro/**tta**/**va**	which is to be told	
luke/a	lue/ttiin	lue/**tta**/**va**	"	read
johta/a	johde/ttiin	johde/**tta**/va	"	led
huomat/a	huomat/tiin	huomat/**ta**/va	"	noticed
pelät/ä	pelät/tiin	pelät/**tä**/**vä**	"	feared
rakenta/a	rakenne/ttiin	rakenne/**tta**/va	"	built
juo/da	juo/tiin	juo/**ta**/va	"	drunk
ajatel/la	ajatel/tiin	ajatel/**ta**/va	"	thought
hävit/ä	hävit/tiin	hävit/**tä**/**vä**	"	lost

The use of these participles will become clearer from the following examples. All the meanings (1—4) are possible, depending on the context.

syö/**tä**/**vä** sieni

an *edible mushroom* ("that can be eaten")

Tämä ei ole suositel/**ta**/**va** kirja.

This is not a book *that can be recommended.*

167

Nämä eivät ole suositel/**ta**/**v**/i/a kirjoja.	These are not books *that can be recommended*.
Onko teillä ilmoite/**tta**/**v**/i/a tuloja?	Do you have any income *to be declared*?
Onko jääkaapissa jotain juo/**ta**/**va**/a?	Is there anything *to drink* in the fridge?
Ei tämä ole mikään pelät/**tä**/**vä** koira!	This is no dog *to be feared* / There is no need to be afraid of this dog.
Onko teillä tarvit/**ta**/**va** pääoma?	Do you have the *necessary* capital?
Ratkais/**ta**/**va**/t kysymykset ovat...	The questions *to be solved* are...
Onko vielä jotain lisät/**tä**/**vä**/ä?	Is there still something *to be added*?
Minulla ei ole muuta sano/**tta**/**va**/a.	I have nothing else *to say*.
Lainat/**ta**/**va**/t kirjat ovat oikealla.	The books *that can be borrowed* are on the right.
Viimeinen suorite/**tta**/**v**/i/sta töistä oli vaikein.	The last of the tasks *to be done* was the most difficult.

'must' The present participle passive is also used in a number of special ways, for instance to express obligation in structures such as the following:

> SUBJECT IN THE GENITIVE + **on, oli, olisi, lienee** + PRESENT PARTICIPLE PASSIVE

minu/**n on** sano/**tta**/**va**
'I must say'

mies/**ten** oli lähde/**ttä**/**vä**
'the men had to leave'

Nyt minun **on** syö/**tä**/**vä**.	Now I *must eat*.
On/ko sinun lähde/**ttä**/**vä** jo?	*Do* you *have to leave* already?
Meidän **oli** tilat/**ta**/**va** taksi.	We *had to order* a taxi.
Kaikkien **on** men/**tä**/**vä** ulos.	Everyone *must go* out.
Pekan **on** usko/**tta**/**va**, että...	Pekka *must believe* that...
Heidän **oli** matkuste/**tta**/**va** Helsinkiin.	They *had to go* to Helsinki.

'can' The present participle passive inflected in the inessive plural, combined with **ol**/**la**, indicates that something can (not) be done.

Onko johtaja tavat/**ta**/**v**/i/ssa?	Is the manager *in* / *available* / "*to be met with*"?
Eikö johtaja ole tavat/**ta**/**v**/i/ssa?	Isn't the manager *available*?
Päätös on teh/**tä**/**v**/i/ssä.	The decision *can be made*.
Tämä asia ei ole muute/**tta**/**v**/i/ssa.	This matter *cannot be altered*.

This participle also occurs in certain fixed expressions.

fixed expressions

Onko teillä huoneita vuokrat/**ta**/**va**/**na**?	Do you have rooms *to let*?
Autoja myy/**tä**/**vä**/**nä**.	Cars *for sale*.
Virka on julistettu hae/**tta**/**va**/**ksi**.	Applications are invited for the post ("The post is declared *to be applied for*").
Paavo on sairaalassa tutki/**tta**/**va**/**na**.	Paavo is in hospital for a check-up / *to be examined*.

§81. THE PAST PARTICIPLES

The past participles occur primarily in the compound tenses, i.e. the perfect and pluperfect, e.g. on sano/**nut** 'has said', on sano/**ttu** 'one has said'; oli sano/**nut** 'had said', oli sano/**ttu** 'one had said'. For the formation of these participles see §§61, 71. By way of recapitulation, here are a few examples of this usage:

PAST PARTICIPLE (perfect tense active)

verbal use	(minä) olen anta/**nut** — I have given
	(sinä) olet anta/**nut** — you have given (sing.)
	Pekka on anta/**nut** — Pekka has given
	(me) olemme anta/**neet** — we have given
	(te) olette anta/**neet** — you have given (pl.)
	he ovat anta/**neet** — they have given
	on anne/**ttu** — one has given

The corresponding pluperfect forms are *(minä) olin anta/nut* 'I had given', *he olivat anta/neet* 'they had given', *oli anne/ttu* 'one had given', etc.

completed action   The past participles indicate completed action *(anta/nut, anne/ttu)*, whereas the present participles indicate incomplete action (cf. §§79, 80).

adjectival use   The past participles also occur as adjectivals, particularly as premodifiers, e.g. *lahjan anta/nut mies* 'the man who gave the present' and *anne/ttu lahja* 'a present that has been / was given'. If a participle has its own objects or adverbials these are placed before the participle (cf. §79).

Examples follow, first of the use of the active participle (-**nut** ~ -**nyt**). The inflectional stem is -**nee**-.

-**nut** ~ -**nyt**	
Paljon matkusta/**nut** ihminen.	A much-*travelled* person.
Koke/**nut** lääkäri.	An *experienced* doctor.
Tunnen koke/**nee**/n lääkärin.	I know an *experienced* doctor.
En tunne koke/**nut**/ta lääkäriä.	I don't know an *experienced* doctor.
Pois juos/**sut** koira.	A dog *that has run* away.
Vietnamissa ol/**lee**/t ihmiset sanovat, että...	People *who have been* in Vietnam say that...
Eilen saapu/**nee**/t matkustajat ovat jo lähteneet.	The travellers *who arrived* yesterday have already left.
Viime syksynä ilmesty/**nee**/t kirjat ovat hyviä.	The books *which were published* last autumn are good.
Pommin löytä/**nyt** koira kuoli.	The dog *which (had) found* the bomb died.
Pommin löytä/**nee**/lle koiralle annettiin mitali.	The dog *which (had) found* the bomb was given a medal.
Näin pala/**nee**/n talon.	I saw a *burnt / burned-down* house.
Pala/**nee**/ssa talossa oli ollut ihmisiä.	There had been people in the *burned-down* house.
Oletteko väsy/**ne**/i/tä?	Are you *tired*?
He ovat hyvin koke/**nee**/i/ta.	They are very *experienced*.

In the same way, the past participle passive -(t)**tu** ~ -(t)**ty** indicates a completed action performed by an unspecified agent.

-(t)**tu** ~ -(t)**ty**	
kaupasta oste/**ttu** kirja	a book *bought* in a shop
syksyllä rakenne/**ttu** talo	a house *built* in the autumn

He asuvat syksyllä rakenne/**tu**/ssa talossaan.	They live in their house *which was built* in the autumn.
hyväksy/**tty** ehdotus	an *accepted* proposal
Hyväksy/**ty**/t opiskelijat voivat jatkaa.	Students *accepted* may continue.
syö/**ty** piirakka	a pie *that has been / was eaten*
Eilen syö/**dy**/t piirakat eivät olleet hyviä.	The pies *that were eaten* yesterday were not good.
anne/**ttu** lahja	a present *that has been / was given*
Anne/**ttu**/j/a lahjoja ei voi ottaa takaisin.	Presents *that have been given* cannot be taken back.
pelaste/**ttu** merimies	a *rescued* sailor
Pelaste/**tu**/t merimiehet olivat hyvässä kunnossa.	The *rescued* sailors were in good shape.
maalat/**tu** seinä	a *painted* wall
Seinät eivät ole maala/**tu**/t.	The walls are not *painted*.

§82. *THE PARTICIPIAL CONSTRUCTION*

The participial construction can be used to contract an affirmative **että** ('that') -clause functioning as the object of certain verbs, e.g. *näh/dä* 'see', *kuul/la* 'hear', *usko/a* 'believe', *sano/a* 'say'. Both present and past participles appear in the participial construction, in both active and passive. The participle in the construction is always in the genitive (-**n**). The following forms occurring in the participial construction can thus be derived from the verb *itke/ä* 'cry':

-n

		BASIC FORM	GENITIVE
PRESENT PARTICIPLE	(active)	itke/**vä**	itke/**vä**/**n**
	(passive)	itke/**ttä**/**vä**	itke/**ttä**/**vän**
PAST PARTICIPLE	(active)	itke/**nyt**	itke/**nee**/**n**
	(passive)	itke/**tty**	itke/**ty**/**n**

These forms are used in context as follows:

	että-CLAUSE		PARTICIPIAL CONSTRUCTION
active is common!	Näen, että Kalle itke/e. I see that Kalle is crying / I see Kalle crying.	~	Näen Kalle/n itke/**vä**/**n**.
	Näen, että Kalle on itkenyt. I see that Kalle has been crying.	~	Näen Kalle/n itke/**nee**/**n**.
passive	Näen, että täällä itke/tään. I see that people are crying here.	~	Näen täällä itke/**ttä**/**vä**/**n**.
	Näen, että täällä on itke/tty. I see that people have been crying here.	~	Näen täällä itke/**ty**/**n**.

The use of the present or past participle is determined by the temporal relation between the **että**-clause and the main clause. The following rule is an important one:

THE PRESENT PARTICIPLES ARE USED IF THE ACTION OF THE että-CLAUSE TAKES PLACE AT THE SAME TIME AS, OR LATER THAN, THAT OF THE MAIN CLAUSE; THE PAST PARTICIPLES ARE USED IF THE ACTION OF THE että-CLAUSE IS EARLIER THAN THAT OF THE MAIN CLAUSE

The subject of an **että**-clause is expressed in the participial construction according to the following rule (which concerns active sentences only, since passive sentences have no subject!). Cf. the subject rule for the inessive structure (§75.1).

subject
rule

THE SUBJECT OF THE että-CLAUSE IS EXPRESSED
a) BY A POSSESSIVE SUFFIX ALONE, IF THE SUBJECT IS THE SAME AS THAT OF THE MAIN CLAUSE;
b) BY A GENITIVE FORM PRECEDING THE PARTICIPLE, IF THE SUBJECT IS DIFFERENT FROM THAT OF THE MAIN CLAUSE (also applies to personal pronouns!)

The examples that follow illustrate first the most common structure, i.e. with the present participle active (**-va/n ~ -vä/n**). This is used when the action of the **että**-clause is simultaneous with or later than the action of the main clause. When part (a) of the above subject rule is applied, the genitive **-n** is dropped (§36).

a) same
subject
-va/n ~
-vä/n

että-CLAUSE	PARTICIPIAL CONSTRUCTION
Usko/**n**, että nuku/**n**. *I believe that I shall sleep.*	Uskon nukku/**va/ni**.
Usko/**t**/ko, että nuku/**t**? Do *you* believe that *you will sleep?*	Uskotko nukku/**va/si**?
Tiedä/**n**, että ole/**n** vanha. *I know that I am old.*	Tiedän ole/**va/ni** vanha.
Pekka luuli, että *hän* oli Kekkonen. *Pekka thought he was Kekkonen.*	Pekka luuli ole/**va/nsa** Kekkonen.
He sanoivat, että *he* tulisivat huomenna. *They said that they would come tomorrow.*	He sanoivat tule/**va/nsa** huomenna.
Hän väittää, että *hän* on sairas. *He claims that he is ill.*	Hän väittää ole/**va/nsa** sairas.
Tuula huomasi, että *hän* itki. *Tuula noticed that she was crying.*	Tuula huomasi itke/**vä/nsä**.
Hallitus tietää, että *se* tulee eroamaan. *The government knows that it will resign.*	Hallitus tietää eroa/**va/nsa**.
Luule/**mme**, että lähde/**mme** huomenna. *We think that we shall leave tomorrow.*	Luulemme lähte/**vä/mme** huomenna.

b)
different
subject

-va/n ∼
-vä/n

Tiedä/**n**, että *hän* on ulkomailla.   Tiedän häne/**n** ole/**va/n** ulkomailla.
I know that *he is* abroad.

Luule/**t**/ko, että tiedä/**n** tämän?   Luuletko minu/**n** tietä/**vä/n** tämän?
Do *you* think that *I know* this?

Näi/**mme**, että *he* lähtivät.   Näimme heidä/**n** lähte/**vä/n**.
We saw that *they left* / saw *them leave*.

Kuuli/**mme**, että *lapsi* huusi.   Kuulimme lapse/**n** huuta/**va/n**.
We heard that *the child was shouting* / heard *the child shout*.

Pekka kuuli, että *juna* saapui.   Pekka kuuli juna/**n** saapu/**va/n**.
Pekka heard that *the train was arriving* / heard *the train arrive*.

He luule/**vat**, että suostu/**t**   He luulevat sinu/**n** suostu/**va/n**
ehdotukseen.   ehdotukseen.
They think that *you will agree* to the proposal.

Note in particular that the personal pronoun subject of an **että**-clause is expressed in the participial construction as a genitive form alone, e.g. ...minu/**n** ole/**va/n**... 'me being'. By contrast, the personal pronoun subject of a **kun** ('when') -clause is expressed in the temporal construction both as a personal pronoun (optionally) and as a possessive suffix, e.g. ...(minu/n) ol/le/ssa/**ni**... 'when being (1st p. sing.)'. Cf. §83.

    The following examples illustrate the use of the past participle active, which is used when the action of the **että**-clause precedes that of the main clause.

että-CLAUSE   PARTICIPIAL CONSTRUCTION

a) same
subject

Luule/**n**, että ole/**n** nukkunut.   Luulen nukku/**nee/ni**.
I think *I have slept*.

Usko/**t**/ko, että nukui/**t**?   Uskotko nukku/**nee/si**?
Do *you* think that *you slept*?

Tiedä/**n**, että oli/**n** sairas.   Tiedän ol/**lee/ni** sairas.
I know that *I was* ill.

He sanoivat, että *he* olivat tulleet jo   He sanoivat tul/**lee/nsa** jo eilen.
eilen.
They said that *they had* already *come* yesterday.

Huomasi/**mme**, että oli/**mme**   Huomasimme myöhästy/**nee/mme**.
myöhästyneet.
We noticed that *we were late*.

Tuula huomasi, että *hän* oli itkenyt.   Tuula huomasi itke/**nee/nsä**.
Tuula noticed that *she had cried*.

TPS tajusi, että *se* oli hävinnyt.   TPS tajusi hävin/**nee/nsä**.
TPS (a sports team) realised that *it had lost*.

b)
different
subject

Tiedä/**n**, että *hän* on ollut ulkomailla.   Tiedän häne/**n** ol/**lee/n** ulkomailla.
I know that *he has been* abroad.

Luule/**t**/ko, että *minä* tiesin tämän?   Luuletko minu/**n** tietä/**nee/n** tämän?
Do *you* think that *I knew* this?

Ymmärsi/**mme**, että *he* olivat lähteneet.
We understood that *they had left* / understood *them to have left*.

Ymmärsimme heidä/**n** lähte/**nee/n**.

Pekka kuuli, että *juna* oli saapunut.
Pekka heard that *the train had arrived*.

Pekka kuuli juna/**n** saapu/**nee/n**.

He luule/**vat**, että suostui/**t** ehdotukseen.
They think that *you agreed* to the proposal.

He luulevat sinu/**n** suostu/**nee/n** ehdotukseen.

Kerrotti/**in**, että *Virtanen* oli kuollut.
It was said that *Virtanen had died* / Virtanen was said *to have died*.

Kerrottiin Virtase/**n** kuol/**lee/n**.

NB: important verbs!

   The participial construction is particularly common with the following verbs: *näky/ä* 'be seen', *näyttä/ä* 'seem', *kuulu/a* 'be heard', *tuntu/a* 'feel, seem'. The subject of the **että**-clause becomes the subject of the main clause, and thus affects the concord of the verb (cf. *Näyttää (siltä), että auto on rikki* 'It seems that the car is broken' → *Auto näyttää olevan rikki* 'The car seems to be broken'). Examples:

Auto näyttää ole/**va/n** rikki.   The car seems *to be* broken.
Sinä näytät ole/**va/n** sairas.   You seem *to be* ill.
Auto näyttää ol/**lee/n** rikki.   The car seems *to have been* broken.
Sinä näytät ol/**lee/n** sairas.   You seem *to have been* ill.
Kekkonen näyttää sano/**va/n**, että...   Kekkonen seems *to be saying* that...
Kekkonen näyttää sano/**nee/n**, että...   Kekkonen seems *to have said* that...
Tilanne tuntuu vaikeutu/**va/n**.   The situation seems *to be getting more difficult*.
Tilanne tuntui vaikeutu/**nee/n**.   The situation seemed *to have got more difficult*.
Tilanne ei tunnu vaikeutu/**va/n**.   The situation does not seem *to be getting more difficult*.
Tilanne ei tuntunut vaikeutu/**va/n**.   The situation did not seem *to be getting more difficult*.
Tilanne ei tuntunut vaikeutu/**nee/n**.   The situation did not seem *to have got more difficult*.

The next examples illustrate passive **että**-clauses. If the action expressed by the verb in the subordinate clause is simultaneous with or later than the action of the main clause, the form -(t)**ta/va/n** ~ -(t)**tä/vä/n** is used, and if the **että**-clause action is earlier the form -**tu/n** ~ -**ty/n** is used.

että-CLAUSE	PARTICIPIAL CONSTRUCTION
-(t)**ta/va/n** ~ -(t)**tä/vä/n**	Tiedän, että Ruotsissa puhu/taan myös suomea.
	I know that in Sweden Finnish *is* also *spoken*.

-(t)**ta/va/n** ~ -(t)**tä/vä/n**

Tiedän, että Ruotsissa puhu/taan myös suomea.
I know that in Sweden Finnish *is* also *spoken*.

Tiedän Ruotsissa puhu/**tta/va/n** myös suomea.

Kuulin, että sano/ttiin, että...
I heard that *it was said* that... / I heard it *said* that...

Kuulin sano/**tta/va/n**, että...

Kalle kuuli, että huoneessa siivot/tiin.
Kalle heard that *someone was cleaning* in the room / heard *someone cleaning*...

Kalle kuuli huoneessa siivot/**ta/va/n**.

173

	Huomasin, että alakerrassa riidel/lään. I noticed that *there is quarrelling* downstairs.	Huomasin alakerrassa riidel/**tä**/**vä**/**n**.
	Tiedän, että ol/laan sitä mieltä että... I know that *people are* of the opinion that...	Tiedän ol/**ta**/**va**/**n** sitä mieltä, että...
-**tu**/**n** ~ -**ty**/**n**	Tiedän, että Virossa on puhu/ttu myös ruotsia. I know that in Estonia Swedish *has* also *been spoken*.	Tiedän Virossa puhu/**tu**/**n** myös ruotsia.
	Kuulin, että oli sano/ttu että... I heard that *it had been said* that...	Kuulin sano/**tu**/**n**, että...
	Huomasin, että oli esite/tty että... I noticed that *it had been proposed* that...	Huomasin esite/**ty**/**n**, että...
NB!	Kalle kertoi, että oli rakenne/ttu talo. Kalle said that a house *had been built*.	Kalle kertoi rakenne/**tu**/**n** talo.
	Kalle kertoi, että talo oli rakenne/ttu. Kalle said that the house *had been built*.	Kalle kertoi talo/**n** rakenne/**tu**/**n**.

NB: definite meaning Note that in the last example above the fact that the object of the passive sentence is definite can be indicated by moving the object before the participle (i.e. to the beginning of its clause) and inflecting it in the genitive.

§83. *THE TEMPORAL CONSTRUCTION*

The temporal construction can be used to contract a **kun** ('when') -clause. If the action of the **kun**-clause is simultaneous with or later than that of the main clause, the form of the verb is the 2nd infinitive inessive, e.g. *sano/e/ssa/ni* 'when I say' (cf. §75.1).

	kun-CLAUSE	TEMPORAL CONSTRUCTION
2nd inf. inessive (§75.1)	Kun Kalle tuli, Pekka lähti. *When* Kalle *came* Pekka left.	Kalle/**n** tul/**le**/**ssa** Pekka lähti.
	Kun tulin, kompastuin. *As* I *came* I stumbled.	Tul/**le**/**ssa**/**ni** kompastuin.

If the action of the **kun**-clause is earlier than that of the main clause, the verb-form in the temporal construction is the past participle passive inflected in the partitive, e.g. *sano/ttu/a* 'having said', *syö/ty/ä* 'having eaten' (cf. §71). The participle does not carry its normal passive meaning here.

past participle passive, partitive (§71)	Kun Kalle oli tullut, Pekka lähti. *When* Kalle *had come* / Kalle *having come*, Pekka left.	Kalle/**n** tul/**tu**/**a** Pekka lähti.
	Kun olin tullut, kompastuin. *When* I *had come* I stumbled.	Tul/**tu**/**a**/**ni** kompastuin.

The table below is a reminder of the formation of the past participle passive.

INFINITIVE		PAST TENSE PASSIVE	PAST PARTICIPLE PASSIVE	PARTITIVE CASE
sano/a	say	sano/ttiin	sano/ttu	sano/**ttu**/**a**
anta/a	give	anne/ttiin	anne/ttu	anne/**ttu**/**a**
juo/da	drink	juo/tiin	juo/tu	juo/**tu**/**a**
ol/la	be	ol/tiin	ol/tu	ol/**tu**/**a**
huomat/a	notice	huomat/tiin	huomat/tu	huomat/**tu**/**a**
pelät/ä	fear	pelät/tiin	pelät/ty	pelät/**ty**/**ä**
ansait/a	earn	ansait/tiin	ansait/tu	ansait/**tu**/**a**

The subject of the **kun**-clause is indicated in the temporal construction according to the same rules as for the 2nd infinitive inessive (§75.1).

<table>
<tr><td>subject
rule</td><td>

THE SUBJECT IS EXPRESSED

a) BY A POSSESSIVE SUFFIX ALONE, IF THE SUBJECT IS IDENTICAL WITH THAT OF THE MAIN CLAUSE;

b) BY AN INDEPENDENT WORD IN THE GENITIVE, IF THE SUBJECT IS DIFFERENT FROM THAT OF THE MAIN CLAUSE;

c) BY THE GENITIVE FORMS OF PERSONAL PRONOUNS (**minun** etc.), ALWAYS FOLLOWED BY A POSSESSIVE SUFFIX ON THE PARTICIPLE (unstressed 1st and 2nd personal pronouns may be omitted)

</td></tr>
</table>

	kun-CLAUSE	PAST PARTICIPLE PASSIVE, PARTITIVE
a) same subject	Kun *Pekka* oli herännyt, *hän* lähti töihin. When *Pekka* had woken up *he* went off to work.	Herät/**ty**/**ä**/**än** Pekka lähti töihin.
	Kun oli/**n** herännyt, lähdi/**n** töihin. When *I* had woken up *I* went off to work.	Hcrät/**ty**/**ä**/**ni** lähdin töihin.
	Tule/**t**/ko ulos, kun ole/**t** juonut kahvia? Will *you* come out when *you* have had some coffee?	Tuletko ulos juo/**tu**/**a**/**si** kahvia?
	Kun oli/**mme** syöneet, lähdi/**mme** kävelylle. When *we* had eaten *we* went for a walk.	Syö/**ty**/**ä**/**mme** lähdimme kävelylle.
	Monet ihmiset ajattelevat paremmin, kun *he* ovat juoneet kahvia. *Many people* think better when *they* have had some coffee.	Monet ihmiset ajattelevat paremmin juo/**tu**/**a**/**an** kahvia.
b) different subject	Kun *Pekka* oli herännyt, *Liisa* lähti töihin. When *Pekka* had woken up *Liisa* went off to work.	Peka/**n** herät/**ty**/**ä** Liisa lähti töihin.
	Kun *Viren* oli tullut maaliin, *Päivärinta* oli vielä loppusuoralla. When *Viren* had arrived at the finish *Päivärinta* wast still on the final straight.	Vireni/**n** tul/**tu**/**a** maaliin Päivärinta oli vielä loppusuoralla.

Kaikki hämmästyivät, kun *Kekkonen* oli sanonut tämän. *Everyone* was surprised when *Kekkonen* had said this.	*Kaikki* hämmästyivät Kekkose/**n** sano/**ttu/a** tämän.

c)
different
subject
(personal
pronoun)

Vaimoni heräsi, kun (*minä*) olin tullut kotiin. *My wife* woke up when *I* had come home.	*Vaimoni* heräsi (minun) tul/**tu/a/ni** kotiin.
Kun oli/**mme** olleet vuoden Ruotsissa, *ajat* huononivat. When *we* had been a year in Sweden *the times* got worse.	(Meidän) ol/**tu/a/mme** vuoden Ruotsissa ajat huononivat.

§84. *THE AGENT CONSTRUCTION*

The agent construction is a way of contracting relative clauses, i.e. those beginning with **joka**, **mikä** 'who, which'; in most cases these clauses then become premodifiers, with the verb functioning as an adjective and the subject (the agent) appearing e.g. in the genitive.

RELATIVE CLAUSE

auto, jonka Kalle osti
the car that Kalle bought

AGENT CONSTRUCTION

Kalle/**n** osta/**ma** auto
the car bought by Kalle

auto, jonka (minä) ostin
the car that I bought

(*minu/n*) osta/**ma**/**ni** auto
the car bought by me

The following rule applies to the verb of the agent construction.

verb rule

> THE VERB OF THE AGENT CONSTRUCTION
> a) USUALLY INDICATES PAST TIME;
> b) IS FORMED FROM THE ENDING -**ma** ~ -**mä**, ADDED TO THE INFLECTIONAL STEM (§76.1);
> c) FUNCTIONS LIKE A NORMAL ADJECTIVE, INFLECTING FOR NUMBER AND ALL CASES (§31)

Point (a) of the rule means that the verb of the construction may correspond to any of the tenses indicating past time (past tense, perfect, pluperfect).

meanings   Kalle/**n** osta/**ma** auto
a) the car which Kalle *bought*
b) the car which Kalle *has bought*
c) the car which Kalle *had bought*

Point (b) means that the verb is formed in the same way as the stem of the 3rd infinitive (§76.1).

	INFINITIVE		3RD PERSON SINGULAR	VERB-FORM IN -ma ~ -mä
formation	anta/a	give	anta/a	anta/**ma**
	vetä/ä	pull	vetä/ä	vetä/**mä**
	kaivat/a	long for	kaipaa	kaipaa/**ma**
	määrät/ä	order	määrää	määrää/**mä**
	syö/dä	eat	syö	syö/**mä**
	valit/a	choose	valitse/e	valitse/**ma**
	mainit/a	mention	mainitse/e	mainitse/**ma**

Point (c) means that the forms in -**ma** ~ -**mä** behave in the sentence like adjectives and are subject to the rules of concord (§31).

adjectival function	sininen auto	the *blue* car
	Kallen osta/**ma** auto	the car Kalle *bought*
	sinise/**n** auto/**n**	of the *blue* car
	Kallen osta/**ma**/**n** auto/**n**	of the car Kalle *bought*
	sinise/**ssä** auto/**ssa**	in the *blue* car
	Kallen osta/**ma**/**ssa** auto/**ssa**	in the car Kalle *bought*
	sinise/**t** auto/**t**	the *blue* cars
	Kallen osta/**ma**/**t** auto/**t**	the cars Kalle *bought*
	sinis/**i**/**llä** auto/**i**/**lla**	with the *blue* cars
	Kallen osta/**m**/**i**/**lla** auto/**i**/**lla**	with the cars Kalle *bought*

The agent in this construction corresponds to the subject of the relative clause (i.e. *Kalle* in the examples above), and is expressed according to the same rules that apply to the subject in the temporal construction (§83).

agent

> THE AGENT IS EXPRESSED
> a) BY A POSSESSIVE SUFFIX ALONE, IF IT IS THE SAME AS THE CORRESPONDING CONSTITUENT IN THE MAIN CLAUSE (generally the subject);
> b) BY AN INDEPENDENT WORD IN THE GENITIVE, IF IT IS DIFFERENT FROM THE CORRESPONDING CONSTITUENT IN THE MAIN CLAUSE;
> c) BY THE GENITIVE FORMS OF PERSONAL PRONOUNS (**minun** etc.), ALWAYS FOLLOWED BY A POSSESSIVE SUFFIX (unstressed 1st and 2nd personal pronouns may be omitted)

Tuula/**n** hankki/**ma** vene maksoi 1000 mk.	The boat *Tuula got* cost 1000 marks.
(Minun) hankki/**ma**/**ni** vene maksoi 1000 mk.	The boat *I got* cost 1000 marks.
Tuula istuu hankki/**ma**/**ssa**/**an** veneessä.	Tuula is sitting in the boat *she got*.
Istun hankki/**ma**/**ssa**/**ni** veneessä.	I am sitting in the boat *I got*.
Miksi ette aja hankki/**ma**/**lla**/**nne** veneellä?	Why don't you go ("drive") in the boat *you got*?
Hankki/**ma**/**mme** veneet eivät maksaneet paljon.	The boats *we got* didn't cost much.

Poik/i/en hankki/ma/t veneet ovat mukavia.
The boats *the boys got* are nice.

Hän ajaa Tuula/n hankki/ma/lla veneellä.
He is going in the boat *Tuula got*.

Particular attention should be paid to expressions such as the following, where the agent construction does not correspond directly to a relative clause.

NB! Ehdotus on Virtase/n esittä/mä.
The proposal was *put forward by Virtanen*.

Tämä runo on Saarikoske/n kirjoitta/ma.
This poem was *written by Saarikoski*.

Nämä runot ovat Saarikoske/n kirjoitta/ma/t ~ kirjoitta/m/i/a.
These poems were *written by Saarikoski*.

Kene/n kirjoitta/m/i/a nämä runot ovat?
By whom were these poems *written*?

19 Comparison of Adjectives

Comparative
Superlative

§85. *COMPARATIVE*

-mpi

The comparative ending is **-mpi**, which is added to the inflectional stem (see ch. 5), e.g. hullu 'mad' : hullu/**mpi** 'madder'. The following sound change occurs before the comparative ending:

> THE SHORT **-a** ~ **-ä** OF DISYLLABIC ADJECTIVES CHANGES
> TO **-e** BEFORE THE COMPARATIVE ENDING

NB:
consonant
gradation

Cf. vahv**a** 'strong' : vahv**e**/**mpi** 'stronger'; selv**ä** 'clear' : selv**e**/**mpi** 'clearer'. The rules of consonant gradation also apply before the comparative ending (§15.6), cf. hel**ppo** 'easy' : helpo/**mpi** 'easier'.

BASIC FORM		COMPARATIVE		CF. INFLECTIONAL STEM §
formation	paksu	thick	paksu/mpi	thicker
	iso	big	iso/mpi	etc.
	kiltti	good-natured	kilti/mpi	
	vanha	old	vanhe/mpi	
	selvä	clear	selve/mpi	
	kova	hard	kove/mpi	
	paha	bad	pahe/mpi	
	jyrkkä	steep	jyrke/mpi	
	tarkka	exact	tarke/mpi	
	nopea	fast	nopea/mpi	
	tärkeä	important	tärkeä/mpi	
	vakava	serious	vakava/mpi	
	suuri	great	suure/mpi	18.3 (suure-)
	pieni	small	piene/mpi	18.3 (piene-)
	uusi	new	uude/mpi	18.4 (uute-)
	terve	healthy	tervee/mpi	19 (tervee-)
	tuore	fresh	tuoree/mpi	19 (tuoree-)
	tavallinen	usual	tavallise/mpi	20.1 (tavallise-)
	punainen	red	punaise/mpi	20.1 (punaise-)
	kaunis	beautiful	kaunii/mpi	20.3 (kaunii-)
	puhdas	clean	puhtaa/mpi	20.3 (puhtaa-)
	raitis	sober	raittii/mpi	20.3 (raittii-)
	voimakas	powerful	voimakkaa/mpi	20.3 (voimakkaa-)
	lyhyt	short	lyhye/mpi	20.8 (lyhye-)
	kevyt	light	kevye/mpi	20.8 (kevye-)

The declension of the comparative forms has one special feature. In the inflectional stem -**mpi** changes to -**mpa**- ~ -**mpä**-, and the consonant gradation rules then change this to -**mma**- ~ -**mmä**-. Before the plural -**i**- the final -**a** ~ -**ä** of these endings is dropped (cf. §16).

COMPARATIVE BASIC FORM			SINGULAR	PLURAL
declension	paksu/**mpi**	thicker	illat. paksu/**mpa**/an	paksu/**mp**/i/in
			ess. paksu/**mpa**/na	paksu/**mp**/i/na
			part. paksu/**mpa**/a	paksu/**mp**/i/a
			gen. paksu/**mma**/n	paksu/**mp**/i/en
			iness. paksu/**mma**/ssa	paksu/**mm**/i/ssa
			elat. paksu/**mma**/sta	paksu/**mm**/i/sta
			adess. paksu/**mma**/lla	paksu/**mm**/i/lla
			ablat. paksu/**mma**/lta	paksu/**mm**/i/lta
			allat. paksu/**mma**/lle	paksu/**mm**/i/lle
			transl. paksu/**mma**/ksi	paksu/**mm**/i/ksi

Similarly, the comparative basic form selve/**mpi** 'clearer' declines as follows: selve/**mpä**/än (illative), selve/**mmä**/n (genitive), selve/**mm**/i/ssä (inessive plural), etc.

hyvä :
pare/mpi

The comparative forms of the adjectives *hyvä* 'good' and *pitkä* 'long' are exceptional: *hyvä : pare/mpi* 'better', and *pitkä : pite/mpi* 'longer'. *Pare/mpi* inflects e.g. pare/**mpa**/an (illative), pare/**mma**/ssa (inessive) and pare/**mm**/i/lla (adessive plural).

In context the comparative forms often co-occur with the word **kuin** 'than'; otherwise they behave like ordinary adjectives.

comparative
kuin X

Minun autoni on iso/**mpi** kuin sinun.
My car is *bigger* than yours.

Ostan iso/**mma**/n auton.
I'll buy a *bigger* car.

Ei iso/**mma**/lla autolla mitään tee!
One can't do anything with a *bigger* car!

Sinä olet nuore/**mpi** kuin minä.
You are *younger* than me.

Mutta minä taas olen vanhe/**mpi** kuin Lauri.
But on the other hand I am *older* than Lauri.

Suomessa on monta suure/**mpa**/a kaupunkia kuin Salo.
In Finland there are many *bigger* towns than Salo.

Uskomme *parempa/an* tulevaisuuteen.
We believe in a *better* future.

Näytät tervee/**mmä**/ltä kuin eilen.
You look *healthier* than yesterday.

Olenkin tervee/**mpi**!
I AM *healthier*!

Pitäisi elää tervee/**mpä**/ä elämää.
One ought to lead a *healthier* life.

Pekka hankki *paremma/n* asunnon.
Pekka got a *better* flat.

Etkö pysty hankkimaan *parempa/a* asuntoa?
Can't you get a *better* flat?

Kaupunki rakentaa *paremp/i/a* asuntoja.
The town is building *better* flats.

Appelsiinit ovat kallii/**mp**/i/a kuin omenat.
Oranges are *more expensive* than apples.

Keltaise/**mma**/t appelsiinit ovat kypse/**mp**/i/ä.
The *yellower* oranges are *riper*.

Ostan nuo keltaise/**mma**/t appelsiinit.
I'll buy those *yellower* oranges.

En osta noita vihreä/**mp**/i/ä appelsiineja.
I shan't buy those *greener* oranges.

Tämä on lue/tu/**mpi** kirja.
This book is *more read*.

The structure *kuin* + nominative can sometimes be replaced by a word in the partitive alone, placed before the comparative form. This structure is used mainly in the written language.

partitive Olet vanhe/**mpi** *kuin minä* = Olet minu/**a** vanhe/**mpi**.
You are *older* than me.

Tämä auto on kallii/**mpi** *kuin tuo* = Tämä auto on tuo/**ta** kallii/**mpi**.
This car is *more expensive* than that one.

§86. *SUPERLATIVE*

-in

NB:
consonant
gradation

NB:
vowel
changes

The superlative ending is **-in**; like the comparative ending, it is added to the inflectional stem, e.g. hullu 'mad' : hullu/**in** 'maddest'. Consonant gradation occurs before the superlative ending (§15.6), e.g. he**lpp**o 'easy' : he**lp**o/**in** 'easiest'.

Before the ending the vowel change rules also apply (§16): a long vowel shortens, short -**a**, -**ä** and -**e** are dropped, and -**i** and -**ii** change to -**e**.

Examples:

BASIC FORM		SUPERLATIVE	CF. INFLECTIONAL STEM §
paksu	thick	paksu/in	
iso	big	iso/in	
kiltti	good-natured	kilte/in	
vanha	old	vanh/in	
selvä	clear	selv/in	
kova	hard	kov/in	
jyrkkä	steep	jyrk/in	
tarkka	exact	tark/in	
nopea	fast	nope/in	
tärkeä	important	tärke/in	
matala	low	matal/in	
suuri	great	suur/in	18.3 (suure-)
pieni	small	pien/in	18.3 (piene-)
uusi	new	uus/in	18.4 (uute-)
tavallinen	usual	tavallis/in	20.1 (tavallise-)
punainen	red	punais/in	20.1 (punaise-)
kaunis	beautiful	kaune/in	20.3 (kaunii-)
raitis	sober	raitte/in	20.3 (raittii-)
vapaa	free	vapa/in	
vakaa	firm	vaka/in	
terve	healthy	terve/in	19 (tervee-)
tuore	fresh	tuore/in	19 (tuoree-)
puhdas	clean	puhta/in	20.3 (puhtaa-)
voimakas	powerful	voimakka/in	20.3 (voimakkaa-)
runsas	abundant	runsa/in	20.3 (runsaa-)
lyhyt	short	lyh(y)/in	20.8 (lyhye-)
ohut	thin	ohu/in	20.8 (ohue-)

The superlative forms also have an unusual declension, which partly resembles that of the comparative (§85). In the inflectional stem -**in** changes to -**impa**- ∿ -**impä**-, which after consonant gradation become -**imma**- ∿ -**immä**-. Before the plural -**i**- the final -**a** ∿ -**ä** is dropped.

SUPERLATIVE BASIC FORM			SINGULAR	PLURAL
paksu/**in**	thickest	illat.	paksu/**impa**/an	paksu/**imp**/i/in
		ess.	paksu/**impa**/na	paksu/**imp**/i/na
		part.	paksu/**impa**/a	paksu/**imp**/i/a
		gen.	paksu/**imma**/n	paksu/**imp**/i/en
		iness.	paksu/**imma**/ssa	paksu/**imm**/i/ssa
		elat.	paksu/**imma**/sta	paksu/**imm**/i/sta
		adess.	paksu/**imma**/lla	paksu/**imm**/i/lla
		ablat.	paksu/**imma**/lta	paksu/**imm**/i/lta
		allat.	paksu/**imma**/lle	paksu/**imm**/i/lle
		transl.	paksu/**imma**/ksi	paksu/**imm**/i/ksi

In the same way, the adjective *selvä* 'clear' has the superlative basic form selv/**in** 'clearest', and declines e.g. selv/**impä**/än (illative), selv/**immä**/stä (elative), selv/**imp**/i/in (illative plural) and selv/**imm**/i/llä (adessive plural).

The partitive singular is normally formed directly from the basic form, by adding the ending -**ta** ∿ -**tä**, e.g. paksu/**in**/ta, selv/**in**/tä, vanh/**in**/ta and voimakka/**in**/ta.

The superlatives of *hyvä* and *pitkä* are exceptional.

BASIC FORM	COMPARATIVE	SUPERLATIVE	
hyvä good	pare/**mpi** better	**paras** or	(gen. parhaa/n)
		parha/**in** best	(gen. parha/**imma**/n, illat. parha/**impa**/an, illat. pl. parha/**imp**/i/in)
pitkä long	pite/**mpi** longer	pis/**in** longest	(gen. pis/**immä**/n)

The partitive singular forms here are *paras/ta* or *parha/in/ta* and *pis/in/tä*, respectively.

In context the superlative forms function like adjectives.

Helsinki on Suomen suur/**in** kaupunki.	Helsinki is Finland's *biggest* town.
Oletko käynyt Suomen suur/**imma**/ssa kaupungissa?	Have you been to Finland's *biggest* town?
Helsinki on kehittynyt Suomen suur/**imma**/ksi kaupungiksi.	Helsinki has developed into Finland's *biggest* town.
Mikä on Suomen vanh/**in** kaupunki?	Which is Finland's *oldest* town?
Rauma kuuluu Suomen vanh/**imp**/i/in kaupunkeihin.	Rauma is one of Finland's *oldest* towns.
Asun kaupungin vanh/**imma**/ssa osassa.	I live in the *oldest* part of the town.
Aion muuttaa kaupungin vanh/**impa**/an osaan.	I'll move to the *oldest* part of the town.

Mitkä ovat kirjan vaike/**imma**/t luvut?
Which are the most difficult chapters of the book?

Viren oli kaikkein nope/**in**, Virtanen taas hita/**in**.
Viren was the *fastest* of all, and Virtanen the *slowest*.

Kuka pojista on *pisin*?
Which of the boys is the *tallest*?

Suomi on yksi maailman pohjois/**imm**/i/sta maista.
Finland is one of the *northernmost* countries in the world.

Note partitive plural! Suomi on maailman pohjois/**imp**/i/a maita.
Finland is one of the *northernmost* countries in the world.

Viren on Suomen nope/**imp**/i/a juoksijoita.
Viren is one of Finland's *fastest* runners.

Annan *parhaa/n (parhaimma/n)* palan sinulle.
I'll give the *best* bit to you.

Liha maistuu *parhaa/lta (parhaimma/lta)* paistettuna.
Meat tastes *best* when it is roasted.

Kalle on *parha/i/ta* ystäviäni.
Kalle is one of my *best* friends.

On halv/**in**/ta syödä puuroa.
It is *cheapest* to eat porridge.

Ostan halv/**imma**/t kengät.
I'll buy the *cheapest* shoes.

Onko Juhannustanssit Suomen luetu/**in** kirja?
Is Midsummer Dance the *most read* book in Finland?

Yrjö Muttinen on Suomen pidety/**imp**/i/ä näyttelijöitä.
Yrjö Muttinen is one of Finland's *most popular* actors.

The structure for the absolute superlative (meaning 'most X' or 'very X') is *mitä* + superlative, eg. *mitä* hullu/*in* 'very mad'.

absolute superlative

Ehdotus on *mitä parhain*.
The proposal is *extremely good*.

Näytät *mitä* terve/**immä**/ltä.
You look *most healthy*.

Hän teki *mitä* syv/**immä**/n vaikutuksen kuulijoihin.
He/she exerted a *most profound* impression on the listeners.

20 Other Word-classes

Adverbs
Prepositions
Postpositions
Conjunctions
Particles

§87. *ADVERBS*

-sti

NB:
consonant
gradation

The most common type of adverb expresses *manner*, and is formed by adding the ending -sti to the inflectional stem of an adjective, e.g. hauska 'nice' : hauska/sti 'nicely'. This ending causes consonant gradation, e.g. helppo 'easy' : helpo/sti 'easily' (§15.6).

BASIC FORM	ADVERB IN -sti	
paksu	paksu/sti	thickly
kiltti	kilti/sti	good-naturedly
nopea	nopea/sti	fast
suuri	suure/sti	greatly
tavallinen	tavallise/sti	usually
kaunis	kaunii/sti	beautifully
puhdas	puhtaa/sti	purely
voimakas	voimakkaa/sti	powerfully

Jussi laulaa kaunii/**sti**.	Jussi sings *beautifully*.
Panen runsaa/**sti** voita leivän päälle.	I put *plenty of* (*"abundantly"*) butter on the bread.
Puhukaa aivan vapaa/**sti**!	Speak quite *freely*!
Nyt täytyy puhua lyhye/**sti**.	Now one must speak *briefly*.
Tavallise/**sti** menen sänkyyn klo 23.	*Usually* I go to bed at 11 o'clock.
Teen työtä tehokkaa/**sti**.	I work *efficiently*.
En pidä tästä erityise/**sti**.	I don't *particularly* like this.

The corresponding comparative and superlative forms are derived by changing the endings -mpi and -in to -mmin (comparative) and -immin (superlative).

ADJECTIVE BASIC FORM		COMPARATIVE ADJECTIVE BASIC FORM	SUPERLATIVE ADJECTIVE BASIC FORM	COMPARATIVE ADVERB IN -mmin	SUPERLATIVE ADVERB IN -immin
helppo	easy	helpo/mpi	helpo/in	helpo/mmin	helpo/immin
selvä	clear	selve/mpi	selv/in	selve/mmin	selv/immin
kova	hard	kove/mpi	kov/in	kove/mmin	kov/immin
matala	low	matala/mpi	matal/in	matala/mmin	matal/immin
tarkka	exact	tarke/mpi	tark/in	tarke/mmin	tark/immin
suuri	great	suure/mpi	suur/in	suure/mmin	suur/immin
tavallinen	usual	tavallise/mpi	tavallis/in	tavallise/mmin	tavallis/immin
kaunis	beautiful	kaunii/mpi	kaune/in	kaunii/mmin	kaune/immin
puhdas	clean	puhtaa/mpi	puhta/in	puhtaa/mmin	puhta/immin
runsas	abundant	runsaa/mpi	runsa/in	runsaa/mmin	runsa/immin
terve	healthy	tervee/mpi	terve/in	tervee/mmin	terve/immin

Yrjö juoksee nopea/**mmin** kuin Lauri.	Yrjö runs *faster* than Lauri.
Aja hitaa/**mmin**!	Drive *more slowly*!
Tuo mies ajaa kaikkein hita/**immin**.	That man drives *the slowest* of all.
Yritä opiskella ahkera/**mmin**.	Try to study *more diligently*.
Bill ääntää selv/**immin**.	Bill pronounces *the most clearly*.
Tavallis/**immin** herään klo 7.	*Most commonly* I wake at 7 o'clock.
Elä tervee/**mmin**!	Live *more healthily*!
Siellä oli runsaa/**mmin** ihmisiä kuin oli odotettu.	There were *more* people there than had been expected.
Kyllä Tyyne laulaa kaune/**immin**, ainakin kaunii/**mmin** kuin Aune.	Tyyne certainly sings *the most beautifully*, at least *more beautifully* than Aune.

paljon The comparative and superlative of *paljon* 'much, many' are exceptional: *enemmän* 'more' and *eniten* 'most'.

Another common group of adverbs is those expressing *place,* such as *alas* 'down', *pois* 'away'. These adverbs often inflect in the three external locative cases (§40) in accordance with the direction of the action of the verb.

place

alas	down
alhaa/lla, -lta, -lle	down, below
ede/ssä, -stä, eteen	in front, before
kaikkia/lla, -lta, -lle	everywhere
kaukana, kaukaa, kauas	far
kotona, kotoa, kotiin	at home
oikea/lla, -lta, -lle	on the right
poissa, pois	away
sie/llä, -ltä, sinne	there (unspecified place)
tuo/lla, -lta, -nne	there (place pointed to)
tää/llä, -ltä, tänne	here
ulkona, ulkoa, ulos	outside
vasemma/lla, -lta, -lle	on the left
ylös	up

Many common adverbs indicate *time*.

time

aikaisin	early	joskus	sometimes
aina	always	kauan	for a long time
eilen	yesterday	kerran	once
ennen	before	kohta	soon
harvoin	rarely	myöhään	late
heti	immediately	nyt	now
huomenna	tomorrow	silloin	then, at that time
		sitten	then, after that
		tänään	today
		usein	often

Another major group are those of *degree, measure* or *quantity*.

degree, measure, quantity

aika	quite, rather	kovin	very
aivan	quite, completely	kyllin	enough
erittäin	extremely	liian	too
hieman	slightly	melko	quite, considerably
hiukan	a little	niin	so
		varsin	exceedingly, quite

185

In addition to those mentioned above there are also other adverbs of *manner*.

manner	hiljaa	quiet(ly)	näin	in this way
	hyvin	well	oikein	right
	ilmaiseksi	free of charge	samoin	in the same way
	itsestään	of itself	siten	in that way
	mielellään	with pleasure	yksin	alone

Also important are the *modal* adverbs, which indicate in a variety of subjective ways the speaker's attitude to what he is saying.

modal	ainakin	at least	muun muassa	among other things
adverbs	ehkä	perhaps	myös	also
	jopa	even	päinvastoin	on the contrary
	juuri	just	tietenkin	of course
	kai	probably	tietysti	of course
	kenties	perhaps	tosin	to be sure
	kyllä	certainly, indeed; yes	tosiaan	really
	mieluummin	rather	vain	only

§88. *PREPOSITIONS*

Prepositions and postpositions (§89) take either the genitive or the partitive. There are many more postpositions than prepositions in Finnish.

Prepositions precede the words whose case they determine, e.g. *ilman* 'without' (*ilman* raha/a 'without money'). The following prepositions take the partitive:

preposi-tion +partitive	ennen	before	lähe/llä, -ltä, -lle	near
	ilman	without	paitsi	besides; except
	keske/llä, -ltä, -lle	in the middle of	pitkin	along
	kohti	towards	päin	towards
			vasten	against

Ennen tois/**ta** maailmansota/**a**.   *Before* the second world war.
Oletko *ilman* raha/**a**?   Don't you have any money? ("Are you *without* money?")

Koira makaa *keskellä* lattia/**a**.   The dog lies *in the middle of* the floor.
Ajan *kohti* Kuopio/**ta**.   I drive *towards* Kuopio.
Paitsi viini/**ä** tarvitsemme oluttakin.   *Besides* wine we need beer, too.
Varas juoksi *pitkin* Eerikinkatu/**a**.   The thief ran *along* Erik's Street.
Kaikki menee *päin* helvetti/**ä**.   Everything is going bloody badly ("*to* hell").

Nojasin *vasten* seinä/**ä**.   I leaned *against* the wall.
Olen *ilman* työ/**tä**.   I have no job. ("I am *without* a job.")

The following prepositions take the genitive; there are not many of these.

preposition + genitive	alle	under (not in locative sense)	läpi	through (temporal)
	halki	through	sitten	since
	kautta	throughout		
	kesken	in the middle of (temporal sense)		

Mies painaa *alle* sada/**n** kilon.

The man weighs *under* 100 kilos.

Kuljen *halki* metsä/**n**.

I walk *through* the wood.

Hänet tunnetaan *kautta* maa/**n**.

He/she is known *throughout* the country.

Kesken tunni/**n** Pekka lähti ulos.

In the middle of the lesson Pekka went out.

Läpi vuotisato/j/**en**.

Through the centuries.

Sitten viime syksy/**n** en ole käynyt ulkomailla.

Since last autumn I have not been abroad.

§89. *POSTPOSITIONS*

Postpositions occur *after* the words whose case they determine, e.g. *yli* 'over, across' (kadu/**n** *yli* 'across the street'). Postpositions taking the **genitive** are very common, and the most important ones are given in the list below. Some of them inflect in three local cases.

post-position + genitive	aikana	during
	a/lla, -lta, -lle	under (place)
	alitse	below
	ansiosta	thanks to
	ede/llä, -ltä, -lle	in front of
	ede/ssä, -stä, eteen	in front of
	eduksi	to the advantage of
	halki	through
	hallu/ssa, -sta, haltuun	in the possession of
	hyväksi	for (the benefit of)
	johdosta	because of
	jäljessä	after, behind
	jälkeen	after, behind
	kanssa	with
	kautta	by means of, via
	kesken	between, among
	keskellä	in the middle of
	keskuude/ssa, -sta, keskuuteen	among
	kohda/lla, -lta, -lle	at, at the point of
	luona	near; at the house of
	luota	from
	luo(kse/en)	to
	lähe/llä, -ltä, -lle	near
	läpi	through
	lävitse	through
	mielestä	in the opinion of
	mukana	with
	mukaan	according to
	ohi	past
	ohitse	past

osalta	as regards
perusteella	on the basis of
perässä	behind, after
poikki	across
puole/lla, -lta, -lle	on the side of
puolesta	on behalf of
pää/llä, -ltä, -lle	on (top of)
päässä	at a distance of
rinnalla	at the side of
sisällä	in, inside
sisään	in, into
taakse	behind (direction towards)
takaa	from behind
takana	behind, at the back of
takia	for the sake of, because of
tähden	for the sake of, because of
viere/ssä, -stä, -en	beside
viere/llä, -ltä,-lle	beside
vuoksi	for the sake of, because of
yli	over, across
ylitse	over, across
ympäri, -llä, -lle	around

Note local cases!	Soda/**n** *aikana* Ryti oli presidenttinä.	*During* the war Ryti was president.
	Koira on pöydä/**n** *alla*.	The dog is *under* the table.
	Koira ryömi pöydä/**n** *alle*.	The dog crawled *under* the table.
	Tule esiin pöydä/**n** *alta*!	Come out *from under* the table!
Note possessive suffixes!	Sinu/**n** *ansiosta/***si** olen nyt täällä.	*Thanks to* you I am here now.
	Talo/**n** *edessä* on koivu.	*In front of* the house is a birch tree.
	Pysäytän auton talo/**n** *eteen*.	I will park the car *in front of* the house.
	Ajammeko kaupungi/**n** *halki*?	Shall we drive *through* the town?
	Auto on Peka/**n** *hallussa*.	The car is *in* Pekka's *possession*.
	Auto joutui Peka/**n** *haltuun*.	The car fell *into* Pekka's *possession*.
	Auto on (minu/**n**) *hallussa/***ni**.	The car is *in* my *possession*.
	Tee jotain Chile/**n** *hyväksi*.	Do something *for* Chile.
	Se/**n** *johdosta*, että...	*Because of* the fact that...
	Tunni/**n** *jälkeen* menen kapakkaan.	*After* the lesson I'm going to the pub.
	Menen tanssimaan Tuula/**n** *kanssa*.	I'm going dancing *with* Tuula.
	Tuletko tanssimaan (minu/**n**) *kanssa/***ni**?	Will you come dancing *with* me?
	Salo/**n** *kautta* pääsee Hankoon.	*Via* Salo one gets to Hanko.
	Näin meidä/**n** *kesken*...	Just *between* ourselves...
	Tori on kaupungi/**n** *keskellä*.	The market-place is *in the centre of* the town.
	Ruotsalais/**ten** *keskuudessa* ollaan sitä mieltä, että...	*Among* the Swedes there is (''one is of'') the opinion that...
	Pekka on Tuula/**n** *luona*.	Pekka is *at* Tuula's.
	Seija on meidä/**n** *luona/***mme**.	Seija is *at* our *place*.
	Tulen Elisa/**n** *luota*.	I'm coming *from* Elisa's.
	Lähdetkö Merja/**n** *luokse*?	Are you going *to* Merja's?
	Naantali on Turu/**n** *lähellä*.	Naantali is *near* Turku.
	Aion muuttaa Salo/**n** *lähelle*.	I intend to move *near* Salo.
	Aurinko paistaa ikkuna/**n** *läpi*.	The sun shines *through* the window.
	Kalle/**n** *mielestä* tämä ei kannata.	*In* Kalle's *opinion* this is not worth it.
	Ukkose/**n** *mukana* tuli sadetta.	*With* the thunder came rain.
	Menen poik/i/**en** *mukaan*.	I'm going *with* the boys.
	Ajoimme kaupa/**n** *ohi*.	We drove *past* the shop.
	Tämä/**n** asia/**n** *osalta* olen eri mieltä.	*As regards* this matter I am of a different opinion.

Sanotu/n *perusteella* väitän, että...	*On the basis of* what has been said I claim that...
Koira juoksi tie/n *poikki*.	The dog ran *across* the road.
Kene/n *puolella* sinä olet?	Whose *side* are you *on*?
Taistelemme isänmaa/n *puolesta*.	We are fighting *for* the fatherland.
Kukkulo/i/**den** *päällä* kasvoi metsää.	*On top of* the hills there were woods ("there grew forest").
Kilometri/n *päässä* on kioski.	A kilometre *away* there is a kiosk.
Talo/n *sisällä* oli lämmintä.	*Inside* the house it was warm.
Lapsi menee ove/n *taakse*.	The child goes *behind* the door.
Lapsi on ove/n *takana*.	The child is *behind* the door.
Lapsi tuli esille ove/n *takaa*.	The child came out *from behind* the door.
Häne/n *takia/an* teen mitä vain.	*For* his/her *sake* I will do anything.
Kirjasto on yliopisto/n *vieressä*.	The library is *next to* the university.
Saanko istua neidi/n *viereen*?	May I sit *next to* you, miss? ("next to miss")
Tällaise/n asia/n *vuoksi* ei pidä riidellä.	One should not quarrel *because of* this sort of thing.
Nyt mennään kadu/n *yli*.	Now let's go *across* the street.
Talo/j/**en** *ympärillä* oli metsää.	*Around* the houses there was forest.
Hän oli purjehtinut maailma/n *ympäri*.	He/she had sailed *round* the world.

When a postposition occurs with a personal pronoun in the genitive a possessive suffix must be added to the postposition, but 1st and 2nd person pronouns themselves may be omitted (§36).

NB: pronoun + possessive suffix!		
	(*minu/n*) kanssa/**ni**	with me
	(*sinu/n*) kanssa/**si**	with you
	(*häne/n* kanssa/**an**	with him/her
	(*me/i/dän*) kanssa/**mme**	with us etc.

The most common postpositions taking the *partitive* are the following:

post-position + partitive				
	alas	down	päin	towards
	kohtaan	towards, to (abstract)	varten	for
	kohti	towards, to (concrete)	vastaan	against
	myöten	along	vastapäätä	opposite
	pitkin	along	ylös	up

Johtaja on hyvin ystävällinen minu/a *kohtaan*.	The manager is very friendly *to* me.
Nyt lähdetään Turku/a *kohti*.	Now let's go *towards* Turku.
Hän kävelee katu/j/a *myöten* ~ *pitkin*.	He walks *along* the streets.
Sinu/a *vartenhan* se hankittiin.	It was *for* you that it was got.
Leena tuli minu/a *vastaan* rautatieasemalle.	Leena came *to meet* me at the railway station ("*against* me").
Onko joku sinu/a *vastassa*?	Is there anyone *meeting* you?
Kirkko/a *vastapäätä* on Elanto.	*Opposite* the church is the Elanto shop.
Nyt täytyy kävellä mäke/ä *ylös*.	Now we have to walk *up* the hill.

The postpositions *asti* 'until, as far as' and *päin* 'towards' take the *illative*.

post- position + illative	Opetus jatkuu ilta/**an** *asti*.	The teaching continues *until* the evening.
	Juna kulkee Helsinki/**in** *päin*.	The train is going *towards* Helsinki.

§90. *CONJUNCTIONS*

Conjunctions are words that link sentences and parts of sentences together, such as **ja** 'and', **kun** 'when'. A list of the most common conjunctions follows below; the most common of all are marked with a plus sign. Some are combinations of a conjunction and the negation verb, e.g. **etten** = *että en*, **ettet** = *että et*, **ettei** = *että ei*, and so on: i.e. they inflect for person.

ei — eikä (en — enkä etc.)	neither — nor (inflects for person)
eli	or, i.e.
ellei (ellen etc.)	if not, unless (inflects for person)
ennen kuin	before
ettei (etten etc.)	that... not (inflects for person)
+ **että**	that
ikään kuin	as though
+ **ja**	and
joko — tai	either — or
jollei (jollen etc.)	if not, unless (inflects for person)
+ **jos**	if
joskin	even if, even though
jotta	in order that, so that
+ **koska**	because, since
+ **kuin**	than
+ **kun**	when, as
kunnes	until
kuten	as, like
mikäli	as far as, in so far as; if
+ **mutta**	but
muttei (mutten etc.)	but... not (inflects for person)
+ **niin**	so
niin että	so that
niin kuin	as, like
niin — kuin -kin	both — and
niin pian kuin	as soon as
nimittäin	namely, you see
näet	namely, you see
paitsi	except, besides
paitsi — myös	not only — but also
samoin kuin	in the same way as
sekä	and
+ **sekä — että**	both — and
sen tähden että	because
+ **sillä**	for, because
+ **tai (~ taikka)**	or (not in questions, cf. **vai**)
toisin kuin	otherwise than
+ **vaan**	but (after a negative)
+ **vai**	or (in questions)
+ **vaikka**	although

Pentti **ja** Pirkko ovat naimisissa.
Ei Pentti **eikä** Pirkko ole tullut vielä.

Pentti *and* Pirkko are married.
Neither Pentti *nor* Pirkko have come yet.

Ellet ole hiljaa, menen ulos.
Ellemme yritä, emme onnistu.
Ellei sää parane, jäämmc kotiin.

Unless you are quiet I shall go out.
If we do *not* try we shall not succeed.
Unless the weather improves we shall stay at home.

Eniten **eli** 450 kappaletta myytiin autoja.
Kesti pitkään **ennen kuin** nukahdin.
Ei kestänyt kauan **ennen kuin** sää kirkastui.
Huomaan, **että** kello on neljä.
Tiedän, **että** Pirkko on täällä.
Väitätkö, **ettei** kello ole neljä?

Väitätkö, **että** kello **ei** ole neljä?

Väitätkö, **etten** tiedä tätä?

Väitätkö, **että en** tiedä tätä?

The highest sales, *viz.* 450 units, were of cars.
It took a long time *before* I fell asleep.
It didn't take long *before* the weather brightened up.
I notice *that* it is 4 o'clock.
I know *that* Pirkko is here.
Are you claiming *that* it is *not* 4 o'clock?
Are you claiming *that* it is *not* 4 o'clock?
Are you claiming *that* I *don't* know this?
Are you claiming *that* I *don't* know this?

Kalle on pitkä **ja** komea.
Matkustan **joko** junalla **tai** autolla.
En matkusta autolla **enkä** junalla.
Tulen **jos** voin.
Tulen, **joskin** saatan myöhästyä hiukan.
Hölkkään **jotta** kunto paranisi.

Kalle is tall *and* handsome.
I travel *either* by train *or* by car.
I travel *neither* by car *nor* by train.
I'll come *if* I can.
I'll come, *although* I might be a bit late.
I go jogging *in order to* get into better condition.

En tule, **koska** olen sairastunut.

I'm not coming, *because* I have fallen ill.

Tulen, **kun** olen terve.
Odotan, **kunnes** hän tulee.
Kuten olen sanonut monta kertaa...
Mikäli Yrjö tulee, lähden kotiin.
Teuvo on pitempi **kuin** minä.
Teuvo on pitkä **mutta** laiha.
Mutta sinähän sanoit, että...
Tulen, **mutten** viivy kauan.
Jos et tule, **niin** rupean itkemään.

I'll come *when* I'm healthy.
I will wait *until* he/she comes.
As I have said many times...
If Yrjö comes I'm going home.
Teuvo is taller *than* me.
Teuvo is tall *but* thin.
But you did say that...
I'll come, *but* I *won't* stay long.
If you don't come, *then* (*"so"*) I shall start crying.

Niin Karjalainen **kuin** Virolainen/**kin** pyrkivät presidentiksi.
Viren on **sekä** nopea **että** kestävä.

Both Karjalainen *and* Virolainen are seeking to become president.
Viren is *not only* fast *but also* has stamina.

Tulen, **sillä** en halua olla yksin kotona.
Otan viiniä **tai** olutta.
Otatko viiniä **vai** olutta?
Otamme **joko** viiniä **tai** vichyä.
Tulen, **vaikka** olen sairas.
En tule, **vaan** jään kotiin nukkumaan.

I'll come, *because* I don't want to be alone at home.
I'll take wine *or* beer.
Will you take wine *or* beer?
We'll take *either* wine *or* Vichy water.
I'll come, *although* I am ill.
I'm not coming, (*but*) I'll stay at home to sleep.

§91. PARTICLES

There are five common enclitic particles: -ko ∼ -kö, -kin, -kaan ∼ -kään, -han ∼ -hän and -pa ∼ -pä. Less common ones are -ka ∼ -kä and -s. As has been said above, enclitic particles always occur last in the word, see the diagrams in sections 12—14.

-ko ∼ -kö

The ending -ko ∼ -kö is used to form direct questions. See §30.1 and the examples below.

Tule/t/**ko**?	*Are* you *coming*?
Et/**kö** tule?	*Aren't* you coming?
Auto/lla/**ko** tulet?	Are you coming *by car*?
Kemi/in/**kö** menet?	Are you going *to Kemi*?
Sa/isi/n/**ko** sipulipihvin?	*Could I have* a steak with onions?
Muutta/isi/t/**ko** Ruotsiin jos voisit?	*Would you move* to Sweden if you could?
Men/nä/än/**kö** ulos?	*Shall we go* out?
Sinä/**kö** sen teit?	Was it *you* who did it?
Jo/**ko** olet korjannut autosi?	Have you repaired your car *already*?

-kin

-kin indicates stress and is often equivalent to 'also' or 'too'. The following examples illustrate its use with nouns:

Olen hankkinut auto/n/**kin**.	I have got *a car, too*.
Minä/**kin** olen hankkinut auton.	*I, too*, have got a car.
Oli hauskaa, että sinä/**kin** tulit.	It was nice that *you* came *too*.
Juotko kahvi/a/**kin**?	Do you drink *coffee as well*?
Olen ollut Espanja/ssa/**kin**.	I have been *to Spain, too*.

-kin is also used with verbs, and then it is difficult to say precisely what meaning it has. It may for instance indicate that some expectation has been fulfilled, or mark a sense of surprise, or strengthen an exclamation.

Odotin häntä ja hän tul/i/**kin**.	I waited for him and he *really did come.*
Olen ollut ui/ma/ssa/**kin**.	I've been *swimming, too*.
Eikö hän ole/**kin** ihana!	*Isn't* he wonderful!
Kalle on/**kin** täällä.	Kalle *is in fact* here.
Etkö lupaa/**kin** apuasi!	*Surely you will promise* your help, *won't you*?
Men/i/n/**kin** kotiin.	I *did go* home.

-kaan ∼ -kään

The particle -kaan ∼ -kään generally corresponds to -kin in negative sentences.

En ole hankkinut auto/a/**kaan**.	I haven't got *a car, either*.
Minä/**kään** en ole hankkinut autoa.	*Neither* have *I* got a car.
Etkö juo kahvi/a/**kaan**?	*Don't/won't* you drink *coffee, either*?
En ole ollut Espanja/ssa/**kaan**.	I *haven't* been to Spain, *either*.
Odotin häntä, mutta hän ei tul/lut/**kaan**.	I waited for him but he *didn't come.*
Kalle ei ole/**kaan** täällä.	Kalle *is not* here, *after all*.
Etkö lupaa/**kaan** apuasi?	*Won't you promise* your help *after all*?

-han ∼ -hän | **-han ∼ -hän** generally indicates that the sentence expresses something that is familiar or known. It may also be used simply to stress the speaker's message. It can only be added to the first element of the sentence.

Tämä/**hän** on skandaali!   *This really* is a scandal!
Ruotsi/**han** on kuningaskunta.   *As we know, Sweden* is a monarchy.
Minä/**hän** rakastan sinua.   I LOVE you!
Rakasta/n/**han** minä sinua.   *Of course* I *love* you.
Sinu/a/**han** minä rakastan.   *You are the one* I love.
Huomenna/**han** lähdemme lomalle.   *Tomorrow* we're going on holiday, *aren't we*?

Viime sunnuntai/na/**han** Kalle syntyi.   *It was last Sunday that* Kalle was born.

Ole/n/**han** minä käynyt Neuvosto-   *Of course*, I've been to the Soviet
liitossakin.   Union as well.

-han ∼ -hän is also used in questions to make them more polite, and to soften commands.

On/ko/**han** Pentti kotona?   *I wonder if* Pentti is at home?
Paljon/ko/**han** pieni kahvi maksaa?   How much *might* a small coffee cost?
Sa/isi/n/ko/**han** laskun?   *Could* I have the bill, *please*?
Ota/**han** vähän lisää!   *Please take* a little more!
Astu/kaa/**han** sisään!   *Please come* in!
Ole/**han** hiljaa!   *Please be* quiet, *will you*?
Vie/**hän** astiat keittiöön!   *Take* the dishes into the kitchen, *could you*?

The particle **-pa ∼ -pä** indicates stress. In the spoken language it is often followed by -s.

On/**pa** hän pitkä!   He *really is* tall!
Kyllä/**pä** sinä olet ahkera!   You *ARE* hard-working, *aren't you*?
Anna/**pa** minullekin vähän kahvia!   *Give* me a little coffee too!
En/**pä** anna!   *No* I won't (''give'')!
On/**pa**(s) täällä kuuma!   It *really is* hot here!
Tuo/ssa/**pa** on iso joukko!   *There's* a *really* big group!

-ka ∼ -kä | The ending **-ka ∼ -kä** is fairly rare. It is mainly used with the negation verb to indicate stress.

En tiedä en/**kä** halua tietää.   I don't know, *and I don't* want to know *either*.

Mormonit eivät käytä kahvia eivät/**kä**   The Mormons don't drink coffee, *nor*
myöskään alkoholia.   alcohol *either*.

Älä heitä paperia älä/**kä** sylje lattialle.   Don't throw paper about *and don't* spit on the floor.

More than one particle may ocasionally be attached to the same word.

several particles | On/**ko**/**han** Sylvi kotona?   *I wonder if* Sylvi is at home?
On/**pa**/**han** täällä kuuma!   It *really is* hot here, *isn't it*!
Tule/**pa**/**han** vähän lähemmäs!   *Come* a bit closer, *will you*?
Geneveriä/**kin**/**kö** vielä otat?   Will you *really* have some more geneva *as well*?

Mene/**pä**/**s** vähän sivummalle!   *Move* over a bit, *will you*?

193

21 Word-formation

General
Derivation
Compounding

§92. GENERAL

derivative suffixes

There are two ways of forming new words from existing words and stems: derivation and compounding. In derivation, new words (word-stems) are made by adding derivative endings or suffixes to the root or to another stem. To the adjective *kaunis* : *kaunii-* 'beautiful', for instance, we can add the ending -**ta** to form the derived verb-stem *kaunis/ta-* 'beautify' (1st infinitive *kaunis/ta/a*). In the same way we can take the verb-stem *aja-* 'drive', and add the ending -*o* to form the derived noun *aj/o* 'drive, chase, hunt', or the ending -**ele**- to form the verb-stem *aj/ele-* 'drive around' (1st infinitive *aj/el/la*).

Derivative suffixes occur immediately after the root but before the inflectional endings, i.e. before number and case endings in nominals, before passive, tense, mood and personal endings in finite verb-forms, and before the infinitive and participle endings in non-finite verb-forms. (See the diagrams in chapter 3.)

Derived nominals and verbs inflect just like non-derived ones. Derived words are subject to the same sound alternations as other words, in particular consonant gradation (§15) and the vowel changes (§16).

Adding derivative suffixes may cause sound alternations in the root: e.g. **kaunii**- : **kaune/us** and aja- : aj/**ele**-. In what follows these alternations will be evident from the examples, and separate rules will not be given. There may also be alternations in the derivative suffixes themselves when further suffixes are added.

chains of suffixes

It is characteristic of Finnish that a given word-form may contain many derivative suffixes, one after the other. Below are some examples. The (non-derived) root is given on the left, the derived word in the middle, and the "basic" or full forms of the derivative suffixes on the right.

STEM	DERIVED WORD		DERIVATIVE SUFFIXES (BASIC FORMS)
aja-	aj/ele/minen	driving about	ele-minen
asee-	asee/llis/ta-	arm (verb)	llinen-ta
asee-	asee/llis/ta/minen	arming (noun)	llinen-ta-minen
aja-	aj/ele/hti-	drift	ele-hti
aja-	aj/ele/hti/va	drifting (adj)	ele-hti-va
lika-	lika/is/uus	dirtiness	inen-uus
koti-	kodi/ttom/uus	homelessness	ton(ttoma)-uus
kuole-	kuole/ma/ttom/uus	immortality	ma-ton(ttoma)-uus
etsi-	etsi/skel/y	search (noun)	skele-y
haukkaa-	hauka/hd/us	yelp (noun)	hta-us
haukkaa-	hauka/ht/el/u	yelping (noun)	hta-ele-u
asu-	asu/nno/ttom/uus	without a house	nto-ton(ttoma)-uus
tuo-	tuo/tta/ma/ttom/uus	unproductiveness	tta-ma-ton(ttoma)-uus

194

Not all derivative suffixes are equally productive. Some are extremely productive, which means they can be added to practically all roots (of a given type). Examples are the suffixes **-ja ~ -jä** 'agent', **-minen** 'verbal noun' and **-ma/ton ~ -mä/tön** 'not', cf. *aja/ja* 'driver', *aja/minen* 'driving', *aja/ma/ton* 'undriven'; *tuli/ja* 'comer', *tule/minen* 'coming', *tule/ma/ton* 'not coming, not come'; *meni/jä* 'goer', *mene/minen* 'going', *mene/mä/tön* 'not going, not gone', etc.

Other suffixes occur primarily or exclusively with certain roots, and are thus more or less unproductive.

§93. DERIVATION

§93.1. Nominal suffixes

Part A of this section deals with denominal suffixes forming new nominals, and part B deals with deverbal suffixes forming new nominals.

-hko ~ -hkö (adjective, indicates 'somewhat')

ROOT (nom.)		DERIVED WORD	
kylmä	cold	kylmähkö	rather cold
kova	hard	kovahko	fairly hard
pieni	small	pienehkö (§18.3)	rather small
iloinen	glad	iloisehko (§20.1)	fairly glad

-inen (adjective)

aika	time	aikainen	early
hiki	sweat	hikinen	sweaty
jää	ice	jäinen	icy
lika	dirt	likainen	dirty
luu	bone	luinen	of bone
puu	wood	puinen	wooden

-isa ~ -isä (adjective)

kala	fish	kalaisa	abounding in fish
leikki	play	leikkisä	playful
raivo	fury	raivoisa	furious

-kko ~ -kkö (collective noun)

aalto	wave	aallokko	the waves, swell
koivu	birch	koivikko	birch grove
kuusi	spruce	kuusikko	spruce grove
pensas	bush	pensaikko	thicket, shrubbery

195

-la ~ -lä (noun, indicates location)

kahvi	coffee	kahvila	café
kylpy	bath	kylpylä	baths
neuvo	advice	neuvola	child health centre
pappi	clergeman, vicar	pappila	vicarage
ravinto	food	ravintola	restaurant
sairas	ill	sairaala	hospital

-lainen ~ -läinen (noun, or noun and adjective, indicates a person)

NB:	apu	help	apulainen	assistant
common!	pako	flight	pakolainen	refugee
	koulu	school	koululainen	schoolchild
cf. §20.1	kansa	people	kansalainen	citizen
	suku	family	sukulainen	relative
	työ	work	työläinen	worker
	kaupunki	town	kaupunkilainen	town-dweller
	Turku	Turku	turkulainen	resident of Turku
	Helsinki	Helsinki	helsinkiläinen	resident of Helsinki
	Ruotsi	Sweden	ruotsalainen	Swede, Swedish
	Suomi	Finland	suomalainen	Finn, Finnish
	Saksa	Germany	saksalainen	German
	Norja	Norway	norjalainen	Norwegian

-lainen ~ -läinen (adjective)

cf. §20.1	eri	separate	erilainen	different
	kaikki	all, everything	kaikenlainen	all kinds of
	tuo	that	tuollainen	that kind of
	tämä	this	tällainen	this kind of
	heikko	weak	heikonlainen	rather weak
	suuri	great	suurenlainen	rather great

-llinen (adjective)

NB:	ase	weapon	aseellinen	armed
common!	hetki	moment	hetkellinen	momentary
	yö	night	yöllinen	nocturnal
cf. §20.1	onni	happiness	onnellinen	happy
	perhe	family	perheellinen	with a family
	isä	father	isällinen	fatherly
	kieli	language	kielellinen	linguistic
	kunta	commune, local council	kunnallinen	municipal, communal
	nainen	woman	naisellinen	womanly, feminine

-mainen ~ -mäinen (adjective)

cf. §20.1	poika	boy	poikamainen	boyish
	tyttö	girl	tyttömäinen	girlish
	ukko	old man	ukkomainen	senile
	sika	pig	sikamainen	swinish, beastly

-nainen ~ -näinen (adjective)

cf. §20.1	koko	whole	kokonainen	whole, total
	eri	separate	erinäinen	particular, certain
	itse	self	itsenäinen	independent
	moni	many	moninainen	various

-nen (diminutive noun)

cf. §20.1	kala	fish	kalanen	little fish
	kirja	book	kirjanen	booklet
	poika	boy	poikanen	little boy; offspring
	kukka	flower	kukkanen	little flower

-sto ~ -stö (collective noun)

lähe-	near	lähistö	neighbourhood
saari	island	saaristo	archipelago
enempi	more	enemmistö	majority
vähempi	less	vähemmistö	minority
elin	organ	elimistö	organism
kasvi	plant	kasvisto	flora
maa	earth, country, land	maasto	terrain
laiva	ship	laivasto	fleet

-tar ~ -tär (feminine noun)

kuningas	king	kuningatar	queen
Pariisi	Paris	pariisitar	Parisian woman
laulaja	singer	laulajatar	female singer
myyjä	salesman	myyjätär	saleswoman

-ton ~ -tön (adjective, indicating 'without')

cf. §20.6	koti	home	koditon	homeless
	nimi	name	nimetön	nameless
	onni	happiness	onneton	unhappy
	työ	work	työtön	unemployed
	lapsi	child	lapseton	childless
	tunne	feeling	tunteeton	unfeeling

-(u)us ~ -(y)ys (abstract noun)

NB: common!	heikko	weak	heikkous	weakness
	vahva	strong	vahvuus	strength
	terve	healthy	terveys	health
cf. §20.4	suuri	great	suuruus	greatness
	korkea	high	korkeus	height
	kaunis	beautiful	kauneus	beauty
	isä	father	isyys	fatherhood, paternity
	nuori	young	nuoruus	youth
	ystävä	friend	ystävyys	friendship
	yksinäinen	lonely	yksinäisyys	loneliness
	syytön	innocent	syyttömyys	innocence
	varovainen	cautious	varovaisuus	caution
	lihava	fat	lihavuus	corpulence

***

197

(B)
verb-to-nominal suffixes

cf. §19

-e (noun)

1ST INFINITIVE		DERIVED WORD	
loista/a	shine	loiste	lustre
katso/a	look	katse	look
kasta/a	wet, dip	kaste	dew
puhu/a	speak	puhe	speech
sata/a	rain	sade	rain
toivo/a	hope	toive	hope, wish, expectation

-i (noun)

syöttä/ä	feed	syötti	bait
kasva/a	grow	kasvi	plant
paista/a	roast	paisti	roast meat
kasvatta/a	bring up, educate	kasvatti	foster child
muista/a	remember	muisti	memory

-in (noun, indicates instrument)

cf. §20.5

avat/a	open	avain	key
puhel/la	talk, chat	puhelin	telephone
soitta/a	play	soitin	(musical) instrument
pakasta/a	freeze	pakastin	freezer

-ja ~ -jä (noun, indicates agent)

NB: common!

myy/dä	sell	myyjä	seller
saa/da	get	saaja	receiver
anta/a	give	antaja	giver
kalasta/a	fish	kalastaja	fisherman
laula/a	sing	laulaja	singer
teh/dä	do	tekijä	doer, maker, author
palvel/la	serve	palvelija	servant
ol/la	be	olija	one who is
tunte/a	know	tuntija	connoisseur

-maton ~ -mätön (negative adjective)

cf. §20.6

kuol/la	die	kuolematon	immortal
ol/la	be	olematon	non-existent
asu/a	live	asumaton	uninhabited
koke/a	experience	kokematon	unexperienced
lyö/dä	hit, beat	lyömätön	unbeaten, unbeatable
näh/dä	see	näkemätön	unseeing, unseen

-nta ~ -ntä (noun)

hankki/a	get, obtain	hankinta	acquisition
etsi/ä	look for	etsintä	search
kysy/ä	ask	kysyntä	demand
ampu/a	shoot	ammunta	shooting

-nti (noun)

saa/da	get	saanti	catch
tuo/da	bring, import, export	tuonti	import
vie/dä	take	vienti	export
myy/dä	sell	myynti	sale
tupakoi/da	smoke	tupakointi	smoking

-nto ~ -ntö (noun)

asu/a	live	asunto	residence
käyttä/ä	use	käytäntö	practice
luo/da	create	luonto	nature

-o ~ -ö (noun)

NB: common!

jaka/a	divide	jako	division
huuta/a	shout	huuto	shout
lentä/ä	fly	lento	flight
levät/ä	rest	lepo	rest
lähte/ä	leave	lähtö	departure
teh/dä	do	teko	a deed, act
pelät/ä	fear	pelko	fear
tietä/ä	know	tieto	knowledge
näh/dä	see	näkö	sight
kuul/la	hear	kuulo	hearing

-os ~ -ös (noun, often indicates result of an action)

cf. § 20.2

kiittä/ä	thank	kiitos	thanks
osta/a	buy	ostos	purchase
tul/la	come	tulos	result
pettä/ä	deceive	petos	deceit
käntä/ä	turn; translate	käännös	turn; translation
piirtä/ä	draw	piirros	drawing

-ri (noun, indicates agent)

leipo/a	bake	leipuri	baker
aja/a	drive	ajuri	driver, cabby
kulke/a	go, walk	kulkuri	tramp
taiko/a	conjure, use magic	taikuri	conjurer, magician

-u ~ -y (noun)

alka/a	begin	alku	beginning
iske/ä	strike	isku	blow, stroke
itke/ä	cry	itku	crying
kylpe/ä	bathe	kylpy	bath
maksa/a	pay	maksu	payment
laula/a	sing	laulu	song
käske/ä	command	käsky	command
sur/ra	grieve	suru	sorrow, grief

-us ~ -ys (noun)

avat/a	open	avaus	opening
hengittä/ä	breathe	hengitys	breathing
kuljetta/a	transport	kuljetus	transportation
metsästä/ä	hunt	metsästys	hunting
kirjoitta/a	write	kirjoitus	writing, article
kalasta/a	fish	kalastus	fishing
puolusta/a	defend	puolustus	defence

-uu (noun)

palat/a	return	paluu	return
taat/a	guarantee	takuu	guarantee
kerjät/ä	beg	kerjuu	begging
kaivat/a	long for	kaipuu	longing
kehrät/ä	spin	kehruu	spinning

-vainen ~ -väinen (adjective)

opetta/a	teach, instruct	opettavainen	instructive
tyyty/ä	be satisfied	tyytyväinen	satisfied
kuol/la	die	kuolevainen	mortal
säästä/ä	save	säästäväinen	economical, thrifty
usko/a	believe	uskovainen	religious

§93.2. *Verbal suffixes*

New verbs can be derived from both verbs and nominals. Deverbal verbs are much more common than denominal ones. The abundance of deverbal verbal suffixes is in fact one of the distinguishing features of Finnish, compared to the Indo—European languages.

(A) verb-to-verb suffixes

-ahta- ~ -ähtä- (momentary verb)

haukku/a	bark	haukahtaa	give a bark
laula/a	sing	laulahtaa	sing for a moment
horju/a	stagger	horjahtaa	stagger (''once'')
istu/a	sit	istahtaa	sit down

-aise- ~ -äise- (momentary verb)

kysy/ä	ask	kysäistä	pop a question
niel/lä	swallow	nielaista	gulp down
vetä/ä	pull	vetäistä	give a pull

-ele-, -ile- (frequentative verb)

aja/a	drive	ajella	drive around
astu/a	step	astella	step, walk around
kysy/ä	ask	kysellä	ask repeatedly
katso/a	look	katsella	look, watch
kalasta/a	fish	kalastella	be fishing
kiistä/ä	deny, contest	kiistellä	dispute, quarrel

-ksi- (frequentative verb)

ime/ä	suck	imeksiä	be sucking
kulke/a	go	kuljeksia	stroll
tunke/a	press, shove	tungeksia	be crowding

-skele- (frequentative verb)

etsi/ä	look for	etsiskellä	be searching
ime/ä	suck	imeskellä	be sucking
ol/la	be	oleskella	stay, be staying
oppi/a	learn	opiskella	study

-skentele- (frequentative verb)

myy/dä	sell	myyskennellä	be selling
käy/dä	go	käyskennellä	stroll about

-tta- ~ -ttä- (has the meaning 'cause to be done' etc.)

teh/dä	do	teettää	have...done
pes/tä	wash	pesettää	have...washed
kasva/a	grow (up)	kasvattaa	grow, bring up
elä/ä	live	elättää	support, provide for

-u- ~ -y- (reflexive verb)

NB: common!	löytä/ä	find	löytyä	be found
	siirtä/ä	move, transfer	siirtyä	move, be transferred
	tunte/a	feel, know	tuntua	feel, be felt, seem
	vaihta/a	change	vaihtua	change, be changed
	tyhjentä/ä	empty	tyhjentyä	empty
	rakasta/a	love	rakastua	fall in love
	pelasta/a	save	pelastua	be saved
	muutta/a	move, change	muuttua	be changed

-utu- ~ -yty- (reflexive verb)

NB: common!	kerät/ä	collect	keräytyä	collect, be collected
	lisät/ä	add	lisäytyä	increase
	elä/ä	live	eläytyä	enter into the spirit of
	vaivat/a	trouble	vaivautua	bother, take the trouble
	jättä/ä	leave	jättäytyä	surrender
	peri/ä	inherit	periytyä	be inherited
	tunke/a	press, shove	tunkeutua	force one's way

(B)
nominal-
to-verb
suffixes

cf. §23.4

-ile-

aika	time	aikailla	delay
pyörä	wheel	pyöräillä	cycle
nyrkki	fist	nyrkkeillä	box
telttä	tent	telttailla	go camping
pallo	ball	palloilla	play ball

-oi- ~ -öi-

tupakka	cigarette	tupakoida	smoke
elämä	life	elämöidä	make a noise
ikävä	longing	ikävöidä	long for, miss
hedelmä	fruit	hedelmöidä	bear fruit
isäntä	master, host	isännöidä	be in charge, act as host

-t- : -ne-

cf. §23.6

halpa	cheap	halvet/a : halpene-	become cheaper
huono	bad	huonot/a : huonone-	become worse
lyhyt	short	lyhet/ä : lyhene-	become shorter
kylmä	cold	kylmet/ä : kylmene-	become colder
tumma	dark	tummeta : tummene-	become darker

-ta- ~ -tä

NB:
common!

cf. §23.2

mitta	measure	mitata	measure
naula	nail	naulata	nail
höylä	plane	höylätä	plane
kuva	picture	kuvata	describe
hauta	grave	haudata	bury

-tta- ~ -ttä-

koulu	school	kouluttaa	educate, train
lippu	flag	liputtaa	put out flags
vero	tax	verottaa	tax
puukko	sheath knife	puukottaa	stab

-u- ~ -y- (reflexive verb)

kuiva	dry	kuivua	(become) dry
tippa	drop	tippua	drip
ruoste	rust	ruostua	rust
kostea	damp	kostua	get damp

The most common type of compound word is made up of two non-derived nouns, e.g. *kirja = kauppa* 'bookshop', *vesi = pullo* 'water-bottle', *pallo = peli* 'ball game', *kirje = kuori* 'envelope' (''letter = cover''), *kivi = katu* 'paved street' (''stone = street''), *kivi = kausi* 'stone age', *kirves = varsi* 'axe handle', *keittiö = kone* 'kitchen machine, appliance'. The first noun of these compounds is often in the genitive, e.g. *meren = ranta* 'seashore', *kirjan = kansi* 'book-cover', *auton = ikkuna* 'car window', *avaimen = reikä* 'keyhole'. The components of a compound may also be derived words themselves: *kaiv/in = kone* 'excavator, digging machine', *lävist/ys = kone* 'punching machine', *pes/u = kone* 'washing machine', *kone = apu/lainen* 'mechanical assistant', *koneen = rakenta/ja* 'machine constructor', *väli/ttä/jä = kone/isto* 'middle-man machinery', *te/o/llis/uus = tuo/ta/nto* 'industrial (''industry'') production', etc. Also fairly common are compounds with more than two elements, such as *maa = talo/us = tuo/ta/nto* 'agricultural production', *el/o = kuva = te/o/llis/uus* 'film industry', *huone = kalu = tehdas* 'furniture factory', *koti = tarve = myy/nti* 'household sale', *kauppa = tase = vaja/us* 'deficit in the balance of trade', *täyde/nn/ys = koulu/t/us = kys/el/y* 'further training inquiry', *el/in = keino = tulo = vero = laki* 'law concerning the taxation of earned income'.

Structurally rather complex compounds are formed when one of the elements is a deverbal noun and/or a word inflecting in a local case: *työn = saa/nti = mahdollis/uus* 'chance of finding work', *tode/llis/uuden = hahmo/-tta/mis = kyky* 'ability to give shape to reality', *oman = voiton = pyy/nti* 'self-interest', *jäsen = hanki/nta = kampanja* 'campaign to recruit members', *nuoteista = laul/u = taito* 'ability to sing at sight', *hallituksessa = ol/o = aika* 'period (''being'') in the government', *pysä/hty/mis = merkin = ant/o = nappi* 'button giving the stop signal'. Structures of this type are quite common and productive, particularly in the written language; cf. also e.g. *prahassa = käy/mä/ttöm/yys = kompleksi* 'complex about not having been to Prague'. Such complex compounds often correspond to complete sentences.

There are also many compound adjectives, especially with a derived adjective as the second element: *asian = muka/inen* 'appropriate', *saman = koko/-inen* 'of the same size', *ala = ikä/inen* 'under-age', *vapaa = miel/inen* 'liberal-minded', *lyhyt = sana/inen* 'taciturn, curt, brief', *moni = mutka/inen* 'complicated', *suomen = kiel/inen* 'speaking Finnish', *kansan = taju/inen* 'popular, easily comprehensible', *kansain = väli/nen* 'international', *pitkä = aika/inen* 'long, long-term', etc.

The first element of a two-part compound may occasionally differ from the basic form. This is particularly the case with nominals ending in -*nen* (§20.1); in compounds these have the same stem as in the partitive singular, e.g. *kokonais = valta/inen* 'holistic' (cf. *kokonainen* 'whole'), *nais = suku = puoli* 'female sex' (cf. *nainen* 'woman'), *yksityis = kohta/inen* 'detailed' (cf. *yksityi-nen* 'individual'), *yleis = kieli* 'standard language' (cf. *yleinen* 'general'), *ihmis = kunta* 'mankind' (cf. *ihminen* 'man'), *hevos = paimen* 'horse herder' (cf. *hevonen* 'horse'), etc. Other special cases include *suur = piirteinen* 'large-scale; broad-minded' (cf. *suuri* 'great'), *kolmi = vuot/ias* 'three-year-old' (cf.

kolme 'three'), *neli = vuot/ias* 'four-year-old' (cf. *neljä* 'four'), *avo = mielinen* 'open-hearted' (cf. *avaa-* '(to) open').

There are not many compound verbs in Finnish. Note however *alle = kirjoittaa* 'sign', *kokoon = panna* 'put together', *laimin = lyödä* 'neglect', *läpi = käydä* 'go through', *yllä = pitää* 'maintain, keep up', *jälleen = vakuuttaa* 'reinsure'.

22 The Colloquial Spoken Language

General
Omission and assimilation of sounds
Differences of form

§95. GENERAL

This book has so far been primarily concerned with the grammar of *standard Finnish*, which is predominantly a written form of the language. However, few Finns actually keep strictly to this norm in their *speech*; it is mostly heard in official, more or less "solemn" situations in which most Finns rarely, if ever, find themselves (speeches, sermons, radio and TV newsreading, rituals such as the opening of Parliament, often in teaching, etc.).

The norms or rules of this spoken standard language are very close to those of the written language. One often hears the claim that "Finnish is spoken the same way as it is written". But this is not literally true. The claim refers to the correspondence between letters and phonemes (§5): one and the same phoneme regularly corresponds to each letter, and vice versa.

In everyday situations not many Finns express themselves in speech exactly as they would in writing. The grammar of colloquial spoken Finnish differs in many ways from that of the written standard and the official spoken form based on this, both in pronunciation and in morphology and syntax. It is not therefore in any way "bad Finnish"; it is merely a form of the language used in *different situations*. In the same way, there have long existed regional dialects which also differ from the (written or spoken) standard language, e.g. the south-western dialects, the Häme dialects, the south-eastern dialects and the northern dialects.

During the past few decades, however, spoken Finnish has been going through a critical transition period caused by rapid changes in society. The most important of these changes have been: the postwar resettlements; changes in the structure of the economy, followed by migration from the countryside and urbanization (particularly the rise of Greater Helsinki); the influence of a uniform, increasingly longer and more thorough education, narrowing not only class differences but also language differences; the nation-wide influence of radio and TV; and the linguistically unifying effect of popular light literature.

The birth of Greater Helsinki, the Helsinki-based broadcasting media, and the status of the capital city have given rise to a widespread form of free spoken Finnish. Many of the features of this spoken language are nevertheless of older stock, originating e.g. in the western dialects of the province of Uusimaa.

Typical of this colloquial speech are certain omissions and assimilations of sounds (§96) and a number of morphological and syntactic features (§97) which are extremely common, especially in the speech of the younger generation.

§96. *OMISSION AND ASSIMILATION OF SOUNDS*

There are several omissions and assimilations which are particularly common in the colloquial spoken language. In the examples that follow, the colloquial spoken language is compared with the "official" pronunciation of the standard language.

1) The final vowels -i and -a, -ä are dropped (and a preceding long consonant is shortened) in certain endings, of which the most important are the inessive -ssa ~ -ssä, the elative -sta ~ -stä, the adessive -lla ~ -llä, the ablative -lta ~ -ltä, the translative -ksi, the second person singular possessive suffix -si, the conditional -isi and the past tense -s/i.

omission of final vowel

"OFFICIAL" PRONUNCIATION		COLLOQUIAL PRONUNCIATION
talossa	in the house	talos
meressä	in the sea	meres
talosta	out of the house	talost
merestä	out of the sea	merest
autolla	by car	autol
häneltä	from him	hänelt
vanhaksi	to (become) old	vanhaks
autosi	your car	autos
hän tulisi	he would come	hän tulis
Pekka sanoisi	Pekka would say	Pekka sanois
meillä on	we have	meil on
Tuula heräsi	Tuula woke	Tuula heräs

2) The final -i of diphthongs (e.g. ai, oi, ui, äi) is dropped in unstressed syllables. This also often applies to the -i of the past tense and the first vowel of the conditional ending -isi.

-i is dropped in diphthongs

punainen	red	punanen
sellainen	such	sellanen
semmoinen	such	semmonen
tuommoinen	that kind of	tuommonen
Kalle sanoi	Kalle said	Kalle sano
Pertti kantoi	Pertti carried	Pertti kanto
hän kestäisi	he would endure	hän kestäs
Keijo antaisi	Keijo would give	Keijo antas

3) When -a and -ä occur after a vowel they often assimilate to the preceding vowel, producing a long vowel (ea and eä become ee, oa becomes oo, etc.).

vowel assimilation

kauhea	terrible	kauhee
nopean	fast (genitive)	nopeen
tärkeä	important	tärkee

kulkea	go	kulkee
en rupea	I do/will not begin	en rupee
väkeä	people (partitive)	väkee
taloa	house (partitive)	taloo
varoa	look out	varoo

4) The final -t of the past participle **-nut** ~ **-nyt** is dropped, or assimilates to the following consonant.

-t is	olen sanonut	I have said	olen sanonu
dropped	olen sanonut sen	I have said it	olen sanonus sen
	Pekka on tullut	Pekka has come	Pekka on tullu
	Pekka on tullut jo	Pekka has already come	Pekka on tulluj jo

5) In some words **-d-** is dropped or changes to **j**.

-d- is	meidän	our	meijän
dropped	teidän	your	teijän
	tehdään	one does	tehään

6) **-n-** and **-l-** are occasionally dropped in the verbs *ole-* 'be', *mene-* 'go', *pane-* 'put', *tule-* 'come'.

-n-, -l-	olen	I am	oon
are	olemme	we are	oomme
dropped	menen	I go	meen
	tulet	you (sing.) come	tuut
	tulette	you (pl.) come	tuutte

§97. DIFFERENCES OF FORM

Some differences of form are closely related to the omissions and assimilations mentioned above (§96).

1) Many common pronoun forms are shortened in the colloquial spoken language.

	"OFFICIAL" PRONUNCIATION		COLLOQUIAL PRONUNCIATION
pronouns			
are	minä	I	mä
shorted	minun	my	mun
	minulla	"at" me	mul(la)
	minulle	to me	mulle
	sinä	you	sä
	sinun	your	sun
	sinulla	"at" you	sul(la)
	tämä	this	tää
	tämän	of this	tän
	tuo	that	toi
	tuon	of that	ton
	tuolla	there	tol(la)
	nuo	those	noi

2) Many numerals become much shorter.

numerals	yksi	1	yks
are	kaksi	2	kaks
shortened	viisi	5	viis
	kuusi	6	kuus
	seitsemän	7	seittemän
	kahdeksan	8	kaheksan
	yhdeksän	9	yheksän
	yksitoista	11	ykstoist
	viisitoista	15	viistoist
	kaksikymmentä	20	kaksky(n)t
	kuusikymmentäviisi	65	kuusky(n)tviis
	seitsemänkymmentä-		
	kahdeksan	78	seitkytkaheksan
	etc.		

3) 1st and 2nd person possessive suffixes are often dropped, and the corresponding pronouns are shortened (cf. §36).

possessive	(minun) kirja/ni	my book	mun kirja
suffixes	(sinun) kirja/si	your (sing.) book	sun kirja
are	(meidän) kirja/mme	our book	meijän kirja
dropped	(teidän) kirja/nne	your (pl.) book	teijän kirja

4) The 3rd person plural ending of finite verbs is not used, being replaced by the 3rd person singular ending (cf. §24). In addition, the pronoun *ne* 'those' often replaces *he* 'they', and similarly in the singular *se* 'it' replaces *hän* 'he, she'.

3rd p. pl.	he tule/vat	they come	ne tulee
= 3rd p.	he anta/vat	they give	ne antaa
sing.	he mene/vät	they go	ne menee

5) The passive forms (§§69—71) are used instead of the 1st person plural ending -**mme**.

passive	me sano/mme	we say	me sanotaan
instead of	me sano/i/mme	we said	me sanottiin
-**mme**	me sano/isi/mme	we would say	me sanottais(iin)
	sano/kaamme	let us say	sanotaan
	emme sano	we do not say	me ei sanota
	emme sano/neet	we did not say	me ei sanottu
	emme sano/isi	we would not say	me ei sanottais(i)
	me mene/mme	we go	me mennään
	me men/i/mme	we went	me mentiin
	me men/isi/mme	we would go	me mentäis(iin)
	men/käämme	let us go	mennään
	emme mene	we do not go	me ei mennä
	emme men/neet	we did not go	me ei menty
	emme men/isi	we would not go	me ei mentäis(i)
	emme ol/isi men/neet	we would not have gone	me ei oltais menty

6) The interrogative particle -**ko** ~ -**kö** often takes the form -**ks** (cf. §30.1).

-**ko** ~ -**kö** = -**ks**	onko(s) teillä palaako täällä vienkö minä	do you have? is it burning here? shall I take?	onks teil palaaks tääl vienks mä

7) The ending -**ma**- ~ -**mä**- of the 3rd infinitive illative (§77) is often dropped.

-**ma**- ~ -**mä**- is dropped	mennään nukku/ma/an lähden tanssi/ma/an tuletko(s) kävele/mä/än	let's go to sleep I'm going dancing are you coming for a walk (''to walk'')?	mennään nukkuun lähen tanssiin tuuks käveleen

The case ending -**Vn** then assimilates to the last vowel of the stem, e.g. *nukku/un*.

Subject Index
(numbers refer to sections)

APPENDIX 2

Inflection Tables

NOMINALS

		SINGULAR	PLURAL	SINGULAR	PLURAL
talo	nom.	talo	talot	kauppa	kaupat
'house'	gen.	talon	talojen	kaupan	kauppojen
kauppa	partit.	taloa	taloja	kauppaa	kauppoja
'shop'	iness.	talossa	taloissa	kaupassa	kaupoissa
	elat.	talosta	taloista	kaupasta	kaupoista
	illat.	taloon	taloihin	kauppaan	kauppoihin
	adess.	talolla	taloilla	kaupalla	kaupoilla
	ablat.	talolta	taloilta	kaupalta	kaupoilta
	allat.	talolle	taloille	kaupalle	kaupoille
	ess.	talona	taloina	kauppana	kauppoina
	transl.	taloksi	taloiksi	kaupaksi	kaupoiksi
tunti	nom.	tunti	tunnit	käsi	kädet
'hour'	gen.	tunnin	tuntien	käden	käsien
(§18.1)	partit.	tuntia	tunteja	kättä	käsiä
käsi	iness.	tunnissa	tunneissa	kädessä	käsissä
'hand'	elat.	tunnista	tunneista	kädestä	käsistä
(§18.4)	illat.	tuntiin	tunteihin	käteen	käsiin
	adess.	tunnilla	tunneilla	kädellä	käsillä
	ablat.	tunnilta	tunneilta	kädeltä	käsiltä
	allat.	tunnille	tunneille	kädelle	käsille
	ess.	tuntina	tunteina	kätenä	käsinä
	transl.	tunniksi	tunneiksi	kädeksi	käsiksi
kieli	nom.	kieli	kielet	liike	liikkeet
'language'	gen.	kielen	kielten	liikkeen	liikkeiden
(§18.3)	partit.	kieltä	kieliä	liikettä	liikkeitä
liike	iness.	kielessä	kielissä	liikkeessä	liikkeissä
'movement'	elat.	kielestä	kielistä	liikkeestä	liikkeistä
(§19)	illat.	kieleen	kieliin	liikkeeseen	liikkeisiin
	adess.	kielellä	kielillä	liikkeellä	liikkeillä
	ablat.	kieleltä	kieliltä	liikkeeltä	liikkeiltä
	allat.	kielelle	kielille	liikkeelle	liikkeille
	ess.	kielenä	kielinä	liikkeenä	liikkeinä
	transl.	kieleksi	kieliksi	liikkeeksi	liikkeiksi
ihminen	nom.	ihminen	ihmiset	ajatus	ajatukset
'person'	gen.	ihmisen	ihmisten	ajatuksen	ajatusten
(§20.1)	partit.	ihmistä	ihmisiä	ajatusta	ajatuksia
ajatus	iness.	ihmisessä	ihmisissä	ajatuksessa	ajatuksissa
'thought'	elat.	ihmisestä	ihmisistä	ajatuksesta	ajatuksista
(§20.2)	illat.	ihmiseen	ihmisiin	ajatukseen	ajatuksiin
	adess.	ihmisellä	ihmisillä	ajatuksella	ajatuksilla
	ablat.	ihmiseltä	ihmisiltä	ajatukselta	ajatuksilta
	allat.	ihmiselle	ihmisille	ajatukselle	ajatuksille
	ess.	ihmisenä	ihmisinä	ajatuksena	ajatuksina
	transl.	ihmiseksi	ihmisiksi	ajatukseksi	ajatuksiksi

taivas	nom.	taivas	taivaat	rengas	renkaat
'heaven'	gen.	taivaan	taivaiden	renkaan	renkaiden
(§20.3)	partit.	taivasta	taivaita	rengasta	renkaita
rengas	iness.	taivaassa	taivaissa	renkaassa	renkaissa
'ring'	elat.	taivaasta	taivaista	renkaasta	renkaista
(§20.3)	illat.	taivaaseen	taivaisiin	renkaaseen	renkaisiin
	adess.	taivaalla	taivailla	renkaalla	renkailla
	ablat.	taivaalta	taivailta	renkaalta	renkailta
	allat.	taivaalle	taivaille	renkaalle	renkaille
	ess.	taivaana	taivaina	renkaana	renkaina
	transl.	taivaaksi	taivaiksi	renkaaksi	renkaiksi
hyvyys	nom.	hyvyys	hyvyydet	avain	avaimet
'goodness'	gen.	hyvyyden	hyvyyksien	avaimen	avaimien
(§20.4)	partit.	hyvyyttä	hyvyyksiä	avainta	avaimia
avain	iness.	hyvyydessä	hyvyyksissä	avaimessa	avaimissa
'key'	elat.	hyvyydestä	hyvyyksistä	avaimesta	avaimista
(§20.5)	illat.	hyvyyteen	hyvyyksiin	avaimeen	avaimiin
	adess.	hyvyydellä	hyvyyksillä	avaimella	avaimilla
	ablat.	hyvyydeltä	hyvyyksiltä	avaimelta	avaimilta
	allat.	hyvyydelle	hyvyyksille	avaimelle	avaimille
	ess.	hyvyytenä	hyvyyksinä	avaimena	avaimina
	transl.	hyvyydeksi	hyvyyksiksi	avaimeksi	avaimiksi
työtön	nom.	työtön	työttömät	askel	askelet
'unem-	gen.	työttömän	työttömien	askelen	askelien
ployed'	partit.	työtöntä	työttömiä	askelta	askelia
(§20.6)	iness.	työttömässä	työttömissä	askelessa	askelissa
askel	elat.	työttömästä	työttömistä	askelesta	askelista
'pace'	illat.	työttömään	työttömiin	askeleen	askeliin
(§20.7)	adess.	työttömällä	työttömillä	askelella	askelilla
	ablat.	työttömältä	työttömiltä	askelelta	askelilta
	allat.	työttömälle	työttömille	askelelle	askelille
	ess.	työttömänä	työttöminä	askelena	askelina
	transl.	työttömäksi	työttömiksi	askeleksi	askeliksi
kolmas	nom.	kolmas	kolmannet	suurempi	suuremmat
'third'	gen.	kolmannen	kolmansien	suuremman	suurempien
(§53)	partit.	kolmatta	kolmansia	suurempaa	suurempia
suurempi	iness.	kolmannessa	kolmansissa	suuremmassa	suuremmissa
'greater'	elat.	kolmannesta	kolmansista	suuremmasta	suuremmista
(§85)	illat.	kolmanteen	kolmansiin	suurempaan	suurempiin
	adess.	kolmannella	kolmansilla	suuremmalla	suuremmilla
	ablat.	kolmannelta	kolmansilta	suuremmalta	suuremmilta
	allat.	kolmannelle	kolmansille	suuremmalle	suuremmille
	ess.	kolmantena	kolmansina	suurempana	suurempina
	transl.	kolmanneksi	kolmansiksi	suuremmaksi	suuremmiksi
suurin	nom.	suurin	suurimmat		
'greatest'	gen.	suurimman	suurimpien		
(§86)	partit.	suurinta	suurimpia		
	iness.	suurimmassa	suurimmissa		
	elat.	suurimmasta	suurimmista		
	illat.	suurimpaan	suurimpiin		
	adess.	suurimmalla	suurimmilla		
	ablat.	suurimmalta	suurimmilta		
	allat.	suurimmalle	suurimmille		
	ess.	suurimpana	suurimpina		
	transl.	suurimmaksi	suurimmiksi		

VERBS

Indicative

Present

sanoa
'say'
(§23.1)

		Affirmative		Negative	
Active					
sing.	1	sanon	I say	en sano	I do not say
	2	sanot	you say	et sano	you do not say
	3	sanoo	etc.	ei sano	etc.
pl.	1	sanomme		emme sano	
	2	sanotte		ette sano	
	3	sanovat		eivät sano	
Passive		sanotaan	one says	ei sanota	

Past

Active					
sing.	1	sanoin	I said	en sanonut	I did not say
	2	sanoit		et sanonut	
	3	sanoi		ei sanonut	
pl.	1	sanoimme		emme sanoneet	
	2	sanoitte		ette sanoneet	
	3	sanoivat		eivät sanoneet	
Passive		sanottiin		ei sanottu	

Perfect

Active					
sing.	1	olen sanonut	I have said	en ole sanonut	I have not said
	2	olet sanonut		et ole sanonut	
	3	on sanonut		ei ole sanonut	
pl.	1	olemme sanoneet		emme ole sanoneet	
	2	olette sanoneet		ette ole sanoneet	
	3	ovat sanoneet		eivät ole sanoneet	
Passive		on sanottu		ei ole sanottu	

Pluperfect

Active					
sing.	1	olin sanonut	I had said	en ollut sanonut	I had not said
	2	olit sanonut		et ollut sanonut	
	3	oli sanonut		ei ollut sanonut	
pl.	1	olimme sanoneet		emme olleet sanoneet	
	2	olitte sanoneet		ette olleet sanoneet	
	3	olivat sanoneet		eivät olleet sanoneet	
Passive		oli sanottu		ei ollut sanottu	

Conditional

Present

Active					
sing.	1	sanoisin	I would say	en sanoisi	I would not say
	2	sanoisit		et sanoisi	
	3	sanoisi		ei sanoisi	
pl.	1	sanoisimme		emme sanoisi	
	2	sanoisitte		ette sanoisi	
	3	sanoisivat		eivät sanoisi	
Passive		sanottaisiin		ei sanottaisi	

Perfect

Active					
sing.	1	olisin sanonut	I would have said	en olisi sanonut	I would not have said
	2	olisit sanonut		et olisi sanonut	
	3	olisi sanonut		ei olisi sanonut	

pl. 1	olisimme sanoneet		emme olisi sanoneet	
2	olisitte sanoneet		ette olisi sanoneet	
3	olisivat sanoneet		eivät olisi sanoneet	
Passive	olisi sanottu		ei olisi sanottu	

Imperative

Present

Active

sing. 2	sano	say	älä sano	do not say
3	sanokoon		älköön sanoko	
pl. 1	sanokaamme		älkäämme sanoko	
2	sanokaa		älkää sanoko	
3	sanokoot		älkööt sanoko	
Passive	sanottakoon		älköön sanottako	

Potential

Present

Active

sing. 1	sanonen	I may say	en sanone	I may not say
2	sanonet		et sanone	
3	sanonee		ei sanone	
pl. 1	sanonemme		emme sanone	
2	sanonette		ette sanone	
3	sanonevat		eivät sanone	
Passive	sanottaneen		ei sanottane	

Perfect

Active

sing. 1	lienen sanonut	I may have	en liene sanonut	I may not have said
2	lienet sanonut		et liene sanonut	
3	lienee sanonut		ei liene sanonut	
pl. 1	lienemme sanoneet		emme liene sanoneet	
2	lienette sanoneet		ette liene sanoneet	
3	lienevät sanoneet		eivät liene sanoneet	
Passive	lienee sanottu		ei liene sanottu	

NON-FINITE FORMS

Infinitives

1st inf.	sanoa	to say
	sanoakseni	
2nd inf.	sanoessa	
	sanoen	
3rd inf.	sanomaan	
	sanomassa	
	sanomasta	
	sanomalla	
	sanomatta	

Participles

Pres. part.		
act.	sanovat	
pass.	sanottava	
Past part.		
act.	sanonut	
pass.	sanottu	

Indicative

Present

hypätä
'jump'
(§23.2)

		Affirmative		Negative	
Active					
	sing.1	hyppään	I jump	en hyppää	I do not jump
	2	hyppäät	etc.	et hyppää	etc.
	3	hyppää		ei hyppää	
	pl. 1	hyppäämme		emme hyppää	
	2	hyppäätte		ette hyppää	
	3	hyppäävät		eivät hyppää	
Passive		hypätään		ei hypätä	

Past

Active					
	sing. 1	hyppäsin	I jumped	en hypännyt	I did not jump
	2	hyppäsit		et hypännyt	
	3	hyppäsi		ei hypännyt	
	pl. 1	hyppäsimme		emme hypänneet	
	2	hyppäsitte		ette hypänneet	
	3	hyppäsivät		eivät hypänneet	
Passive		hypättiin		ei hypätty	

Perfect

Active					
	sing. 1	olen hypännyt	I have jumped	en ole hypännyt	I have not jumped
	2	olet hypännyt		et ole hypännyt	
	3	on hypännyt		ei ole hypännyt	
	pl. 1	olemme hypänneet		emme ole hypännet	
	2	olette hypänneet		ette ole hypänneet	
	3	ovat hypänneet		eivät ole hypänneet	
Passive		on hypätty		ei ole hypätty	

Pluperfect

Active					
	sing. 1	olin hypännyt	I had jumped	en ollut hypännyt	I had not jumped
	2	olit hypännyt		et ollut hypännyt	
	3	oli hypännyt		ei ollut hypännyt	
	pl. 1	olimme hypänneet		emme olleet hypänneet	
	2	olitte hypänneet		ette olleet hypänneet	
	3	olivat hypänneet		eivät olleet hypänneet	
Passive		oli hypätty		ei ollut hypätty	

Conditional

Present

Active					
	sing. 1	olisin hypännyt	I would have jumped	en olisi hypännyt	I would not have
	2	olisit hypännyt		et olisi hypännyt	jumped
	3	olisi hypännyt		ei olisi hypännyt	
	pl. 1	olisimme hypänneet		emme olisi hypänneet	
	2	olisitte hypänneet		ette olisi hypänneet	
	3	olisivat hypänneet		eivät olisi hypänneet	
Passive		olisi hypätty		ei olisi hypätty	

Imperative

Present

Active				
sing. 2	hyppää	jump	älä hyppää	do not jump
3	hypätköön		älköön hypätkö	
pl. 1	hypätkäämme		älkäämme hypätkö	
2	hypätkää		älkää hypätkö	
3	hypätkööt		älkööt hypätkö	
Passive	hypättäköön		älköön hypättäkö	

Potential

Present

Active				
sing. 1	hypännen	I may jump	en hypänne	I may not jump
2	hypännet		et hypänne	
3	hypännee		ei hypänne	
pl. 1	hypännemme		emme hypänne	
2	hypännette		ette hypänne	
3	hypännevät		eivät hypänne	
Passive	hypättäneen		ei hypättäne	

Perfect

Active				
sing. 1	lienen hypännyt	I may have jumped	en liene hypännyt	I may not have jumped
2	lienet hypännyt		et liene hypännyt	
3	lienee hypännyt		ei liene hypännyt	
pl. 1	lienemme hypänneet		emme liene hypänneet	
2	lienette hypänneet		ette liene hypänneet	
3	lienevät hypänneet		eivät liene hypänneet	
Passive	lienee hypätty		ei liene hypätty	

NON-FINITE FORMS

Infinitives

1st inf.	hypätä	to jump
	hypätäkseni	
2nd inf.	hypätessä	
	hypäten	
3rd inf.	hyppäämään	
	hyppäämässä	
	hyppäämästä	
	hyppäämällä	
	hyppäämättä	

Participles

Pres. part.		
act.	hyppäävä	
pass.	hypättävä	
Past part.		
act.	hypännyt	
pass.	hypätty	

217

Indicative

Present

		Active		Negative	
saada	sing. 1	saan	I get.	en saa	I do not get.
'get'	2	saat	etc.	et saa	etc.
(§23.3)	3	saa		ei saa	
	pl. 1	saamme		emme saa	
	2	saatte		ette saa	
	3	saavat		eivät saa	
	Passive	saadaan		ei saada	

Past

	Active		Negative	
sing. 1	sain	I got	en saanut	I did not get
2	sait		et saanut	
3	sai		ei saanut	
pl. 1	saimme		emme saaneet	
2	saitte		ette saaneet	
3	saivat		eivät saaneet	
Passive	saatiin		ei saatu	

Perfect

	Active		Negative	
sing. 1	olen saanut	I have got	en ole saanut	I have not got
2	olet saanut		et ole saanut	
3	on saanut		ei ole saanut	
pl. 1	olemme saaneet		emme ole saaneet	
2	olette saaneet		ette ole saaneet	
3	ovat saaneet		eivät ole saaneet	
Passive	on saanut		ei ole saatu	

Pluperfect

	Active		Negative	
sing. 1	olin saanut	I had got	en ollut saanut	I had not got
2	olit saanut		et ollut saanut	
3	oli saanut		ei ollut saanut	
pl. 1	olimme saaneet		emme olleet saaneet	
2	olitte saaneet		ette olleet saaneet	
3	olivat saaneet		eivät olleet saaneet	
Passive	oli saatu		ei ollut saatu	

Conditional

Present

	Active		Negative	
sing. 1	saisin	I would get	en saisi	I would not get
2	saisit		et saisi	
3	saisi		ei saisi	
pl. 1	saisimme		emme saisi	
2	saisitte		ette saisi	
3	saisivat		eivät saisi	
Passive	saataisiin		ei saataisi	

Perfect

	Active		Negative	
sing. 1	olisin saanut	I would have got	en olisi saanut	I would not have got
2	olisit saanut		et olisi saanut	
3	olisi saanut		ei olisi saanut	
pl. 1	olisimme saaneet		emme olisi saaneet	
2	olisitte saaneet		ette olisi saaneet	
3	olisivat saaneet		eivät olisi saaneet	
Passive	olisi saatu		ei olisi saatu	

Imperative

Present

Active				
sing. 2	saa	get	älä saa	do not get
3	saakoon		älköön saako	
pl. 1	saakaamme		älkäämme saako	
2	saakaa		älkää saako	
3	saakoot		älkööt saako	
Passive	saatakoon		älköön saatako	

Potential

Present

Active				
sing. 1	saanen	I may get	en saane	I may not get
2	saanet		et saane	
3	saanee		ei saane	
pl. 1	saanemme		emme saane	
2	saanette		ette saane	
3	saanevat		eivät saane	
Passive	saataneen		ei saatane	

Perfect

Active				
sing. 1	lienen saanut	I may have got	en liene saanut	I may not have got
2	lienet saanut		et liene saanut	
3	lienee saanut		ei liene saanut	
pl. 1	lienemme saaneet		emme liene saaneet	
2	lienette saaneet		ette liene saaneet	
3	lienevät saaneet		eivät liene saaneet	
Passive	lienee saatu		ei liene saatu	

NON-FINITE FORMS

Infinitives

1st inf.	saada	to get
	saadakseni	
2nd inf.	saadessa	
	saaden	
3rd inf.	saamaan	
	saamassa	
	saamasta	
	saamalla	
	saamatta	

Participles

Pres.		
part. act.	saava	
pass.	saatava	
Past		
part. act.	saanut	
pass.	saatu	

Indicative

Present

		Affirmative		Negative	
tarvita 'need' (§23.5)	Active				
	sing. 1	tarvitsen	I need	en tarvitse	I do not need
	2	tarvitset	etc.	et tarvitse	etc.
	3	tarvitsee		ei tarvitse	
	pl. 1	tarvitsemme		emme tarvitse	
	2	tarvitsette		ette tarvitse	
	3	tarvitsevat		eivät tarvitse	
	Passive	tarvitaan		ei tarvita	

Past

	Active				
	sing. 1	tarvitsin	I needed	en tarvinnut	I did not need
	2	tarvitsit		et tarvinnut	
	3	tarvitsi		ei tarvinnut	
	pl. 1	tarvitsimme		emme tarvinneet	
	2	tarvitsitte		ette tarvinneet	
	3	tarvitsivat		eivät tarvinneet	
	Passive	tarvittiin		ei tarvittu	

Perfect

	Active				
	sing. 1	olen tarvinnut	I have needed	en ole tarvinnut	I have not needed
	2	olet tarvinnut		et ole tarvinnut	
	3	on tarvinnut		ei ole tarvinnut	
	pl. 1	olemme tarvinneet		emme ole tarvinneet	
	2	olette tarvinneet		ette ole tarvinneet	
	3	ovat tarvinneet		eivät ole tarvinneet	
	Passive	on tarvittu		ei ole tarvittu	

Pluperfect

	Active				
	sing. 1	olin tarvinnut	I had needed	en ollut tarvinnut	I had not needed
	2	olin tarvinnut		et ollut tarvinnut	
	3	oli tarvinnut		ei ollut tarvinnut	
	pl. 1	olimme tarvinneet		emme olleet tarvinneet	
	2	olitte tarvinneet		ette olleet tarvinneet	
	3	olivat tarvinneet		eivät olleet tarvinneet	
	Passive	oli tarvittu		ei ollut tarvittu	

Conditional

Present

	Active				
	sing. 1	tarvitsisin	I would need	en tarvitsisi	I would not need
	2	tarvitsisit		et tarvitsisi	
	3	tarvitsisi		ei tarvitsisi	
	pl. 1	tarvitsisimme		emme tarvitsisi	
	2	tarvitsisitte		ette tarvitsisi	
	3	tarvitsisivat		eivät tarvitsisi	
	Passive	tarvittaisiin		ei tarvittaisi	

Perfect

Active						
sing. 1	olisin tarvinnut	I would have	en olisi tarvinnut	I would not have
2	olisit tarvinnut	needed	et olisi tarvinnut	needed
3	olisi tarvinnut		ei olisi tarvinnut	
pl. 1	olisimme tarvinneet		emme olisi tarvinneet	
2	olisitte tarvinneet		ette olisi tarvinneet	
3	olisivat tarvinneet		eivät olisi tarvinneet	
Passive	olisi tarvittu		ei olisi tarvittu	

Imperative

Present

Active						
sing. 2	tarvitse	need	älä tarvitse	do not need
3	tarvitkoon		älköön tarvitko	
pl. 1	tarvitkaamme		älkäämme tarvitko	
2	tarvitkaa		älkää tarvitko	
3	tarvikoot		älkööt tarvitko	
Passive	tarvittakoon		älköön tarvittako	

Potential

Present

Active						
sing. 1	tarvinnen	I may need	en tarvinne	I may not need
2	tarvinnet		et tarvinne	
3	tarvinnee		ei tarvinne	
pl. 1	tarvinnemme		emme tarvinne	
2	tarvinnette		ette tarvinne	
3	tarvinnevat		eivät tarvinne	
Passive	tarvittaneen		ei tarvittane	

Perfect

Active						
sing. 1	lienen tarvinnut	I may have needed	en liene tarvinnut	I may not have needed
2	lienet tarvinnut		et liene tarvinnut	
3	lienee tarvinnut		ei liene tarvinnut	
pl. 1	lienemme tarvinneet		emme liene tarvinneet	
2	lienette tarvinneet		ette liene tarvinneet	
3	lienevät tarvinneet		eivät liene tarvinneet	
Passive	lienee tarvittu		ei liene tarvittu	

NON-FINITE FORMS

Infinitives

1st inf.	tarvita	to need
	tarvitakseni	
2nd inf.	tarvitessa	
	tarviten	
3rd inf.	tarvitsemaan	
	tarvitsemassa	
	tarvitsemasta	
	tarvitsemalla	
	tarvitsematta	

Participles

Pres.		
part. act.	tarvitseva	
pass.	tarvittava	
Past		
part. act.	tarvinnut	
pass.	tarvittu	

APPENDIX 3

BIBLIOGRAPHY

Aaltio, Maija-Hellikki, *Finnish for foreigners.* Otava, Keuruu 1973.

Branch, Michael & Niemikorpi, Antero & Saukkonen, Pauli, *A Student's Glossary of Finnish.* WSOY, Helsinki 1980.

Hakulinen, Auli & Karlsson, Fred, *Nykysuomen lauseoppia.* Suomalaisen Kirjallisuuden Seura, Helsinki 1979.

Hakulinen, Lauri, *Suomen kielen rakenne ja kehitys.* Fourth, revised and enlarged edition. Otava, Helsinki 1979.

Hämäläinen, Eila, *Suomen harjoituksia.* I. Second edition. Suomalaisen Kirjallisuuden Seura, Helsinki 1979.

Ikola, Osmo, toim., *Nykysuomen käsikirja.* Weilin & Göös, Espoo 1977.

Kallioinen, Vilho, *Suomen kielen rakenneharjoituksia ulkomaalaisille.* Tietolipas 57. Suomalaisen Kirjallisuuden Seura, Helsinki 1972.

— —, *Finnish Conversational Exercises.* Suomalaisen Kirjallisuuden Seura, Helsinki 1974.

Karlsson, Fred, *Finskans struktur.* LiberLäromedel, Lund 1976.

— —, *Suomen kielen äänne- ja muotorakenne.* WSOY, Helsinki 1983.

Karlsson, Göran, *Finsk formlära.* Second edition. Söderströms, Helsingfors 1978.

Loman, Bengt & Pulkkinen, Paavo, *Finskt uttal.* Studentlitteratur, Lund 1966.

Nuutinen, Olli, *Suomea suomeksi.* I + II. Second, revised edition. Suomalaisen Kirjallisuuden Seura, Helsinki 1979.

Saukkonen, Pauli & Haipus, Marjatta & Niemikorpi, Antero & Sulkala, Helena, *Suomen kielen taajuussanasto.* WSOY, Helsinki 1979.

Siro, Paavo, *Suomen kielen lauseoppi.* Tietosanakirja, Helsinki 1964.

Stenberg, Anne-Marie, *Finsk satslära.* Söderströms, Helsingfors 1971.

Vesikansa, Jouko, *Johdokset.* WSOY, Helsinki 1977.